11/10/2(

As o...
Thomas Cook are the experts in travel.

For more than 135 years our
guidebooks have unlocked the secrets
of destinations around the world,
...th travellers a wealth of
experience a... ...for travel.

**Rely on Thomas Cook as your
travelling companion on your next trip
and benefit from our unique heritage.**

Thomas Cook **driving** guides

LOIRE VALLEY

Andrew Sanger, Fiona Nichols,
Gillian Thomas and John Harrison

Thomas
Cook

Your travelling companion since 1873

Written by Andrew Sanger, Fiona Nichols, Gillian Thomas and John Harrison,
updated by Andrew Sanger
Original photography by Ethel Davies

Published by Thomas Cook Publishing
A division of Thomas Cook Tour Operations Limited
Company registration no. 3772199 England
The Thomas Cook Business Park, Unit 9, Coningsby Road,
Peterborough PE3 8SB, United Kingdom
Email: books@thomascook.com, Tel: + 44 (0) 1733 416477
www.thomascookpublishing.com

Produced by Cambridge Publishing Management Limited
Burr Elm Court, Main Street, Caldecote CB23 7NU
www.cambridgepm.co.uk

ISBN: 978-1-84848-359-0

© 2005, 2007, 2009 Thomas Cook Publishing
This fourth edition © 2011
Text © Thomas Cook Publishing
Maps © Thomas Cook Publishing/PCGraphics (UK) Limited

Series Editor: Karen Beaulah
Production/DTP: Steven Collins

Printed and bound in India by Replika Press Pvt Ltd

Cover photography © Claire Takacs/Alamy

About the authors

Andrew Sanger is a well-established travel writer who has contributed many hundreds of travel articles to a wide range of British newspapers and magazines. He has also written over 30 guidebooks, most about regions of France, which have been translated into several languages. His most recent titles for Thomas Cook are *driving guides Provence and the Côte d'Azur* and *driving guides Burgundy and the Rhône Valley*. Andrew was editor of French Railways' travel magazine *Rail Europe*, and has twice been the winner of the prestigious Travelex Travel Writers' Award in London, in 1994 and 1996.

Fiona Nichols has contributed travel and lifestyle articles to magazines and newspapers in various parts of the world. She is a co-author of some dozen or so travel guides, and author-photographer of eight travel books. Fiona lives in the south of France, near the Spanish border, where she continues to write and photograph travel-related features and books. This is her first contribution to a Thomas Cook publication.

Gillian Thomas and **John Harrison** are freelance travel writers who started their careers at the BBC, where Gillian worked in the Paris news office. Married, with three grown-up children, they are frequent visitors to France for camping, walking, cycling and canal-boating holidays. They wrote the *driving guides Languedoc and Southwest France* for Thomas Cook.

Acknowledgements

Andrew Sanger would like to thank Rail Europe and the Regional Tourist Board of Centre-Val de Loire for their assistance. Gillian Thomas and John Harrison would like to thank Brittany Ferries and the tourist boards of the Central Loire Valley and Western Loire regions for their assistance. Fiona Nichols would like to thank all the tourist offices concerned, who were extremely kind and informative.

Contents

About driving guides

Thomas Cook's driving guides are designed to provide you with a comprehensive but flexible reference source to guide you as you tour a country or region by car. This guide divides the Loire Valley into touring areas – one per chapter. Major cultural centres or cities form chapters in their own right. Each chapter contains enough attractions to provide at least a day's worth of activities – often more.

Ratings

To make it easier for you to plan your time and decide what to see, every area is rated according to its attractions in categories such as Architecture, Entertainment and Children.

Chapter contents

Every chapter has an introduction summing up the main attractions of the area or town, and a ratings box, which will highlight its appeal – some places may be more attractive to families travelling with children, others to wine lovers visiting vineyards, and others to people interested in finding castles, churches or nature reserves.

Each chapter is then divided into an alphabetical gazetteer, and a suggested tour or walk. You can select whether you just want to visit a particular sight or attraction, choosing from those described in the gazetteer, or whether you want to tour the area comprehensively. If the latter, you can construct your own itinerary, or follow the authors' suggested tour, which comes at the end of every area chapter.

The gazetteer

The gazetteer section describes all the major attractions in the area – the villages, towns, historic sites, nature reserves, parks or museums that you are most likely to want to see. Maps of the area highlight all the places mentioned in the text. Using this comprehensive overview of the area, you may choose just to visit one or two sights.

One way to use the guide is to find individual sights that interest you, using the index or overview map, and read what our authors have to say about them. This will help you decide whether to visit the sight. If you do, you will find plenty of practical information, such as the telephone number for enquiries.

Alternatively, you can choose a hotel, with the help of the accommodation recommendations contained in this guide. You can then turn to the overall map on pages 8–9 to help you work out which chapters in the book describe regions closest to your base.

Symbol Key

ⓘ Tourist Information Centre

ⓦ Website

ⓔ Advice on arriving or departing

ⓟ Parking locations

ⓖ Advice on getting around

⊃ Directions

ⓝ Sights and attractions

ⓒ Accommodation

ⓝ Eating

ⓞ Shopping

ⓢ Sport

ⓔ Entertainment

Practical information

The practical information in the page margins will help you locate the services you need as an independent traveller – including the tourist information centre, car parks and public transport facilities. You will also find the opening times of sights, museums, churches and other attractions, as well as useful tips on shopping, market days, cultural events, entertainment, festivals and sports facilities.

Driving tours

The suggested tour is just that – a suggestion, with plenty of optional detours and one or two ideas for making your own discoveries, under the heading 'Also worth exploring'. The routes are designed to link the attractions described in the gazetteer section, and to cover outstandingly scenic landscapes. The total distance is given for each tour, and the time it will take you to drive the complete route; but bear in mind that this indication is just for driving time: you will need to allow extra time for visiting attractions along the way.

Many of the routes are circular, so that you can join them at any point. Where the nature of the terrain dictates that the route has to be linear, the route can either be followed out and back, or you can use it as a link route, to get from one area in the book to another.

As you follow the route descriptions, you will find names picked out in bold capital letters – this means that the place is described fully in the gazetteer. Other names picked out in bold indicate additional villages or attractions worth a brief stop along the route.

Accommodation and food

In every chapter you will find lodging and eating recommendations. These are designed to cover a range of price brackets and concentrate on more characterful small or individualistic hotels and restaurants. In addition, you will find information in the 'Travel facts' chapter on chain hotels, with an address to which you can write for a guide, map or directory.

The price indications used in the guide have the following meanings:

€	budget level
€€	typical/average prices
€€€	de luxe

Argentan

Alençon

Laval

Page 192

Pag

Chart

Château

Page 170

Page 146

Page 162

Le Mans

**PAYS
DE LA LOIRE**

La Flèche

Vendôme

Page 126

Page 52

Page 136

Angers

Blois

Page 202

Page 68

Page 42

Tours

CENTR

Page 102

Page 90

Saumur

Page 116

Page 80

Chinon

Loches

Châtellerault

**POITOU
CHARENTES**

Poitiers

Le Blanc

ILE DE FRANCE

Evry

Melun

Fontainebleau

Sens

Page 248

Orléans

Montargis

Page 240

Auxerre

Page 212

BOURGOGNE

Page 228

omorantin-
nthenay

Vierzon   Page 268

Page 260

Bourges

Nevers

Châteauroux

La Châtre

Moulins

Above
Statue of Joan of Arc, Orléans

Introduction

The Loire Valley today is one of the world's greatest tourist areas, enjoyed by visitors throughout the year. This is not just a recent phenomenon, however. Long before the advent of mass tourism, its mild climate and natural beauty attracted royalty and pleasure-loving nobility from far and wide.

These first visitors built mighty castles to protect themselves in an era of almost constant feuding. Then, in the 16th century, as life in France gradually became more peaceful and the influence of the Renaissance began to spread, the need for fortification declined. Instead, comfort and decoration became the priorities. Beautiful country houses were built, carefully positioned to make the most of the landscape, and furnished sumptuously.

The legacy of those times is an astonishing mixture of châteaux open to the public. These range from ruined castles to elegant mansions that are still family homes. Most are architectural masterpieces with striking exteriors, often rich in detail. Some of the interiors are bare, some decorated with just a few token items which hint at their past, and some fully furnished – often overwhelmingly so to modern eyes! Adding further to the pleasure of a visit, many have extensive gardens that are a delight to stroll around.

In some châteaux the visitor is free to wander alone; in others a guided tour is compulsory. Some are further brought to life by imaginative *son-et-lumière* presentations. In many there is far more to see than can be absorbed in a single visit, especially if something particular catches the eye and sets the imagination racing; perhaps a dainty turret, a grand staircase, a secret door, a voluptuous portrait or a dank dungeon. Who knows what pageantry, feasting, intrigues and passion each château must have witnessed over the centuries?

But exploring châteaux is only one of the pleasures of a stay in the Loire Valley. The countryside may be largely flat but there are beautiful views to enjoy. The area is well endowed, too, with historic towns and tranquil villages, magnificent churches and a remarkable diversity of museums whose collections range as widely as masks, mushrooms, military tanks and – inevitably – wine. Most unusual of all is the underground life in some of the old *tuffeau* (tufa) caves, originally quarried to provide stone for building the châteaux but now used inventively as homes, museums or restaurants.

Throughout the area, there is accommodation to suit every taste, from grand château-hotels to small, family-run inns. Everywhere, too, the local love of good food, particularly fish and cheeses, is obvious, complemented of course by the excellent local wines. Pausing at wineries to do some sampling, and perhaps to invest in a case or two, is an essential part of most visitors' itinerary.

So the Loire Valley certainly deserves its popularity. Indeed, for most people, a single visit is not enough. Many return again and again, including the large number of Parisians who regard it as the ideal location for a holiday home.

Most important of all is the Loire itself, the longest river in France. Its influence on the areas through which it flows is reflected by the fact that no fewer than six of France's *départements* include it in their name: Loire, Haute-Loire, Loire-Atlantique, Indre-et-Loire, Maine-et-Loire and Saône-et-Loire. And countless towns and villages on its banks proudly call themselves 'sur-Loire'. Starting far to the south, high in the mountains of the Cévennes, it flows in a great semicircle – first north, then west – to the Atlantic. On the way it is joined by more than a hundred tributaries, including several that are important rivers in their own right like the Cher, Vienne, Maine and Sarthe. By the time it reaches the area covered in this book, it is often as wide as a lake. For centuries much of the adjoining land was prone to devastating floods. Even in towns, people had to resort to boats, many were drowned and buildings were washed away. Today, however, its flow is much more controlled, thanks largely to the long embankments built beside it.

Until the arrival of railways, the Loire was an important highway, busy with cargo boats. Similarly, the construction of bridges across it, often architectural gems in their own right that remain to this day, put paid to the many little ferries that once linked its banks. Now, by comparison, the water seems quiet and tranquil – but ever picturesque. For the touring traveller in this region, that special combination of peacefulness and beauty is a recurring one, making for many enduring memories of time spent in discovering the delights of the Loire Valley.

Below
Saumur

Travel facts

Accommodation

France (for Loire Valley websites, see pages 17–18):
France (for Loire
www.francetourism.com
(French Tourist Office site
in the USA with useful
accommodation and trip-
planning pages);
www.holidayfrance.org.uk
(UK tour operators
specialising in France);
www.gites-de-france.fr
(Gîtes de France site);
www.logishotels.com
(Logis de France site).

Accommodation in the Loire Valley ranges from stylish 5-star hotels to country campsites, and everything in between. There are hundreds of small, moderately priced independent family-run hotels. A particular feature of the region is privately owned châteaux that take paying guests. Almost every little town, and many a tiny village, has at least one clean, adequately comfortable, unpretentious hotel (or, sometimes, *restaurant avec chambres*, restaurant with rooms). Standards range from the extremely basic to the height of elegance. Pricing is normally for the room, not per person. A star system is in force, but some traditional hotels in both town and country fall short of even a single star, while others far exceed the requirements for the maximum grade '4-star Luxe'. Most are 2–3 stars. Self-catering *gîtes* – usually country cottages – are often a bargain, though facilities can be basic. In this region, it is always wise to book ahead, and if you want to visit during high season (July–August), it's wise to plan everything a couple of months in advance.

The major international hotel chains are represented in the Loire region. The big French chains, all with several hotels in the region, include:
• **Campanile** – popular national chain of motels with restaurant; reliable, all identical, mid-price.
• **Formule 1, Etap Hotel, Balladins, Bonsaï, Première Class** – all economy motels, modern but minimalist.
• **Ibis** – modern, functional, town hotels, mid- to low-budget.
• **Le Méridien** – smart, modern high-quality chain.
• **Sofitel** – luxurious modern hotels.

Useful French hotel and restaurant federations include:
• **Relais & Châteaux** – independently owned, top of the market, old-fashioned luxury and (especially those designated as *Relais Gourmand*) with excellent food. Free handbook from French Government Tourist Offices abroad. *www.relaischateaux.com*
• **Relais Routiers** – truckdrivers' stops; inexpensive roadside restaurants, often with a few basic rooms above. Recognisable by a blue and red circular sign outside. *www.relais-routiers.com*
• **Relais du Silence** – good-quality hotels in especially quiet locations. Bookable online at *www.silencehotel.com*
• **Logis de France** – over 3,000 small, unpretentious, family-run independent hotels, nearly all with a good, inexpensive restaurant

Conversion tables

Distances

Metric	Imperial
1m	3ft 3in
5m	16ft 6in
10m	33ft
50m	164ft
100m	330ft
1km	0.75 mile
2km	1.5 miles
5km	3 miles
10km	6 miles
20km	12.5 miles
50km	31 miles
100km	62 miles

Weight

Kg	Lb
1	2
2	4.5
5	11
10	22
20	45
50	110
75	165
100	220

Fluid measures

Litres	Imperial gallon
5	1.1
10	2.2
20	4.4
50	11

Area

1 hectare = 2.471 acres
1 acre = 0.4 hectares

(half of them specialise in regional dishes); rooms are adequate and reasonably priced. Free handbook from French Government Tourist Offices abroad. *www.logishotels.com*

• **Château Acceuil** or **Chambres d'Hôtes en Châteaux et Demeures Privés** is an alternative B&B in the Loire where the 'guesthouses' are privately owned châteaux and mansions. Details of them can be found in a variety of handbooks available from local regional tourism authorities (CRTs) or from French tourist offices abroad.

• **Gîtes de France** are simple cottages rented as inexpensive self-catering holiday accommodation. Some are bookable in the UK from Brittany Ferries, *tel: 08703 665 333*. For more information, visit the Gîtes de France website, *www.gites-de-france.fr*, which is in French and English and allows online booking of some *gîtes*.

• **Villages de Vacances (holiday villages)**, either for all the family or for children only, are popular with the French. Details from national and regional tourist offices. *www.ternelia.com*

Other options include:

• **Chambres d'Hôtes** ('guest rooms'), often announced by a simple handmade sign on a front gate, are homely B&B stopovers (often with evening meal too), usually in ordinary family homes in rural areas. *www.chambres-hotes.org* and *www.bedbreak.co.uk*

• **Meublés** (literally, 'furnished') are short-let apartments suitable for holidays. There are some in all the major towns. Contact local tourist offices for a list, and they can also make bookings.

• **Campsites** – France has over 11,000 approved campsites. They're graded with stars: anything above 2 stars will have hot showers and good facilities. *Camping à la Ferme*, campsites on farms, tend to be more basic. Four-star and the even better 4-star 'Grand Comfort' sites have excellent amenities, a play area, shop and sports facilities, often including a swimming pool. *Castels et Camping*, mainly in superb locations, is a federation of top-quality campsites (*www.les-castels.com*).

Airports

Nantes Airport is the principal airport for the western Loire. It receives flights from London and, in summer, from Montreal, operated by both full-service carriers and budget airlines from the UK. Low-cost airlines also serve the other Loire Valley regional airports, Angers and Tours. The rest of the Loire Valley region is within easy reach of Paris Orly. Nantes Airport is to be replaced by the new Aéroport du Grand Ouest, at Notre-Dame-des-Landes, with a projected opening date in 2015.

Children

Children in France strike their British, American and Australasian counterparts (and their parents) as very well behaved and fairly strictly disciplined. Children are expected to sit quietly at the table and eat grown-up food. On the other hand, there are plenty of facilities and entertainments for children and they are welcomed everywhere.

Climate

The Loire Valley is known as the 'Garden of France', and gardens need watering. Humid conditions and rain are possible all year. The region enjoys a long, warm summer, from around May to September, with daytime temperatures often reaching above 20°C. Autumn is bright, mild and comfortably warm. Occasional heavy downpours are a feature of the later summer and autumn. Spring is mild and pleasant. In winter it can be damp, though not especially cold, and in the larger valleys even milder.

Currency

France is part of the eurozone, throughout which the currency is the euro, divided into 100 euro cents (which in France only are also officially known as centimes). There are notes of 5, 10, 20, 50, 100, 200 and 500 euros, and coins of 1 and 2 euros, and of 1, 2, 5, 10, 20 and 50 cents. Euros are readily available from all ATMs (Cash Dispensers) using credit cards and bank cards displaying the appropriate international symbols. If entering or leaving France with more than €7,600 in cash, it must be declared to Customs.

Customs regulations

Non-EU citizens, aged over 16 and spending less than 6 months in France, may be able to reclaim VAT (*TVA* in French) on any items costing over €175 purchased for export. At the time of the purchase, present your passport and ask for a *bordereau* form. On leaving France, you should be sure to have the *bordereau* validated by French Customs. *www.douane.gouv.fr*
• For travellers returning to the **UK and other EU countries**, there are no restrictions except that all goods brought back must be for personal consumption and must be legal for private possession. In the UK HM Customs & Excise still maintain (unenforceable) limits on the amount of alcoholic drinks and tobacco that will be considered reasonable 'for personal use'. These propose up to 90 litres of wine, 10 litres of spirits and 3,200 cigarettes. More information can be found at *www.hmce.gov.uk*
• Travellers returning to the **USA** have an allowance on goods for personal use of up to $800, but most plants or foods are prohibited. You will find US Customs listed in the 'US Government' section of your local phone directory under the Treasury Department listing.

Electricity

The power supply in France is 220 volts. Circular 2-pin plugs are used.

Entry formalities

Travellers from the UK, USA, Australia, New Zealand and Canada do not need a visa for visits of less than 90 days. South Africans must apply for a visa from a French embassy. You can check visa requirements at www.diplomatie.gouv.fr

Festivals

Mar:
• *Festival de Pâques*, Chartres;
• *Festival de Jazz*, Chartres;
• *Conteries Mars* (carnival and festival), Blois;
Easter Sat: Easter Vigil (at 2200), St-Benoît-sur-Loire;
Easter weekend: St-François Fair, Sully-sur-Loire;
Easter Mon: Easter Egg Festival, Pagode de Chanteloup.

Apr:
• International Guitar Festival, Vendôme;
• 24-hour motorcycle race, Le Mans.
End Apr:
• Horsemanship Competitions, Saumur;
• Evening Carnival Parade, Cholet.
Whitsun:
• Wine Fair, Vouvray;
• Wine Fair, Sancerre;
• Rhododendron Festival, Châteauneuf-sur-Loire.

May:
Weekend nearest 1 May:
• *Fête du Crottin de Chavignol*, Sancerre;
• Harpsichord Festival, Chartres;

You may also call US Customs in Washington, DC; *tel: (202) 927-6724*. For US Treasury customs information, consult *www.cbp.gov*
• For **Australia**, the allowance is up to $900-worth of goods, including 250 cigarettes and 2.25 litres of alcoholic drinks. Foods and anything containing wood or plant material may be prohibited. *www.customs.gov.au*
• For **New Zealand**, the allowance is $700-worth of goods, including 200 cigarettes and 6 bottles of alcoholic drinks. Foods and anything containing wood or plant material may be prohibited. *www.customs.govt.nz*
• In general, all goods brought back to **Canada** must be declared. *Tel: 1-800-461-9999* for more information or see *www.cbsa-asfc.gc.ca*
• **South Africans** can bring back goods for personal use, including gifts, tax-free including 1 litre spirits, 2 litres wine and 450 cigarettes. Other goods up to a value of R12,000 may be brought in but are taxed at 20 per cent.

For visitors entering France from the UK or any other EU country, there are no limits on legal articles for ordinary personal use. For those entering from outside the EU, the limits are explained on the website *www.ambafrance-us.org*

Drinking

The Loire Valley is famous for its fine wines, but everyday drinking in the region's homes and bars is similar to elsewhere in France. Even here, the Loire's great wines are reserved for special occasions or an evening out. Of the local wines, the most common and least expensive are fruity white Sauvignon de Touraine and sweeter Rosé d'Anjou. Drink plays a vital part in life, but it is rare to see a local person drunk. The French do not usually drink with the intention of getting drunk at all, but to enhance appetite, conversation and companionship. In any bar or brasserie, not only alcoholic and soft drinks are served but also coffee (including decaffeinated), hot chocolate, tea and herbal teas.

Drinks

de l'eau minérale – mineral water
de l'eau gazeuse ou plate – sparkling or still water
une bière – any name-brand German or Belgian beer
un demi or *une bière à la pression* – a glass of draught lager-style beer
un café – espresso (the French keep going with frequent shots all day)
un café-crème (usually *un grand crème*) – coffee with milk (the French usually drink this only for breakfast)
un déca – decaffeinated coffee
un thé (*nature, citron* or *au lait*) – tea (black, with lemon or with milk)
une tisane – herbal tea

5–6 May: *Grande Brocante* street market, Orléans; **7–8 May:** *Fêtes Johanniques* (Joan of Arc festival), Orléans.

Jun:
• International Jazz Festival, Orléans;
• 24-hour motor race, Le Mans;
• International Classical Music Festival (at weekends), Sully-sur-Loire.
Last weekend in Jun: solstice bonfire and market, Chaumont-sur-Loire.
End Jun:
• *Les Orientales* music festival, St-Florent-le-Viel;
• Touraine Music and Dance Festivals, region around Tours;
End Jun–mid-Jul: Anjou Festival (one of France's main arts festivals), Angers and throughout Anjou.
Jun–Oct: International Garden Festival, Chaumont-sur-Loire.

Jul:
Loir Music Festival, Montoire-sur-le-Loir;
First weekend Jul: *Les Scénomanies* (street theatre), Le Mans.
Early Jul: *Les Affranchis* (festival of street entertainment), La Flèche;
Third weekend Jul: Carnival, Gien;
Last weekend Jul: Military Tattoo, Saumur;
Jul–Aug: International Organ Festival, Chartres.

Aug:
First weekend Aug: Rabelais Market, Chinon;
Mid-Aug:
• Wine Fair, Vouvray;
• World Folklore Festival, Montoire-sur-le-Loir;

Right
Wine museum, Tours

un chocolat chaud – hot chocolate
un Miky – cold chocolate drink
un kir – an aperitif of dry white wine and *crème de cassis* (blackcurrant liqueur)
Suze, Noilly Prat, Dubonnet and Martini – popular brand-name aperitifs
un panaché – shandy (mixed beer and lemonade)
un coca/un coca light – Coca Cola/Diet Coke
un diabolo menthe (green) or *diabolo grenadine* (red) – lemonade mixed with brightly coloured mint- or pomegranate-flavoured syrup
un jus d'ananas or *un jus de poire* – pineapple juice or pear juice, both of which are popular
un jus d'orange – bottled orange juice
une orange pressée – freshly squeezed orange juice
un Orangina – fizzy orange drink
sirop – fruit-flavoured sweet drink served in either still or fizzy water
du vin (*rouge/blanc/rosé/doux/mousseux*) – wine (red/white/rosé/sweet/sparkling). No need to ask for dry – it's all dry unless you specify sweet.
un pichet/demi-pichet (*d'eau/de vin blanc/de vin rouge/de vin rosé*) – 1-litre carafe/half-litre carafe (of water/white wine/red wine/rosé wine)
See also The wines of the Loire (*page 35*).

Eating out

Most French eating places offer a choice of about three *menus*, that is, *prix fixe* (fixed price) set meals, as well as the *à la carte* menu, a list of individually priced dishes. The price difference reflects not differences in quality but in the number of courses and difficulty of preparation. In general, to get the best out of a French restaurant, order one of the *menus*. Prices will usually be higher if you pick and choose from the *carte*. The day's menus are always displayed outside the restaurant.

Prices must include service and all taxes. It's not necessary to give any extra tip, though a few cents is often left for the waiter on a café table. Vin compris means wine included (usually about a quarter or third of a litre of house wine per person).

Away from resorts and big cities, it can be difficult to find something to eat outside normal mealtimes. The lunch break lasts from 1200 to about 1400. Sunday lunch, often taken *en famille* at a local restaurant, lasts until 1500. A little more flexibility comes into dinner hours, from 1900 to 2200, though 2000 is still the usual time to start dinner. Brasseries are bars that generally serve food at any time. A *salon de thé* serves pastries and other light snacks with tea or coffee.

- Wine Fair, Pouilly-sur-Loire;
End Aug: Wine Fair, Sancerre.

Sept:
8 Sept: pilgrimage, St-André-de-Cléry;
Mid–end Sept: Annual Jazz Festival, Montlouis-sur-Loire.

Oct:
Rockomotives, Vendôme;
End Oct: Oyster Fair, Sancerre.

Mid-Nov: Wine Fair, Vouvray.

24 Dec:
- *Messes des Naulets* (mass in dialect), different Anjou church each year;
- Christmas vigil and Mass (at 2200), St-Benoît-sur-Loire.

Useful websites

France:
www.holidayfrance.org.uk – UK-based site of tour operators specialising in France.

www.francetourism.com – French Tourist Office in USA has useful accommodation and trip-planning pages.

The Loire Valley:
www.visaloire.com (Centre Val de Loire).

www.regioncentre.fr (Centre region).

www.berrylindre.com (Berry and Indre).

www.chartres-tourisme.com (Chartres and its region).

www.berrylecher.com (Berry region, Cher and Indre *départements*)

Right
Tourist office, Montrichard

Health

It's usually possible to see a general practitioner quickly without an appointment, or to phone to request a visit. For doctors, medicines and hospital treatment, payment must be made on the spot. Keep doctors' and pharmacists' receipts – you will need them when claiming reimbursement, whether through your EHIC Card (European Health Insurance Card, available free from *www.ehic.org.uk*, by phoning *0845 606 2030*, or from post offices) or from your travel insurance.

Information

For French tourist office websites worldwide, including email addresses, see *www.franceguide.com*. These are now:
- **Australia:** Maison de la France (French Government Tourist Office), *Level 13, 25 Bligh Street, Sydney, NSW 2000; tel: 02-9231 5244; fax: 02-9221 8682; email: info.au@franceguide.com*
- **Canada:** Maison de la France (French Government Tourist Office), *1981 av. McGill College, Suite 490, Montreal H3A 2W9; tel: (514) 288-2026; fax: (514) 845-4868; email: canada@franceguide.com*
- **Ireland:** Maison de la France (French Government Tourist Office), *no office open to the public; tel: 01 560 235235; email: info.ie@ franceguide.com*
- **UK:** Maison de la France (French Government Tourist Office), *The French Travel Centre, Lincoln House, 300 High Holborn, London WC1V 7JH; tel: 09068 244123 (premium rate); email: info.uk@ franceguide.com*
- **USA:** Maisons de la France (French Government Tourist Offices) can all deal with enquiries emailed to *info.us@franceguide.com* or by phone on *514 288 1904*. The offices are located at: *444 Madison Ave, New York, 10022 NY; fax: 212 838 78 55. 9454 Wilshire Blvd – Suite 715, Beverly Hills, 90212 CA; fax: 310 276 28 35; email:*

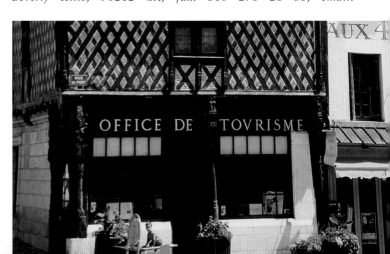

www.loire-france.com (the Loire Valley from Sancerre to St Nazaire).

www.tourism-touraine.com (Touraine district, Loire Valley).

www.chambordcountry.com (Loir-et-Cher département, Loire and Loir Valleys).

www.tourismloiret.com (Loiret département).

www.coeur-de-france.com – useful promotional site for Centre region; in French.

www.paysdelaloire.fr (Pays de la Loire).

www.loiredeschateaux.com (Blois-Chambord area).

info.losangeles@franceguide.com. *Consulate General of France, 205 N. Michigan Ave, Suite 3770, Chicago 60601, IL; email: info. chicago@franceguide.com*

• **Comité Régional du Tourisme (Regional Tourism Committee) in the Loire Valley:** CRT Centre (covering central and eastern parts of the region): *37 av. de Paris, Orléans; tel: 08 10 24 02 40; fax: 02 38 79 95 10; email: crtl.centre@crtlcentre.com; www.loirevalleytourism.com* CRT Pays de la Loire (covering western parts of the region): *2 r. de la Loire, Nantes; tel: 02 40 48 24 20; www.paysdelaloire.fr*

Maps

Tourist offices can provide city and country maps printed in French and sometimes also in English. City brochures usually have a map of the city printed inside.

Michelin regional maps 517 (Pays de Loire) and 518 (Centre Berry-Nivernais) cover most of the Loire Valley in detail. For Eure-et-Loir *département*, including Chartres, map 514 (Ile-de-France) is needed. The annual Michelin motoring atlas is useful for touring in the Loire region and further afield. The *Michelin Atlas Autoroutier* (Motorway Atlas) is a handbook detailing facilities, junctions, etc on the *autoroutes*. IGN regional maps are an alternative to Michelin, and IGN local large-scale maps are ideal for walking.

Museums

Basic opening times for most museums in the region are *0900–1200, 1400–1800, closed Mon or Tue and some national holidays*, with many variations (sometimes with different opening times on different days and different months). Hours are often extended in July and August.

Below
Bridge over the Loire at Blois

Opening times

Shops: typically *Tue–Sat 0900–1200 or 1230, and 1500–1900*. Food shops may open earlier in the morning, but later in the afternoon, and some (especially *pâtisseries*) open on Sun am. In cities, tourist centres or resorts, shops may keep longer hours or stay open all day every day.
Department stores: *Mon–Sat 0900–1830* (often with one or more later evenings per week).
Hypermarkets: *Mon–Sat 0900–2200.*
Banks: either *Mon–Fri* or *Tue–Sat 0900–1200 and 1400–1700*, with local variations. Banks always close on local and national holidays.
Petrol stations: usually around *0700–2200 daily.*
Post offices: *Mon–Fri 0800–1900, Sat 0800–1200*. Stamps and envelopes can usually be bought from newsagents.

Insurance

UK citizens should travel with the EHIC Card (see page 17) entitling reimbursement of part of any medical expenses incurred, as well as travel insurance covering medical emergencies. All others are advised to have full medical cover as part of their travel insurance policy. For motorists, third-party insurance is compulsory. Comprehensive motor insurance issued by UK insurers is valid in the EU (a 'Green Card' is no longer required, though some insurers wish to be informed that you are going abroad).

Regional Nature Parks

Regional Nature Parks control and oversee development in unique or threatened natural and cultural environments. The Loire region contains one Regional Nature Park, Loire-Anjou-Touraine, lying between Angers and Tours, and reaching south as far as Richelieu. For information, contact the Park's office at: *Maison du Parc, 7 r. Jeanne d'Arc, 49730 Montsoreau; tel: 02 41 53 66 00; fax: 02 41 53 66 09; email: info@parc-loire-anjou-touraine.fr; www.parc-loire-anjou-touraine.fr*

Tourist offices: usually *Mon–Sat 0900–1200 and 1400–1800.* Longer hours, and no midday closing, in season.
Businesses: *Mon–Fri 0900–1200 and 1400–1800.*
Bars: *0700 or 0800 to 2300 or 2400.* Some stay open later, especially in resorts.
Restaurants: *1200–1400 and 1900–2200.* Most restaurants have one or more days off per week.
Churches: usually *daily 0900–1700.*

Packing

Bring a hat, sunglasses, light clothes, cool footwear, plus a sweater and light raincoat. If you're planning to visit upmarket nightspots or classical concerts, a smart dress or jacket or smart casual wear could be appropriate. It can be cool even on summer evenings, and if you are attending outdoor evening events such as a *son-et-lumière*, it's wise to be prepared. In winter take a thick sweater and warm coat.

Postal services

Postcards and letters are charged at the same rate for all EU destinations, with delivery within a few days. Stamps are available in newsagents. Airmail rates for letters to other destinations are much higher and items have to be weighed at a post office (indicated by a *La Poste* sign). Letter boxes are yellow.

Sport

River cruising – most of the Loire is too difficult for inexperienced sailors, but certain sections of the river, as well as the region's other rivers, provide plenty of scope for river cruising, especially along the Cher and the Loir. Several foreign and local hire companies and package operators provide craft and make all arrangements.
Walking – the region is criss-crossed by marked footpaths, especially through the forests and along the riverbanks. The Angers, Tours and Orléans tourist offices have information for ramblers.
Cycling – a relatively easy region for cycling, this is a popular way to explore the forests and along the major rivers.
Golf – there are around 20 excellent golf courses in the Loire Valley.
Riding – there are several riding schools and centres, notably the National Riding School at St-Hilaire-St-Florent, near Saumur. For information on riding holidays, contact the **Association Régionale de Tourisme Equestre** at the following addresses:
for Val-de-Loire Océan region (western *départements*) – *La Senserie, 44522 La Roche-Blanche; tel: 02 40 98 41 87;* for Val de Loire Centre (central and eastern *départements*) – *Maison des Sports, 32 r. Alain Gerbault, 41000 Blois; tel: 02 54 42 95 60.*

National holidays

I Jan: New Year's Day
Mar/Apr: Easter Monday
I May: Labour Day
8 May: VE Day
May: Ascension
May/Jun: Pentecost (Whit
Monday)
14 Jul: National Day
15 Aug: Assumption
I Nov: All Saints
II Nov: Armistice Day
25 Dec: Christmas Day
When a national holiday
falls on a Sunday, the next
day is taken as a holiday
instead.

Public transport

Town buses (called *bus*)
are available in all cities
from about *0700–2100*.

Trains are useful for
excursions, with stations in
almost all towns.

Taxis are available in all
towns; these are licensed
private cars, which usually
have to be called by phone.

Safety and security

All towns and rural areas
included here are generally
very safe. However, it is
wise to take certain
precautions: do not wear
ostentatious jewellery,
openly handle large sums
of cash, or leave anything
of value on view in cars.
To call the police, dial *17*.

Opposite
Kayaking on the Loire at
Château des Ormeaux

Telephones

With few exceptions, public phones in France require a pre-paid
phonecard (*une télécarte*), available from newsagents, tabacs and other
shops.
Directory Enquiries: *12*
International Directory Enquiries: *3212*
Operator: *13*
Police: *17*
To call the UK from France, the international dialling code is 00 44.
The code for Australia is 00 61, USA and Canada 00 1, New Zealand
00 64. Calling from the UK and most other countries, the code
for France is 00 33. From the USA and Canada, the code is 001 33.
For more information about using the phone in France, visit
www.francetelecom.fr/en

Time

France uses Central European Standard Time and Central European
Daylight Saving Time. These are 1 hour ahead of UK time and 5 hours

Tipping

Restaurants – included, not necessary.
Bars – included, not necessary, but you could leave a few cents.
Taxis – up to €1.
Hotels, room service – included, not necessary.
Tour guides – €1–2.
Toilet attendants – a few cents.

Toilets

Usually called WC (pronounced *veh-seh*) or *toilettes*. Free or small charge in bars. Small charge for attended public toilets; no charge if not attended. Many are automatic self-cleaning (these can be unsafe for children).

ahead of US Eastern Standard Time. Central European Daylight Saving Time ('Summer Time') starts at 0200 on the last Sunday in March and ends at 0300 on the last Sunday in October.

Travellers with disabilities

For parking, use your Europe-wide blue card just as in the UK. Vehicles modified for a disabled driver and showing 'disabled' on the registration document are entitled to lower *autoroute* tolls.
Accessibility information for tourists available from:
Association des Paralysés de France *17 blvd Auguste Blanqui, 75013 Paris; tel: 01 40 78 69 00; www.apf.asso.fr*
CNRH *236bis r. de Tolbiac, 75013 Paris; tel: 01 53 80 66 66.*
RADAR *12 City Forum, 250 City Rd, London EC1V 8AF; tel: 020 7250 3222; email: radar@radar.org.uk; www.radar.org.uk.* Also check out *www.yanous.com/English.html* for helpful hints.

World Heritage Site

The Loire Valley was declared a World Heritage Site in the year 2000.

Driver's guide

Automobile clubs

Members of UK motoring organisations (AA or RAC) can extend their accident insurance and breakdown services to France. Both organisations offer a wide range of information and advice as well as suggesting itineraries and routes. *www.theaa.com* offers a free, turn-by-turn route map of your journey. See also *www.rac.co.uk* and *www.viamichelin.co.uk*

Autoroutes

Most of the French *autoroutes* are toll roads. The most common system of charging (*péage*) involves taking a ticket from a machine at the start of the toll section, which raises an automatic barrier. On leaving the system, or at an intermediate tollbooth, the ticket is presented and the amount to pay is displayed on an illuminated sign. Payment may be made in euros or by credit card. Signatures are not normally required. Traveller's cheques cannot usually be used for tolls. On *autoroutes* speed is sometimes automatically computed from time of entry and distance covered on arrival at the tollbooth. If a speeding offence is disclosed you may be prosecuted.

Accidents

You must STOP after any accident. You can be in serious trouble if you don't. Call *15, 17* or *18* to alert the Ambulance, Police or Fire Service as appropriate, or use the EU universal emergency number *112*. On an *autoroute* or main road, use one of the bright-orange free SOS emergency roadside telephones located at frequent intervals.

Give whatever aid you are capable of to any person injured or in peril. It is an offence not to do this if it lies within your ability. This applies whether you are driver, passenger or witness. Safeguard against a secondary accident. Hazard lights – warning triangle – signal to other traffic. Exchange details of vehicles, drivers' insurance, etc. (French cars display insurance details on a windscreen sticker.) Complete a 'European Accident Statement' form – ask your insurers for this before you leave; the French driver will almost certainly have one. This forms a factual record. It is not an admission of fault. Note as many details as you can. Photographs? Witnesses? If someone has been injured, you must inform the police. If you have damaged someone else's vehicle or property and you are unable to give the owner your details, you must inform the police. The police will not usually take details where an accident involves material damage only, unless there is evidence of an offence such as dangerous or drink driving. Inform your insurers as soon as possible.

Breakdowns

If you are on an *autoroute*, stop your vehicle on the hard shoulder, getting it as far to the right as possible. On ordinary roads, consider using the verge but beware of roadside ditches. Hazard lights on. Place a warning triangle at least 30m from the scene, visible from 100m away. (Remember, it can be very dangerous to walk on the hard shoulder of any motorway.) You and your passengers are probably safer out of the vehicle and well up the verge away from the traffic.

If you need assistance on an *autoroute* you must use one of the free roadside telephones to connect you with the police. You cannot arrange recovery yourself, even if you are a member of a breakdown service. No garage will send a recovery vehicle on to an *autoroute* without police permission. There is a fixed scale of charges (€112 from 0800–1800 on weekdays, €168 outside these hours and at weekends). You may not carry out a DIY tow on an *autoroute* and you may only do so on an ordinary road for 'a few metres' in an emergency. Makeshift towing is strongly discouraged and usually voids French car insurance.

Documents

Members of EU countries and US citizens only need a valid national driving licence, but an international driving licence is essential for other nationals. Provisional licences are not valid and drivers must be over the age of 18. UK photo card licences are best. Paper licences are lawful but further proof of ID may be required. Registration papers (a logbook) and a letter of authorisation if the car is not registered in your name, insurance papers and Test Certificate (MoT) (originals – photocopies are not valid) and a nationality plate must be carried. The above documents must be produced at the time on request by police. An immediate fine may be imposed if they are not to hand. For UK drivers, a 'Green Card' is not required in France for car insurance. Your certificate of insurance issued in Britain conforms to French legal needs. However, this is minimum legal cover. You should ask your insurers to extend your normal, full cover for use abroad for the period of your stay. Continental breakdown insurance is recommended. Should you visit the state of Andorra in the Pyrenees you will require a 'Green Card'. Holders of US insurance must take out a European policy.

Continental breakdown insurance is strongly recommended and one phone call is all it takes to hand the whole problem over to multi-lingual operators who are experts in sorting things out.

Caravans and camper vans (Trailers and RVs)

France is probably the most 'camping and caravanning friendly' country in Europe and there are numerous attractive campsites from economical to de luxe in the area covered by this guide. Booking ahead is really only necessary at the height of the season. The Alan Rogers' campsite guides are very useful. *Camping sauvage* ('wild' camping) is completely banned. Camping in State Forests or any wooded area is virtually always prohibited because of the serious risk of fire. Overnight parking of motorhomes is frequently permitted (and often free) in the central square of smaller towns and villages where water and toilet facilities are available. There are no formalities about bringing a caravan into France if your stay is for less than six months.

Motorhomes and cars towing trailers have to pay a higher toll on *autoroutes*. Some caravanners use the facilities of the *autoroute aires de repos* (rest areas) for an overnight stop. This is quite lawful, as your *autoroute* ticket lasts for at least 24 hours. If you do this, you are advised to use common sense and stop in a well-lit spot, in view of passers-by. Thefts and break-ins are, unfortunately, not unknown.

Speed limits for cars towing trailers or caravans are the same as solo vehicles. Occasionally, there may be a reduced speed limit for caravans on long declines. This is to reduce the danger of instability when the caravan is being neither pulled nor braked but is 'floating' behind the towing vehicle.

If you intend driving in the Pyrenees or the Alps (and particularly if you are towing a trailer) you should remember that engine efficiency decreases with altitude, by about 10 per cent per 900m. This can mean that a heavily laden non-turbo car, just coping with the additional load at sea level, may not manage the incline as it climbs higher.

Driving in the Loire Valley

There are three classes of road – motorway (*autoroute* – A); national road (*route nationale* – RN or N); and departmental road (*route départementale* – D). Major roads also have an E number in green indicating that they are part of the European route network. The French Ministry of Transport has transferred responsibility for most former N roads to *départements* and these have been reclassified as D roads.

Autoroutes are of excellent quality with frequent rest and service areas, offering the fastest means of covering long distances by car. The A10 (Paris–Bordeaux) runs between Orléans and Tours. The A11

Drinking and driving

The French limit is 50mg of alcohol per 100ml of blood and penalties increase sharply if an 80mg limit is exceeded. There is a determined campaign to reduce incidents of drinking and driving, and penalties are severe, with heavy fines and imprisonment. Random breath tests are common and you should not underestimate the powers of the police or the consequences of failing a test. A large fine may be demanded on the spot and your vehicle may be impounded until it is paid. Any disqualification is immediate. If you are the sole driver, you will be stranded and any 'get-you-home' insurance will be invalidated by reason of you having committed an illegal act.

Essentials

You *must* have a red warning triangle and hazard lights in case of accident, a headlight dip adjusted to the right, a first-aid kit, a high-visibility jacket and spare bulbs. You'll also need nationality (GB, IRL, etc) plates (or a sticker, usually supplied with Channel crossing tickets), a torch and a petrol container.

Petrol = *Essence*
Unleaded = *Sans plomb 95 and 98 octane*
4-star = *Super*
Diesel = *Gazole, Gasoil* or *Diésel*
LPG = *GPL*

(Paris–Nantes) gives access to Chartres and Angers and the western part of the region. The A71 runs from Orléans to Bourges. A short stretch of the valley west of Tours has no *autoroute* access; the A85 then starts and continues to Angers and Nantes.

While the *autoroutes* offer virtually the shortest distance between two points, the RN (*route nationale*) and D (*départmentale*) roads are well maintained and make it easy to avoid busy main highways. Roads in town may be of a poor standard, and are often cobbled. While locals may drive normally over cobbles, it would be wiser to protect your car's suspension by driving gently on these streets. Some country lanes may be of a poor standard, too.

Driving rules

Traffic drives on the right in France. A fundamental driving rule is that traffic from the right has priority at junctions. In practice, priority from the right applies mostly in towns and on rural roads. Main roads are clearly signed as such by a yellow and white diamond sign, which is repeated every 5km, or the conventional triangle showing a broad vertical black stripe with a narrow horizontal line crossing it (*see page 27*). Junctions marked with a simple X, or not marked at all, are governed by the 'Priority from the Right' rule. Any unmarked junction in a town or village must be treated as subject to this rule.

The rule applies to junctions and does not mean giving way to vehicles coming out of lay-bys, driveways, garages, parking spaces, etc. You should, however, give way to buses moving away from a bus stop.

Traffic on roundabouts has priority and drivers entering the system must wait for a safe opportunity. Unfortunately, French drivers are very haphazard about signalling their intentions on roundabouts and care is needed.

Pedestrians have right of way when on marked crossings, but the practice of stopping for a pedestrian waiting to use a crossing is unknown. If you decide to display such courtesy, remember that following drivers may not anticipate your action.

Fuel

Service stations are open all day but are normally closed on Sundays and national holidays. If a national holiday falls on, say, a Thursday, it is common practice to take the Friday off as well, rather than spoil a good weekend. This can mean that petrol stations are closed for four days, especially in the country. In rural areas petrol stations can be few and far between, especially on *départementale* roads.

Fuel is cheapest at big supermarkets in out-of-town retail parks (*Centres Commerciaux*) and, not surprisingly, most expensive on motorways. Keeping the fuel tank well filled is good practice.

Fines

The police/*gendarmes* have wide powers to impose on-the-spot fines for a variety of motoring offences. Speed checks are frequent and merciless. Payment must be in cash and should you not be able to pay there and then, for instance if the banks are closed and there is no ATM nearby, your vehicle and your passport may be impounded until you do. The fine is, in fact, a part payment (*amende forfaitaire*) and you may receive notification of a higher penalty later. At present such extra fines cannot be enforced abroad but EU legislation is being contemplated to make this possible.

Speed-trap detection devices are illegal, whether in use or not. The device is invariably seized and a heavy fine imposed.

In practice, if you drive sensibly, you are no more likely to be stopped or prosecuted in France than in any other country. It is the *consequences* of such a prosecution that should be considered, especially when you are on holiday.

'Inforoute'

If your car radio is equipped with RDS this will work in France, interrupting radio programmes with road news flashes (in French). You may also receive traffic news on 'Inforoute' on 107.7 MHz FM. These low-power transmitters cover the motorway routes and provide local up-to-date traffic reports, in French.

Information

You should take an up-to-date map with you. Changes in road numbers and motorway interchanges can booby-trap old editions. The Michelin 1:200 000 'yellow' maps are ideal. Free *Bison Futé* (Crafty Bison) maps, showing alternative routes using secondary roads to avoid traffic problems, are available from the French Government Tourist Office or information offices in France. These routes are well signposted, make a pleasant change from main roads and are a great help in avoiding the predictable traffic problem zones. If you want to be a 'Crafty Bison' yourself, you could try taking an early or late lunch and stay on the road between 1200 and 1400. The French drop everything for lunch and the roads become much quieter.

Parking

The Loire Valley region is predominantly rural, with few busy urban areas other than along the River Loire itself. Parking is not usually a problem outside large towns. However, in town centres, especially Tours, Amboise, Blois and Orléans, cars left in no-parking zones are generally quickly towed away without warning – often within 10 minutes of parking. Kerbside signs always make it clear what the parking regulations are in each street.

There is some free parking in Disc Parking zones, where the bays are marked out in blue. Purchase a disc (*Disque de stationnement*) at petrol stations or supermarkets. Setting your arrival time on the disc automatically displays the expiry time in a cut-out window. Meter or ticket parking follows the usual pattern. Very often parking is free 1200–1400. These times are displayed on the ticket machine.

If parking in the street, you *must* park facing the direction of travel, i.e. on the right in two-way streets. It is, in any case, bad practice to park on the left, as you may drive off forgetting to move to the correct side of the road.

It is illegal to leave a vehicle parked in the same place for more than seven days, and a lesser time in some cities. Obstructive or illegal parking, especially in cities, often results in the offending vehicle being uplifted and taken to a pound. Foreign number plates will not save you.

Some parking zones work on the basis of parking on the odd-numbered side of the street for the first fortnight of a month (1st–15th) and on the even-numbered side for the second. A special sign indicates the entry to the zone. (*See page 27*.) Changeover time is between 2030 and 2100 on the last day of each fortnight.

Headlights

All traffic must use headlights in rain or poor visibility. Right-hand-drive cars must have their headlight beam modified to prevent dazzle. This can take the form of masking off part of the headlamps (which unfortunately reduces the light output) or stick-on optical beam deflectors, which cause the headlight to dip to the right. Some vehicles with quartz-iodine headlamps cannot be modified in these ways and you should check with the car dealer. Driving with defective lights can result in a fine. The fine is less likely if you can remedy the defect right away. It is a legal requirement to carry a spare set of bulbs. Motorcycles must display headlights at all times.

Mobile phones

The use of a hand-held phone when driving is specifically forbidden. The use of hands-free phones is strongly discouraged. The only safe and legal way for the driver to use a mobile is to stop and switch off the engine beforehand.

Seat belts

Wearing of seat belts for front and rear passengers is compulsory when the vehicle engine is running. Children under ten must occupy the rear seats but an infant up to nine months may travel in the front seat if secured in an approved rear-facing seat, *but not if a passenger air bag is fitted.*

Security

Sensible care should be taken, particularly where vehicles are left for long periods in vulnerable places such as tourist site car parks. Do not leave items on view inside the car, even if you know they are of little or no value; a potential thief does not.

In the large cities it is wise to keep car doors locked and windows up, if in slow-moving traffic or while stationary at traffic lights, as thieves on motorcycles occasionally reach inside to steal valuables. If hot weather means you must have the window open, be sure that handbags, wallets, cameras, etc are well out of sight and reach and, above all, never on a passenger's lap.

Should you have the misfortune to become a victim of crime, your insurers will require you to report the circumstances to the police and obtain a record that you have done so. In rural areas go to the *Gendarmerie* and in larger towns the *Commissariat de Police.*

Speed limits

Autoroutes – 130kph (110kph in rain). If windscreen wipers are needed it's 'raining'.
Dual carriageways – 110kph (100kph in rain).
Other roads – 90kph (80kph in rain).
All built-up areas – 50kph on roads between the entrance sign to a town and departure sign (place name crossed with diagonal bar).
There's a 50kph limit on any road when visibility is less than 50m.
Drivers with less than two years' experience must not exceed the 'rain' speed limits even in fine weather.

Road signs

All major routes are clearly signed; even most minor roads have their destinations and route numbers marked. International European traffic signs are used throughout France.

accôtement non-stabilisé – soft verge
aire de repos – rest area
cédez le passage – give way
chaussée déformée – uneven surface
défense de stationner – no parking
dépassement interdit – no overtaking
déviation – diversion
gravillons – loose chippings
passage protégé – right of way
péage – toll
priorité à droite – priority to traffic from the right
priorité aux piétons – give way to pedestrians
ralentir/ralentissez – slow down
rappel – reminder of previous restriction
renseignements – information
route barrée – road closed
sens interdit – no entry
sens unique – one way
seulement riverains – residents only
sortie de camions – HGV exit
station d'essence – petrol station
stationnement gratuit – free parking
stationnement interdit – no parking
stationnement payant – paid parking
toutes directions – route for through traffic
un train peut en cacher un autre – one train may hide another
virage – bend
vous n'avez pas la priorité – you do not have priority

FRENCH ROAD SIGNS

(A)

You have Priority at *all* junctions on this road.

(B)*

You have Priority at *next* junction. (Note: important difference with A.)

(C)*

Be prepared to *Give Way* to traffic from right at next junction.

End of Priority road.

CÉDEZ LE PASSAGE

'Give Way'.

*Signs B and C may indicate a junction from either side, not necessarily a full crossroads.

VOUS N'AVEZ PAS LA PRIORITE

You do not have Priority. *Give Way* at roundabout.

Signs attached to traffic lights are valid only if lights are OFF or yellow light is flashing.

Flashing yellow light = Proceed with caution. *Give Way* to traffic on right.

BERGERAC

The red border on a town sign *means start of 50kph limit*. If surmounted by 'Priority' sign (as here), you are on the Priority road through the town.

PARKING

Disc Parking.

Parking on payment at meter.

Entry to zone where Parking is allowed first fortnight on odd-numbered side of street – second fortnight on even-numbered side.

WARNINGS

RISQUE DE VERGLAS

Risk of black ice.

Snow chains obligatory.

ALLUMEZ VOS FEUX

Switch on Headlights.

70m

Minimum distance between vehicles.

Itinéraire Bis

Alternative Route.

Déviation

Diversion.

Frequently found at tunnels.

Getting to the Loire Valley

From the UK

Option one: just get in your car and go

France's impressive and ever-increasing network of *autoroutes* (motorways) makes driving to the area straightforward. The shortest route from the UK is via St-Malo, from where Angers is only a 3hr drive.

For those travelling from the north or west of the UK, any of the western Channel crossings to Caen, Cherbourg, Le Havre or St-Malo from Portsmouth, Poole or Plymouth have the advantage of avoiding London and Paris, although they involve a longer crossing by day or overnight.

On the shorter sea route from England, the French ferry ports at the eastern end of the Channel – Boulogne, Calais and Dunkerque – all have easy links to the *autoroute* network.

Eurotunnel's car-carrying rail service through the Channel Tunnel from Folkestone takes 35 minutes and operates 24 hours a day with up to four departures an hour at peak times (when booking is recommended). Its terminal near Calais is directly linked with the *autoroute* network.

Calais to Paris is 290km. From Paris, the A10/A11 *autoroute* goes to Chartres (85km) and Le Mans (206km), both on the northern borders of the area. The A10 continues to Orléans (130km) and then southwest through Blois to Tours (236km).

Option two: rail and drive

Eurostar passenger trains run through the Channel Tunnel from London St Pancras International (some stopping at Ebbsfleet and Ashford in Kent) to Lille (1hr 30min) and to Paris (2hr 20min), where they link with SNCF's high-speed TGV trains.

- Paris to Le Mans about 1hr, Lille to Le Mans about 2hr
- Paris to Angers 1½hr, Lille to Angers 3hr
- Paris to Nantes 2hr, Lille to Nantes 4hr
- Paris to St-Pierre-des-Corps (1hr) for Tours (10min shuttle).

Reservations must be made in advance with Rail Europe (*tel: 08708 371 371; www.raileurope.co.uk*) or, in France, with SNCF (*tel: 0892 35 35 35; www.sncf.com*). Other express services go from Paris to Chartres (about 1hr), Orléans (1hr), Blois (2hr), Amboise (2½hr) and Tours (2½hr). Local services go to Bourges, Chartres and Saumur.

Cross-Channel services

Brittany Ferries *tel: 0871 244 0744; www.brittanyferries.com*

Eurostar *tel: 08432 186 186; www.eurostar.com*

LD Lines Transmanche *tel: 0810 630 304; www.transmancheferries.com*

Norfolk Line Ferries *tel: 0844 847 5042; www.norfolkline-ferries.com*

P&O Ferries *tel: 08716 645 645; www.poferries.com*

Rail Europe *tel: 08448 484 064; www.raileurope. co.uk; or in person at Rail Europe's Travel Centre, 1 Regent Street, London W1.*

SeaFrance *tel: 0871 423 7119; www.seafrance.com*

For up-to-date details of long-distance bus, ferry and rail services, consult the *Thomas Cook European Rail Timetable*, published monthly.

Option three: fly and drive

Nantes International Airport is served by direct flights from Gatwick in the UK and elsewhere in Europe. Though west of the region, it is less than an hour from Angers by road or rail. Keep an eye on routes offered by budget airlines, sometimes including London–Tours direct flights. Airlines offer fly-drive arrangements and airports have car-hire desks. Car hire is relatively expensive in France.

Option four: a package holiday

Several British tour operators offer holidays in the Loire area, including travel and accommodation. Most are members of the Association of British Tour Operators to France (ABTOF), whose easy-to-use consumer website is a useful tool for finding the right company for your preferred holiday (*www.holidayfrance.org.uk*). On offer is every type of holiday from luxury château hotels to homely *chambres d'hotes*, and from gastronomic tours to walking and cycling. Eurocamp and others feature pre-erected tents or mobile homes (*tel: 0844 406 0456; www.eurocamp.co.uk*). Holidays by rail are offered by French Travel Service (*tel: 0844 84 888 43; www.f-t-s.co.uk*). A selection of Gîtes de France, Chambres d'Hôtes and other accommodation is bookable through Brittany Ferries (*tel: 0870 9 076 103; www.brittany-ferries.co.uk/holidays*). Other operators featuring villas, apartments and houses include VFB (*tel: 01452 716840; www.vfbholidays.co.uk*). For walking or riding holidays, and also short breaks at small hotels (often Logis de France), try Inntravel (*tel: 01653 617949; www.inntravel.co.uk*). The free *Traveller in France* brochure from the French Government Tourist Office, *Lincoln House, 300 High Holborn, London WC1V 7JH* (*tel: 09068 244 123* – premium line; *email info.uk@franceguide.com; www.franceguide.com*), gives details of companies and holiday ideas.

From other regions of France

Autoroutes and *routes nationales* link the Loire Valley with other regions of France, although most routes from the north are via Paris (*see opposite*). From other directions:

- A11 from Nantes to Angers, Le Mans and Chartres
- A10 from Bordeaux to Tours
- A20 from Montauban to Vierzon
- A71 from Clermont-Ferrand to Orléans
- N7 then N76 from Lyon to Tours
- A40, N79 then N76 to Bourges and Tours

From outside Europe

There are frequent direct scheduled flights to Paris from North America, Australia and New Zealand. On arrival, there are fast and simple TGV rail connections, as well as car hire and road links, as described above.

Maps

Maps of the *autoroute* network, also showing service stations and their facilities, are available free from the Association des Sociétés Françaises d'Autoroutes, *3 r. Edmond Valentin, 75007 Paris* (tel: *01 47 05 90 01*; email: *asfa@autoroutes.fr*). Three of Michelin's Regional Maps (1:200,000) cover the area, numbers 232, 237 and 238. Michelin's Departmental Maps, which are smaller but have the same scale and information, are numbers 60 (Le Mans area), 63 (west of Angers), 64 (Angers to Orléans) and 65 (east of Orléans). Michelin also offers an internet route-planning service: *www.michelin-travel.com*

Setting the scene

The Loire – Valley of the Kings

The 'Valley of the Kings' merits its epithet, for on its banks and along its tributaries are many reminders of the region's significant role in the regal history of France. Early invaders tried their luck in this fertile land before the crown established its authority in the 16th century. When the kings of France chose to bring their courts to the banks of the Loire, they built castles and lodges without parallel and invited the best artists to decorate their domains. Even the great Leonardo da Vinci lived out his last years here. It was in the Loire Valley that the French Renaissance flowered, and its artistic importance was to continue until the Revolution – even, in the case of its literary exponents, into the 20th century.

Spanning eight *départements*, and extending over one-fifth of the country, the Loire Valley is one of France's best-loved and most-visited regions. Within the area covered by this guide there are hundreds of medieval villages, scores of old towns and a handful of cities. Le Mans is the largest, with 145,000 inhabitants, closely followed by Angers with some 142,000, Tours with 130,000 citizens and Orléans with 105,000. Most famous for its glorious châteaux, the Loire Valley has much more besides to lure its visitors, to keep them entranced, and to have them return time and again.

Below
A château in the Loire Valley

Hills, valleys and plains

Little of the area covered by the scope of this book rises to any great height. By definition the Loire Valley is an area of lower lands, undulating through the central plains of France. It rises in the south to the Central Massif, in which the Loire itself has its source, and again slightly in the eastern parts of the Berry, where the Sancerrois hills rise to around 250m. Westwards from the city of Tours, the land slopes gently all the way to the sea. Either side of the valley cut by the river, there are gentle hills which, in the Touraine area, are particularly noted for viticulture.

The River Loire runs for 1,020km, flowing northwards from the foot of Mont Gerbier-de-Jonc, in the Ardèche, turning westwards at Orléans and continuing west to the Atlantic Sea at Saint-Nazaire, beyond the port of Nantes. Its waters are composed of run-off from other rivers, the most important of which are the Nièvre, Allier, Beuvron, Cher, Indre, Vienne, Maine, Layon, Esure, Sèvre, Nantaise and the Erde, but the Loire also transports meltwater from the Central Massif, and carries a large quantity of sand and other fluvial material. To prevent the risk of flooding where the Loire has low banks, levees were constructed to contain the water – great for viewing the river and its wildlife. As another measure against the risks of rising water, and to join the various rivers within this vast basin, a number of parallel and transversal canals were built beginning in the early 17th century, and proved a boon to transport. Of these, the Canal Latéral à la Loire, Canal de Briare, Canal d'Orléans and the smaller Canal de la Dive are the most important.

Because of the rich alluvial deposits laid down by the mighty river's course, the area around the Loire has developed as prime agricultural land. And, with the successful cultivation of cereals, root vegetables, seeds, medicinal plants (yes, those poppy-like flowers in some parts really are opium), asparagus, strawberries, mushrooms, rape and sunflower seeds, apples and pears, the region has earned another sobriquet as the 'Garden of France'.

Who goes?

One of this region's greatest assets is that it is a year-round destination. Its appeal knows no seasons. The breadth of its sights and attractions enables the first-time visitor to sample many quintessential elements of the country while holidaying here, and travellers who come to explore France's culture or history will find more than enough to satisfy their quest for knowledge. Nature lovers will adore its watery and wooded delights, while gourmets can take pleasure in fine cuisine and good wines, often served in a delightful setting. And it's good to know that children are more than welcome and often particularly well catered for: water activities, zoos and animal breeding centres, and themed amusement parks ensure there is much to entertain the Loire's younger visitors.

When to go

Below
Inside a dovecote

A landlocked area of forests and agricultural land, where the hills rarely breach the 300m limit, the Loire basin is generally mild in climate. Its winters are tempered in the west by the proximity to the Atlantic, from where the rainfall comes, and the summers are warm but rarely too hot. It can rain at any time of the year, although there is less precipitation in July and August, sometimes only falling as brief thunderstorms. In the southeastern part of the Berry, around Bourges and Sancerre, the climate is slightly more extreme. Temperatures in the hills around Sancerre will drop on cold winter nights to less than 4°C. Tours seems to have the warmest summers, averaging 19.1°C in July, and only receiving 690mm of annual rainfall. Summer months are inevitably the most popular (French school holidays, from the first week in July to the end of August, mean that all those child-friendly sights are saturated), though late April to early June, when the leaves unfurl and fields of brilliant yellow mustard and rapeseed splash the countryside with colour, are delightful. So, too, are the mellow months of early autumn. Late September and October are often warm and dry, and the gentle tones of a countryside closing down for winter can be magical. Plus, of course, the annual wine harvest enlivens the region and is cause for celebration. Although winters can be dull, weather-wise, the lack of crowds visiting monuments and dining out makes this also an appealing time to visit.

History

The Loire Valley, the geographical and cultural dividing line between north and south, has played a central, turbulent role in French history. For many centuries the power of the local nobility rivalled that of the throne, and the region was the scene of bloody and repeated territorial conflict.

Early times

Imposing prehistoric tombs and sacred sites testify to a thriving Neolithic culture in the Loire Valley as early as the third millennium BC. Celtic tribes founded settlements at Blois, Orléans and Chartres around 800 BC, and came under the umbrella of the Roman Empire in 51 BC when France (known as Gaul) was conquered by Julius Caesar. Under the *pax romana* the region experienced 300 years of peace and prosperity. Latin speech and Roman law prevailed and a distinct Gallo-Roman civilisation developed.

The spread of Christianity coincided with Rome's decline and successive waves of barbarian invasions. Franks and Visigoths fought for domination until the Frankish king Clovis won the day in 507. His successors' endless fratricidal quarrels caused economic, social and political fragmentation. In a rare episode of national unity, Charles Martel repulsed the Moors in a battle south of Tours in 732, but the French soon took a battering from repeated Viking raids and this period was characterised by the weakness of central authority.

Barons and battles

The decline of royal authority was a major reason for the development of feudalism, a service-and-protection social system that enabled local warlords to establish enormous power bases staffed by their own private armies. From the 9th century onwards the Loire Valley was dominated by factious feudal magnates, of whom the most famous was Foulques Nerra of Anjou. His inheritance passed to the Plantagenets, rulers of territory from Normandy to Aquitaine, who also gained control of England when Henri of Anjou inherited the English crown in 1154.

The fact that the English kings were also French nobles, holding or claiming vast fiefs in France, brought the two nations into centuries of conflict, culminating in the period known as the Hundred Years War.

This flared intermittently between 1337 and 1453, and major battles between France and England were fought in the Loire region. At one point the English held most of France, including Paris, but their decision to besiege the key city of Orléans in 1428 was thwarted by the teenage Joan of Arc, who helped relieve the city and inspired a French recovery.

During the 16th century the region became the playground of kings and dukes. Prolonged wars with Italy gave successive French kings, particularly François I, a taste for Italian art and architecture, and the Loire Valley became a great Renaissance building site. Amboise, Blois and Chambord were transformed into dazzling centres of culture and court life. But artistic and intellectual renewal was followed by nearly 40 years of ferocious religious war (1562–98) between Catholics and the Protestant Huguenots, which brought the French state close to disintegration.

The French court moved to Paris at the end of the 16th century and a strong, centralised monarchy, epitomised by Louis XIV, developed. The Loire ceased to be at the centre of French politics and turned into a quiet backwater. But political and religious peace permitted slow, steady economic growth. Market gardens and the wine trade expanded, and textile manufacturing prospered. Canals were dug to connect the wealthy port of Nantes and the River Loire directly with Paris, with the Loire remaining a key transportation route until the advent of the railway in the 19th century.

However, the Loire Valley remained essentially conservative and agricultural, and during the French Revolution the Vendée became the centre of a violent popular uprising against the Republicans. The Grand Royal and Catholic Army (the Whites) used guerrilla tactics to gain control of nearly all the Vendée and won several battles against Republican forces (the Blues) until defeated at Cholet on 17 October 1793. Republican reprisals decimated the Vendée and, in all, more than 250,000 locals died.

Modern times

After the Revolution the region once more took a back seat, but during World War II the Loire Valley was the demarcation line between occupied and unoccupied France and became a centre of French Resistance. Many of the Loire's cities came under German control and were also bombed. Post-war, the region has traded on its rich architectural legacy, as well as its climate, its beautiful landscapes and its varied wildlife, to become one of the most important tourist destinations in France. The inauguration in 1989 of high-speed train services brought the region within fast commuting distance of Paris, and in 2000 a large zone was designated a *Patrimoine mondial*, a national heritage area, by UNESCO.

Navigating the river

The Loire's importance was acknowledged by the Romans. As a source of transport it was invaluable, for its waters were navigable from as far up as Saint-Thibault right down to the coast – a distance of over 500km. During the Middle Ages its staging points grew into villages, gradually becoming small towns where crafts and trades were closely linked to the river. A number of interesting museums outline riverine life along its course. As we see through many of the following chapters, the Loire, its man-made canals and its major tributaries – the Cher, Loir, Sarthe and Vienne – still play an important role in transport. Working barges and boats may have reduced in numbers but, instead of cargo, the river now carries an increasing quantity of visitors and locals in leisure cruisers of all kinds.

The wines of the Loire

What to bring home

Wines head the shopping list but other bargains should include the myriad styles of porcelain, the unusual sweets and dried fruits.

Thanks to the River Loire, the climate of the surrounding hills is tempered, providing an even range of temperatures – ideal for viticulture. Chenin noir (also known as Pineau d'Aunis) has been growing in the valley for over 11 centuries. Some 60 per cent of wine produced is white: the Muscadet and Folle Blanche cultivars from around Nantes; Chenin blanc (sometimes called Pineau de la Loire) around Anjou and Touraine; Sauvignon around Sancerre and Pouilly. Thirty per cent is made up of the reds: Cabernet Franc, Cabernet Sauvignon and a lesser proportion of Gamay are all grown around Touraine, while Pinot noir is used around Sancerre. Some 10 per cent of red cultivars are used for rosé wines. A smaller still percentage of vines is used to create sparkling wines, of which the AOC Saumur is the undisputed king.

Wines to look out for include Chinon, Rosé d'Anjou, Sancerre (possibly the finest of the Loire's white wines), Saumur, Vouvray, Muscadet de Sèvre-et-Maine, Reuilly, Quincy and Pouilly. Some châteaux, such as Cheverny and Valençay, have their own appellations. A wine guide is an invaluable companion to the better wine estates.

You're likely to discover good local wines with a gourmet meal, but visitors are usually welcome to visit local wine estates; tourist offices in each area can provide addresses. Various wine routes are marked, notable in Touraine and

Right
Ripe Cabernet Franc grapes on the vine in the Loire Valley

Right
The Canal de Briare, linking the
Loire and the Seine

Opposite
Château de Villandry

around Sancerre, and visitors are welcome to stop wherever they see the sign *dégustation* (tasting). Although there is no obligation to buy, *politesse* dictates that you should perhaps purchase a bottle as goodwill. If you come across some real finds, the wine estates will be happy to ship your wines home. Note, too, that the northern part of this area is known for its cider, a powerful brew when produced in its *artisanale* form but toned down when mass-produced. Lastly, that much-loved liqueur, Cointreau, is produced in Angers.

Gastronomic temptations

It is far from easy to characterise the gastronomy of an area as vast, and as varied, as the Loire basin. Although it is not best known for its cuisine, the area does have plenty of interesting specialities to offer, and the marriage of wine sauces and fresh local produce invariably creates some culinary distinction.

Truffles

Diamants noirs, or black diamonds, are the recipe for success in Marigny-Marmande. This town has styled itself as the capital of the truffle trade, and the lucrative business of growing these black diamonds has been filling the town coffers for over a century. There are more than 30ha of truffle beds and the cultivation is celebrated each 21 December with a truffle market of national importance.

Touraine is known for its *charcuterie* (pork cookery): pork *rillons* (*rilles* means little snips of pork) and *rillettes* from Tours and Vouvray are made from practically any and all parts of a pig, stewed for hours with herbs and sometimes vegetables, then poured into little pots and sealed with pork dripping. Touraine is also noted for *andouillettes* (sausages made with tripe). Anjou is known for its *rillauds* (similar to *rillettes*) and *pâtés de prunes*, while Pithiviers has a reputation for a *pâté d'alouette* (lark's liver pâté), usually padded out with other livers. Elsewhere, especially in the Sologne and Berry, *terrines de gibier* (game pâté) is a firm winter favourite.

Vegetables in this area are plentiful – it is one of the country's prime areas of cultivation – but are rarely used for more than soups (lentil and pumpkin in particular) or for dressing a main dish. A little *salade composée* (mixed salad) is usually the French answer to eating vegetables, although seasonal new potatoes, beetroot and asparagus are particularly delicious. Mushroom cultivation is also important,

Above
Halle du Marché

especially in those chalky caves along the river-banks. *Champignons de Paris* (round white mushrooms), *girolles* (chanterelles) and *morilles* (morels) are all favourites, while the popular but difficult-to-translate *bolets rude*, *shiitakes* and *cèpes* all appear on the dining table, often accompanying game and frequently served lightly fried in butter and garlic with a sprinkling of parsley.

Inevitably, the rivers provide many a main course. Carp, perch, eel and salmon are all fished and served with sauces such as the *beurre blanc* of Nantes, or rich reductions made from local wines. Locally reared meat includes beef, though probably the area is best known for its *gibier* or game: *chevreuil* (young buck) or *venaison* (venison), *sanglier* (wild boar) or *faisan* (pheasant) are usually roasted or stewed slowly. *Lapin farci* (stuffed rabbit) and *lièvre* (hare) can also be found on winter menus. Other main courses include *chapons* or capons and fattened chickens from La Flèche. *Poulet George Sand*, named after the author, is a Berry speciality in which chicken or young capons are served with a sauce made from freshwater crayfish.

The Loire produces a number of cheeses, predominantly from goat's milk. The whiter the exterior, the younger and usually milder the cheese. Yellowing crusts denote a drier cheese and a far more pungent taste. Some cheeses have been elevated to AOC (*appellation d'origine contrôlée*) status, ensuring a continuing quality. Look out for the *Crottin de Chavignol*, a small, round cheese from near Sancerre; the pyramids from Selles-sur-Cher, St-Aignan and Valençay; the *pavé de Sologne* and ash-covered goat's cheeses from Vendôme.

On a sweet note, the area is known for its pears, strawberries and Golden Delicious apples. Locally collected honey is an important ingredient in many desserts and *pâtisseries*. Favourite dishes include *tarte Tatin* (*see page 218*), an upside-down apple tart, *prunes de Tours* (plums steeped in red wine), *fromentée* (a wheat cake with almond milk), almond biscuits, *pruneaux de Tours* (dried prunes), *sanciaux* (honey-filled doughnuts from the Berry) or *cotingnac* (a quince compote), sold in a little box.

Markets

Part of the French experience is to stroll through the *marchés* (markets). Market day has traditionally been one of the week's highlights, a chance to purchase freshly picked fruit and vegetables, fill up with locally produced cheeses, sample wines or pâtés and cold cuts, replace the chicken or rabbit stock, buy saucepans and exchange gossip. In days gone by, market folk were often the heralds of news and, although the media now fulfils this role, market day is still an excuse to get out and meet people. Today's markets tend to bring household appliances and cheap clothing into the sales place but there is also a growing demand for locally produced breads, cheeses, jams and handicrafts. That enticing tag, *artisanale*, may not mean quality but it does mean hand-made and should invite consideration.

Snacks, treats, self-catering – and where to buy a picnic

On non-market days head for a popular *boulangerie*, where bread will be freshly baked. A stick-like *baguette* is the usual request, though you might like to try *pain au seigle* (rye bread) or *pain complet*, a rather pale wholemeal bread. A *boulangerie* may also function as a *pâtisserie* selling delicious *friandises*: croissants, *pains au raisins* (raisin-filled pastry wheels), *pains au chocolat* or *chocolatines*. However, for the best pastries and tarts, head for a dedicated *pâtissier* – a professional pastry chef. If you're stuck for bread but see a sign for a *depôt de pain*, that means the shop sells bread and pastries, but they aren't baked on the premises. For those little extra goodies, you can spend hours in a *confiserie* where an amazing array of sweet confections and imaginative chocolates is often hand-created.

A *supermarché* or *hypermarché* will have all you require, and more, though it's not quite as much fun as buying in small shops. However, their range of cheeses, cold cuts and wines is usually excellent. Bread, by contrast, is not such a good buy here. If you are after a bottle of wine, don't waste time looking for an off-licence: away from the largest cities, they hardly exist. Everyone heads for the supermarket where the choice is good and the prices are fair.

Chances are that you will not want a *boucherie* (butcher's) if all you are buying is picnic food. But French meat is excellent in quality, and often the *boucher* will also sell cold meats, pre-cooked cold dishes and some tinned foods. For a wider range of cooked meats and other prepared dishes, visit a *charcuterie* (a pork butcher) or a *traiteur* (delicatessen). Watch out, though, for the *boucherie hippophragique* or *boucherie chevaline*: these butchers deal only in horse meat.

Tourist offices

Tourist offices have a confusing number of names in France. They are usually known as:
- Office de (or du) Tourisme;
- Bureau de (or du) Tourisme;
- Syndicat d'Initiative;
- OTSI (standing for Office du Tourisme/Syndicat d'Initiative).

In this book we have called them all 'Tourist Office'. As a general rule, they are *open Mon–Sat 0900–1200, 1400–1800*, but with longer hours in July and August. Note that the departmental tourism offices, listed as the *Comité départemental de tourisme,* are not open to members of the public, but are happy to answer queries by phone, letter or email.

Below
River Loire skiff

Highlights

Best cathedrals
- Cathédrale Notre-Dame, Chartres (*see page 184*)
- Cathédrale de St-Etienne, Bourges (*see page 261*)
- Cathédrale St-Gatien, Tours (*see page 44*)
- Cathédrale St-Julien, Le Mans (*see page 164*)
- Cathédrale Ste-Croix, Orléans (*see page 242*)

Best churches
- Cunault (*see page 105*)
- St-Benoît, St-Benoît-sur-Loire (*see page 254*)

Best châteaux
- Château d'Angers (*see page 138*)
- Château d'Azay-le-Rideau (*see page 68*)
- Château de Brézé (*see page 105*)
- Château de Chambord (*see page 232*)
- Château de Chenonceau (*see page 57*)
- Château de Grand-Lucé (*see page 175*)
- Château de Saumur (*see page 118*)
- Château de Serrant, St-Georges-sur-Loire (*see page 132*)
- Château de Villandry (*see page 77*)
- Château du Lude (*see page 150*)
- Château d'Ussé (*see page 74*)
- Château Royal, Amboise (*see page 52*)
- Château Royal de Blois (*see page 204*)
- Château de Sully-sur-Loire (*see page 256*)

Best museums
- Musée Bertrand, Châteauroux (*see page 271*)
- Musée des 24h Circuit de la Sarthe (*see page 176*)
- Musée Jean Lurçat et de la Tapisserie Contemporaine, Angers (*see page 143*)
- Musée Maurice Dufresne, Marnay (*see page 72*)

Best towns
- Briare (*see page 248*)
- Le Mans old town (*see page 162*)
- Loches (*see page 96*)
- Romorantin-Lanthenay (*see page 218*)

Best villages
- Asnières-sur-Vègre (*see page 171*)
- Crissay-sur-Manse (*see page 78*)
- Montrésor (*see page 98*)

Best for wine tasting
- Angers (*see page 136*)
- The Grands Châteaux: Tours–Blois route (*see page 52*)
- Saumur (*see page 116*)
- Upper Reaches route (*see page 248*)

Best for caves
- Chinon–Saumur route (*see page 102*)
- Le Loir: Vendôme–La Flèche route (*see page 146*)

Best for children
- Château d'Ussé (*see page 74*)
- Doué-la-Fontaine zoo (*see page 107*)
- Grottes Pétrifiantes de Savonnières (*see page 75*)
- Musée Maurice Dufresne, Marnay (*see page 72*)
- Musée du Masque, St-Hilaire-St-Florent (*see page 112*)
- St-Aignan zoo (*see page 221*)

Best son-et-lumière
- Bourges (*see page 260*)
- Château d'Azay-le-Rideau (*see page 68*)
- Château de Chenonceau (*see page 57*)
- Château de Montsoreau (*see page 110*)

Tours

Ratings

Architecture	● ● ● ● ●
History	● ● ● ● ●
Restaurants	● ● ● ● ●
Street life	● ● ● ●
Entertainment	● ● ● ●
Children	● ● ●
Museums	● ● ●
Shopping	● ● ●

The city of Tours, capital of the Loire Valley region, has no great Renaissance château of its own. Yet, to the French mind, Tours is the very essence of what these palatial, aristocratic Renaissance homes are all about. The city has a long reputation for civilisation, culture and refinement. It has great restaurants, chic shopping, style and flair in abundance and, even in today's France, the Tours accent is considered the 'best' in the land. The old quarter down by the riverside, with a grid of streets laid out by the Romans, remains attractive and atmospheric. Even its appearance (apart from some hasty building to repair wartime damage) seems elegant, a black and white city, smart in tufa and slate. The more modern quarter has benefited in recent years from some stylish, attention-grabbing new architecture. There's a cheerful, bright quality to the light, and Tours is still, as Balzac described it, 'a smiling city'.

Getting there and getting around

① Tours Tourist Office 78–82
r. Bernard Palissy (opposite railway station); tel: 02 47 70 37 37; fax: 02 47 61 14 22; email: info@ligeris.com. Open mid-Oct–mid-Apr Mon–Sat 0900–1230 and 1330–1800, Sun & hols 1000–1300; rest of year Mon–Sat 0830–1900, Sun & hols 1000–1230 and 1430–1700.

The tourist office provides information, maps and bookings for events, hotels, excursions, etc.

By road
Autoroute A10 (Paris–Bordeaux) and major roads N152/D952 (Loire Valley), N10 (from Chartres) and D938 (from Le Mans) enter into the city. The city centre lies on the south bank of the Loire between the Mirabeau and Napoleon bridges.

By rail
TGV direct from Paris or Lille (same-station connection with Eurostar from London) stops at St-Pierre-des-Corps station, 3km from the city centre. A shuttle train into the central station runs every few minutes.

Parking
There are car parks on the perimeter of the old central quarter, close to pl. Jean Jaurès, pl. des Halles, pl. de la Préfecture and near the main station at pl. Général de Gaulle.

www.ligeris.com (the tourist office site, in French and English. Informative and useful); www.tours.fr (the town's official site, mainly in French, some English); www.agglo-tours.fr (website of the communes of Greater Tours).

Guided tours

The tourist office organises, or can book, a choice of guided tours of the city and surrounding area. A small 'tourist train' gives a 45min tour of the city centre, leaving from the tourist office every 40–50min throughout the day in summer.

Sights

Carte Multi-Visites

The Carte Multi-Visites from the tourist office gives entry to all major monuments and sights, and a lecture tour. It is valid for one year.

Basilique St-Martin

The present church, built in the early 20th century in a mock Romanesque-Byzantine style, replaces a vast basilica, famed throughout Christendom, erected in 1175 and destroyed in 1802. For centuries St Martin was revered in Tours. A Roman legionnaire, Martin was noted for the decisive moment of his life when he saw a shivering pauper by the road. Taking out his sword, he cut his cloak in two and gave one half to the poor man. The act caused Martin to become convinced of the rightness of Christianity, and he devoted the rest of his life to spreading its teaching, converting much of France, demolishing pagan shrines and building churches. In Poitou he founded the first monastery in Gaul, and became the symbol of French Christianity. Although Martin had little connection with

① **Basilique St-Martin**
€ *pl. de Châteauneuf
(off r. des Halles). Open
daily.*

Tours – he was from Hungary, and the cloak incident occurred at Amiens, in northern France – his relics were stolen from his Poitou monastery and brought here to encourage pilgrims to visit the city, which they did in great numbers. The importance of Tours goes back to the St-Martin pilgrimage, and his relics can still be seen in the crypt. The street outside the church, r. des Halles, roughly follows the huge nave of the original building. Lighter-coloured cobbles pick out the position of the capitals.

① **Cathédrale St-
Gatien** *pl. de la
Cathédrale, on r. Lavoisier;
tel: 02 47 70 21 00. Open
approx 0830–1230 and
1400–2000.*

Cloître de la Psalette €
*pl. de la Cathédrale, on
r. Lavoisier; tel: 02 47 47 05
19. Open daily (except Mon
and Tue Dec–Mar, and
some hols) approx 0930–
1230 and 1400–1800
(1700 in winter). Not open
for visits during services.*

Cathédrale St-Gatien

The 19th-century architect and restorer Viollet-le-Duc described the cathedral at Tours as 'a book of architecture'. It is especially a book about French Gothic, tracing the style through all its stages from the lovely 13th-century choir through the 14th-century nave to the amazingly elaborate 15th-century Flamboyant west façade, with its three doorways, crowned with Gothic-Renaissance lantern towers that mark the first move into the next architectural style. The two towers rise from Romanesque bases standing on Gallo-Roman foundations.

Inside, the building is white, with a very narrow nave giving an illusion of height. Despite the evolving style, the building creates an impressive sense of unity. Although much of the glass was blown out in World War II, several exceptional stained-glass windows of the 13th, 14th and 15th centuries around the choir managed to survive. Note especially the superb 14th-century rose windows in the transept. Most of the original statuary destroyed during the Revolution has been replaced with 19th-century replicas. There is also a fine Renaissance organ.

The cathedral gives access to the **Cloître de la Psalette**, an exquisite 15th- to 16th-century Gothic-Renaissance structure with three galleries, including an open Renaissance staircase. La Psalette was originally for the use of the cathedral choir. Up the stairs are a former scriptorium and a vaulted library. The round stone tower beside the building is a restored remnant of the city's Roman wall.

Since 1996 the cathedral has been beautifully floodlit every night; the lighting is by Bideau (a native of Tours), who designed the acclaimed Year 2000 lighting for the Eiffel Tower.

St Martin

The pious, ascetic ex-soldier is the most popular saint in France, with more than 450 towns and villages bearing his name. Fittingly for a man who turned away from war, his feast day is 11 November, Armistice Day.

Opposite
Musée des Beaux-Arts, Tours

Atelier Histoire de Tours € *Château Royal; tel: 02 47 70 88 59. Open Wed and Sat pm.*

Château Royal

Although Tours is the capital of 'chateaux country', it lacks a real château of its own. Little survives of Henri II's fortress at Tours, apart from the 12th-century Tour de Guise, altered in the 15th century, and the Pavillon de Mars, added in the 18th century. The Guise connection comes from the tower's most famous prisoner, the son of the Duke de Guise, who had been assassinated in Blois. Today, the Château Royal is home to the **Atelier Histoire de Tours**, a permanent exhibition on the history of the town. Although open only two afternoons a week, it can also be visited on guided tours. Look out, too, for temporary art exhibitions that are held here.

Hôtel Gouin / Musée Archéologique € *25 r. du Commerce; tel: 02 47 66 22 32; www.musee-gouin.fr. Open 1000–1300 and 1400–1730 (longer pm opening hours Apr–Sept). Closed Mon. The museum is currently closed for restoration.*

Hôtel Gouin / Musée Archéologique

A Gothic house with rich Renaissance decoration, the Gouin mansion is set back within its courtyard on Tours' historic main street. Although much damaged by wartime bombing, this is a good example of a prosperous 15th-century private home transformed in the Renaissance by the addition of a lavishly carved south façade and a staircase tower on the north side. Inside, the museum displays a wide variety of local relics illustrating the whole period of human habitation in the Tours area. The Gallo-Roman, medieval and Renaissance periods are well represented, and a special attraction is Jean-Jacques Rousseau's physics laboratory (18th century), brought from Chenonceau. Interesting temporary exhibitions are also held here.

Musée des Beaux-Arts

Musée des Beaux-Arts €€ 18 pl. F. Sicard; tel: 02 47 05 68 73. Open Wed–Mon 0900–1245 and 1400–1800. Closed hols.

Beside the cathedral, in the 17th- to 18th-century former Archbishops' Palace, the works of the Fine Arts Museum are displayed in a grand setting of wood-panelled walls, fine silks, tapestries and furnishings of the period. The round tower on the street side of the building is a remnant of the town's Gallo-Roman fortifications. In the centre of the courtyard stands a vast cedar of Lebanon, planted in 1809. Also in the courtyard, under shelter to one side, is the remarkable stuffed circus elephant Fritz, which had to be killed here in 1904. (Part of the Barnum & Bailey touring circus, he had turned 'rogue' and dangerous.) The treasures of the museum are mainly 17th- to 19th-century paintings and sculpture, with works by Rubens, Rembrandt, Degas and Delacroix. Striking is Louis Boulanger's portrait of Balzac in his dressing gown. Older works represented are some Italian Primitives and Mantegna's *Christ in the Garden of Olives* and *The Resurrection*.

Musée du Compagnonnage

Musée du Compagnonnage €€ Cloître St-Julien, 8 r. Nationale; tel: 02 47 21 62 20; www.musee-du-compagnonnage.info. Open daily 0900–1200 and 1400–1800 (mid-Jun–mid-Sept open until 0030); Sept–Jun closed Tue. The other sights have the same address, phone number and entry times.

Compagnonnage means craft guilds, the historic brotherhoods of artisans qualified in a trade. An early form of trade union, a guild defended the rights, status, interests and wage levels of its members. This intriguing and unusual museum gathers together a variety of documents, tools and finished work to illustrate the guilds of such ancient trades as roofers, ropemakers, clogmakers and woodturners.

The museum is housed within the 15th- to 16th-century guestroom and dormitory of the monks of St-Julien abbey. The 13th-century Gothic **St-Julien abbey church** (founded as long ago as the 5th century) has older, Romanesque sections, including the west tower, as well as being lit through modern stained-glass windows by Max Ingrand. Another of the abbey buildings, the superbly vaulted 12th-century Celliers St-Julien in the chapterhouse, contains a fascinating **Touraine museum of wine**, dealing with the history, cultivation and tradition of wine. Exhibits include an original Gallo-Roman wine press from nearby Azay-le-Rideau.

Right
Hôtel Gouin Musée Archéologique

Accommodation and food in Tours

Le Petit Patrimoine € *58 r. Colbert; tel: 02 47 66 05 81.* There are several informal and inexpensive eating places along r. Colbert, in the old quarter. This is one of the very best of them. Enjoy good, low-priced eating here, with simple, classic menus well prepared. Local specialities are strongly featured, such as *Tourte Tourangelle*, pastry with pork.

Le Bistrot de la Tranchée €€ *103 av. de la Tranchée; tel: 02 47 41 09 08; fax: 02 47 41 80 95; email: charles-barrier@yahoo.fr.* This relaxed, pleasant and satisfyingly traditional bistrot, with its maroon panelling and blackboard menu, belongs to Charles Barrier's smart fine-dining restaurant right next door. Here, though, unpretentious brasserie fare is the order of the day, with classic dishes such as *blanquette de veau à l'ancienne* and *confit d'agneau pommes boulangères*, all prepared to a high standard.

La Deuvalière €€ *18 r. de la Monnaie; tel: 02 47 64 01 57; fax: 02 47 64 01 57; email: ladeuvaliere@wanadoo.fr; www.restaurantladeuvaliere. com.* In a handsome 16th-century mansion in the heart of Vieux Tours, with a calm, refined atmosphere, the Deuvalière has quickly made a name for itself under the young Israeli chef Emmanuel Deuval, who specialises in inventive, light, fresh and elegant menus, changed to suit the season. Deuval worked at several restaurants around France before choosing Tours as the right place to open his own place.

Hôtel des Châteaux de la Loire €€ *12 r. Gambetta; tel: 02 47 05 10 05; email: hoteldes chateaux.tours@wanadoo.fr; www.hoteldeschateaux.fr.* Not far from the sights of the old town, this unpretentious mid-range hotel has adequate, well-kept rooms with TV and bath,

Right
Rillettes and Touraine wine

plus private parking, at a modest price. There's a breakfast buffet, but no restaurant.

Les Tuffeaux €€ *19 r. Lavoisier; tel: 02 47 47 19 89. Tuffeau* is the French name for tufa, the Loire's white stone, and this small, appealing restaurant has bare walls of it as well as a fireplace in the middle, and a friendly atmosphere. Excellent food and good wine are served, with fish dishes skilfully prepared.

Charles Barrier €€–€€€ *101 av. de la Tranchée; tel: 02 47 54 20 39; fax: 02 47 41 80 95.* A great classic gastronomic restaurant that pleasantly overlooks a garden. Barrier and his team offer traditional dishes perfectly prepared with imaginative touches. Seafood is a speciality, with an interesting use of spices in some dishes. Excellent local wines, superb desserts. The restaurant is on the Loire's north bank, about 10 minutes' drive from the city centre.

Hôtel Univers (and Restaurant La Touraine) €€€ *5 blvd Heurteloup; tel: 02 47 05 37 12; fax: 02 47 61 51 80; email: hotel-univers-sa@wanadoo.fr; www.oceaniahotels.com/lunivers-tours.php.* Around the corner from the railway station, adjacent to the pl. Jean Jaurès, with its flowers and fountains and wonderfully florid neo-Baroque town hall, this is the best hotel in the town centre. Quiet, comfortable and professional, the hotel is also known for an impressive frieze in the large reception area depicting all the illustrious guests who have stayed here since 1846 (including several heads of state). Good breakfasts. The long-established restaurant serves classic French gastronomic dishes expertly prepared. Expensive.

Shopping

The main shopping street is r. Nationale. For a wide selection of high-quality local specialities, try *Les Douceurs Tourangelles, 104 r. du Commerce.* Antique lovers should browse r. de la Scellerie.

Markets

There are street markets every day of the week in different parts of the city centre.
• **Daily produce market** (covered market) – *Les Halles, r. des Halles; all day (am only on Sun).*
• **Evening produce market** – *pl. de la Résistance; 1800–2000 on the first Fri of every month.* An unusual, atmospheric market.
• **Flower market** – *blvd Béranger; Wed and Sat.*
• **Antiquarian books** – *blvd Heurteloup; Sat.*
• **Antiques** – about three markets are held each month.

Entertainment

The city enjoys a full programme of concerts, exhibitions and shows. Ask the tourist office for *Tours Spectacles*, detailing current and forthcoming events. Several city-centre bars have live music in the evening.

Suggested walk

Total distance: About 2km.

Time: About half a day.

Links: Tours is the starting point for two driving tours: The Grands Châteaux: Tours–Blois (*see page 52*) and The Grands Châteaux: Tours–Chinon (*see page 68*).

Route: Start at the **CATHEDRAL ST-GATIEN** ❶. Beside it is the **MUSEE DES BEAUX-ARTS** ❷. Round the back of the cathedral in r. de la Psalette is the house of the priest as described by Balzac in *Le Curé de Tours*. Walk the few paces up r. Lavoisier to r. Colbert.

Detour: Continue on r. Lavoisier across r. Colbert to the **CHATEAU ROYAL** ❸, beside the main through road on the riverbank. A pedestrian suspension bridge, the Pont de Fil, crosses the river just here, and there is a waterside walkway (*end of detour*).

Below
Place Plumereau

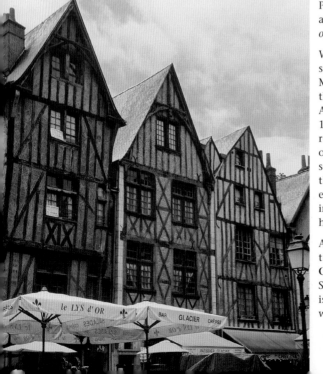

Walk west along r. Colbert, the main street of Tours in medieval times. Mainly pedestrianised, it is a pleasant thoroughfare with many restaurants. Architecturally, every period from the 15th century to the present day is represented, including several very old half-timbered houses, as well as some ugly post-war houses. Some of the older doorposts or lintels – for example, at Nos 25–27 – have interesting carvings. Joan of Arc had her armour made at 39 r. Colbert.

At the intersection with r. Nationale turn right for the **MUSEE DU COMPAGNONNAGE** ❹, in the old St-Julien abbey church. R. Nationale is the modern main street of Tours, which was largely rebuilt after the war, connecting pl. Jean Jaurès to pont Wilson, the main Loire bridge. Balzac was born at No 39, but the house has disappeared. Return to r. Colbert.

Further along, r. Colbert becomes r. du Commerce, where the **HOTEL GOUIN / MUSEE ARCHEOLOGIQUE** ❺ stands within its courtyard. R. Colbert enters the old quarter, known as Vieux Tours or Quartier St-Martin, and arrives at **pl. Plumereau**, a popular focal point, filled with café tables and enclosed by historic buildings, mainly 15th century. The mulberry tree in the centre is a reminder that Tours (with Lyon, its rival) was the capital of the medieval silk industry. Explore the lanes off the square, in which several medieval houses have external staircases and other interesting features. One of the more striking old streets is **r. du Grand-Marché**. Off the north side of the square, in picturesque little **pl. St-Pierre le Puellier**, remnants of Roman homes have been uncovered.

A few paces away is **BASILIQUE ST-MARTIN** ❻. The old tower that you will pass on the way is the Tour Charlemagne, a remnant of the original St-Martin basilica that was destroyed in 1802. As you are walking in r. des Halles on the approach to the basilica, notice that differently coloured cobbles pick out the position of the capitals of the nave of the original building.

The Grands Châteaux: Tours–Blois

For some 30km, the capricious Loire and gentle Cher flow alongside each other, almost parallel, gradually coming to a meeting point west of Tours. The old heart of Tours itself stands on a narrow spit of land between the two rivers, which both run through the city. The countryside to the east, as far as Chaumont on the Loire and Montrichard on the Cher, forms a narrow peninsula that feels enclosed by these majestic waterways. The area is exceptionally rich in European history, art and civilisation. An unhurried journey from Tours to Blois, with a detour along the valley of the River Cher, captures among the best that the Loire Valley region can offer. Not only the loveliest château of them all, at Chenonceaux, but the finest wines, from Vouvray, and one of the most agreeable and interesting towns, at Amboise, are here, together with an abundance of other châteaux, sights and attractions.

AMBOISE

🌐 *www.amboise-valdeloire.com* (the town's tourism site, in several languages).

🚗 The main road into (and through) Amboise is the D751, running along the waterfront. The heart of the town lies south and west of the Loire bridge.

The **Château Royal** of Amboise, standing firmly on its riverside rock facing the Loire, was home to every king or queen of France for 160 years, up to the end of the 16th century. Charles VIII – who was born and died in the castle – added the first Renaissance decoration to the old Gothic fortress that Louis XI had already greatly enlarged and improved. It was here that the first Italian influence was seen in French art and architecture, when Charles returned from Italy in 1495. Louis XII continued the work with a new wing. Although François I is so closely linked with the vast château he constructed at Chambord, he lived at Amboise from the age of 7 to 27 (he became king at 24). The early years of his reign were associated with constant parties and dances and complete immersion in art and luxury, to the point of employing a team of prostitutes to service the young men of the court. In those days the castle area was six times larger than now, and a second river ran behind it, along present-day r. Victor Hugo and pl.

There are small pay-and-display car parks beside and opposite the tourist office and beside the château. There is a much larger, free car park signposted *Parking du Château* near the château.

Amboise Tourist Office *quai Général de Gaulle; tel: 02 47 57 09 28; fax: 02 47 57 14 35; email: contact@amboise-valdeloire.com. Open low season Mon–Sat 0930–1230 and 1400–1830, Sun, hols & eve of hols am only; intermediate season Mon–Sat 0930–1230 and 1330–1900, Sun, hols & eve of hols 0930–1230 and 1500–1800; high season Mon–Sat 0900–2000, Sun and hols 1000–1800. Closed 25 Dec & 1 Jan.*

Debré (where the visitors' entrance is now). Inherited by Gaston d'Orléans (Louis XIII's brother), who involved himself in conspiracies against the crown, the huge château was largely demolished in 1631, with further damage done after the Revolution. But what remains of the château still dominates this lively, popular town, and makes an impressive view from the Loire bridge.

From the château entrance, a steep ramp turns up to reach the high terrace overlooking the Loire. The little white Flamboyant chapel here is dedicated to St Hubert, patron saint of huntsmen – note the antlers on the spire, and the extraordinary carved animal frieze above the entrance. Extending away from the terrace are the attractive park and gardens, with a memorial to Leonardo da Vinci. On his death in 1519, Leonardo was buried in the château grounds. Despite claims that his grave is in the chapel, the exact location of his body is unknown.

The château interior feels bare and spacious inside, and has almost no furniture or decoration; a few 15th-century pieces survive, some brought from other locations. The lovely Salle du Conseil has a white fireplace, red-brick walls and a white vaulted ceiling, supported by four slender columns decorated with the ermine tail emblem of Anne of Brittany, twice queen of France. From its balcony ironwork, hundreds of Huguenots were hanged in 1560. In the Salle de l'Echanson – a kind of dining room – fine medieval tapestries depict

🖈 Guided tours are organised by the tourist office, including (weekends only) a young guide in period costume who acts out the story of Amboise. *A guided tour by Little Train runs Apr–Oct from beside the tourist office and from the château, 1000–1900.*

🎭 **Son-et-Lumière**
For the 1hr *son-et-lumière* at the château, called *A La Cour du Roy François*, 250 actors bring to life the world of François I and Leonardo da Vinci. *Tel: 02 47 57 14 47, www.renaissance-amboise. com; performances Wed and Sat at 2230 in Jun–Jul, 2200 in Aug–Sept.*

🏰 **Château Royal €€**
Entrance in pl. Debré; tel: 02 47 57 00 98; www.chateau-amboise.com. Open Jan & Dec 0900–1200 and 1400–1645 (closed 25 Dec & 1 Jan); Nov, Feb–Mar 0900–1200 and 1330–1730; Apr–Jun 0900–1830; Jul–Aug 0900–1900; Sept–Oct 0900–1800.

Château du Clos Lucé
€€ av. du Clos Lucé; tel: 02 47 57 00 73; fax: 02 47 30 54 28; www.vinci-closluce. com. Open Jan 1000–1700; Nov–Dec & Feb–22 Mar 0900–1800; 23 Mar–Jun & Sept–Oct 0900–1900; Jul–Aug 0900–2000.

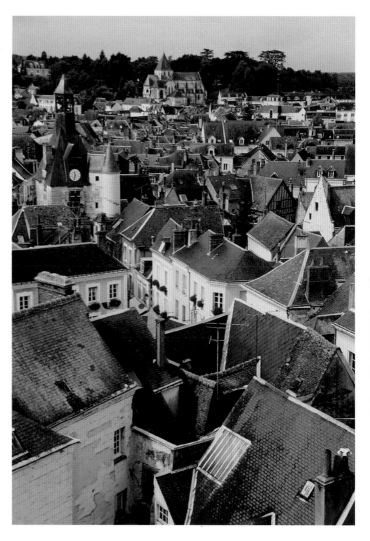

Above
Amboise, view from the Château Royal

biblical scenes. Climb to the roof of the Tour des Minimes for a view across the bridges, sandy banks and wooded islands of the Loire. The tower has a spiral ramp allowing horsemen to ride to the top, as does Tour Hurtault, on the other side of the terrace.

From the château, a 400m walk leads to the extensive Renaissance gardens of the Parc Leonardo da Vinci, in which stands the **Château du Clos Lucé**, the grandly elegant red-brick and white stone mansion that was Leonardo da Vinci's home for the last four years of his life. On the way there, notice several houses on the left carved into the rock face, although they have modern façades. Leonardo moved to

Parc Mini-Châteaux €€€ *route de Chenonceaux; tel: 02 47 23 44 57; www.mini-chateaux.com. Open Apr–Jun & Sept–Oct 0900–1900; Jul–Aug 0900–2000 (2300 on Sat and Sun); rest of year shorter hours, closes 1700. Closed Dec–Mar and part of Nov.*

Parc Le Fou de l'Ane €€ *route de Chenonceaux; tel: 08 36 68 69 37. Open Apr–Jun & Sept–Oct 1000–1900; Jul–Aug 0900–2000; rest of year 1000–1700.*

Aquarium du Val de Loire €€€ *On D283, near Lussault-sur-Loire; tel: 02 47 23 44 44; www. aquarium duvaldeloire.com. Open Apr–Jun & Sept–Oct 0900–1900; Jul–Aug 0900–2000 (2300 on Sat and Sun); rest of year shorter hours, closes 1700. Closed Dec–Jan and part of Nov & Feb.*

Amboise from Florence in 1516 at the invitation of François I, and was given a pension as well as lodgings in this royal possession. Leonardo brought with him four of his most treasured paintings, one of them the *Mona Lisa*. It appears that he did no painting in France, instead working on his scientific ideas, which are emphasised in the displays within the house. Especially interesting are IBM's computer-engineered working models of Leonardo's 'machines'. Also worth seeing are the historic kitchens.

There are many other sights, entertainments and family attractions in and around Amboise. On the outskirts of town, the children's attraction **Parc Mini-Châteaux** entertains and educates visitors of all ages. The 2ha park contains accurate scale models of every one of the great Loire châteaux and their parks, at 4 per cent of their actual size. Amusing touches are figures in 15th-century dress, miniaturised trees and working-model TGVs and other trains. At night the châteaux are illuminated and have mini-firework displays to scale. Close by, on the same road, and run by the same company, **Parc Le Fou de l'Ane** gives a chance to admire donkeys from Egypt, Ireland and France. Just out of town in the direction of Bléré stands the curious **Pagode de Chanteloup** (*see page 64*), while 10km west of Amboise, the **Aquarium du Val de Loire** holds Europe's largest freshwater collections, with a huge variety of species from around the world. There are some sea creatures, too, including sharks.

Accommodation and food in and around Amboise

Hôtel-Restaurant Le Blason €–€€ *11 pl. de Richelieu; tel: 02 47 23 22 41; fax: 02 47 57 56 18; www.leblason.fr.* Excellent value for good, classic cuisine with local wines. The hotel, too, in a half-timbered house in the heart of town, is plain and simple but good value for money.

Château de Pray €€€ *route de Chargé, off D751, 2km east of Amboise; tel: 02 47 57 23 67; fax: 02 47 57 32 50; email: chateau.depray@wanadoo.fr; http://praycastel.online.fr.* An interesting, well-preserved Gothic and Renaissance mansion of the 13th and 16th centuries, with round corner turrets topped with black spires, de Pray was among the first family-home châteaux to open its doors to paying guests. The public rooms are

Right
Château Royal, Amboise

filled with historical furnishings, decorations and memorabilia, but the house is no museum – it has been altered and modernised in every century. The bedrooms are adequately comfortable, with many period touches. Attractive gardens include a large vegetable plot and a swimming pool, and have a view down to the Loire. The cosy main dining room, done up in medieval style, has wooden beams, framed portraits, a big old tapestry and crossed swords over the fireplace. The food is elegant, tasty and well prepared. An excellent breakfast is served in the château's curious orangerie, a 'room' carved out of the tufa rock (concerts are also held here).

CHAUMONT-SUR-LOIRE

ⓘ Chaumont Tourist Office *24 r. du Maréchal Leclerc; tel: 02 54 20 91 73; fax: 02 54 20 90 34; www.chaumont-sur-loire.eu. Open daily.*

Ⓐ Festivals *Last weekend in Jun – Solstice Bonfire, and market. Jun–Oct – Festival International des Parcs et Jardins; details from Conservatoire International des Parcs et Jardins, Chaumont-sur-Loire, tel: 02 54 20 99 22; www.domaine-chaumont.fr*

Ⓑ Château de Chaumont €€ *Chaumont-sur-Loire; tel: 02 54 51 26 26; fax: 02 54 20 91 16. Open mid-Mar–end Oct 0930–1830; rest of year 1000–1700. Closed some hols.*

From the small, pretty village of Chaumont, beside the south bank of the Loire, a path leads steeply up through extensive château parkland to the impressive cliff-top château. With massive round towers in white tufa, under pointed black slate roofs, and with a working drawbridge, the château stands picture-perfect on its table of flat green turf. It commands a magnificent view of the river. The **Château de Chaumont** is an excellent example of a feudal Gothic fortress, with Renaissance decoration inside and out. Catherine de Medici, Henri II's queen, acquired Chaumont after the king died, and was able to force Diane de Poitiers, who had been the king's mistress, to accept Chaumont in exchange for her beloved Chenonceau. Although a royal castle, Chaumont eventually came into the hands of Mademoiselle Say, heiress to a huge fortune made in the sugar trade. She married the Prince de Broglie, and became a princess. The last private individual to own the château, her legacy is the rich decoration of the residential apartments, including fine furniture, glazed tiles and tapestries. Of particular note is the Council Room, in which hang some fine Flemish tapestries. It is paved with 17th-century majolica tiles taken from a Sicilian palace. The portrait medallions on display were made in the 18th century by the Italian engraver Nini, whose workshop was in the old stables. Preserved there today are the fine 19th-century stables fitted out by the Princess de Broglie to the highest possible standard. These now house a riding centre. At a little distance is the château's farmhouse, today home to the Conservatoire International des Parcs et Jardins, a study and information centre on landscaping. The Conservatoire organises Chaumont's remarkable annual garden festival.

Accommodation and food in and around Chaumont-sur-Loire

Restaurant La Chancelière €–€€ *1 r. de Bellevue; tel: 02 54 20 96 95; fax: 02 54 33 91 71; www.restaurant-lachanceliere.fr.* Inevitably touristy, but this charming, simple, friendly place beside the Loire serves generous, tasty, classic French cooking at very modest prices.

Relais des Landes (and Restaurant La Closerie) €€–€€€ *N of Ouchamps on D7; tel: 02 54 44 40 40; fax: 02 54 44 03 89; www.relaisdeslandes.com.* A 13km drive from Chaumont, this pretty, flowery 17th-century farm estate is a perfect haven of unpretentious peace and comfort in tranquil open countryside 15km south of Blois. Swans swim in the lake, and there are 10ha of grounds, a swimming pool, and comfortable rooms arranged around gardens. There's also an excellent restaurant.

The Chaumont International Garden Festival

Weeds, lawns, pests and flowerbeds are not the issue, beauty and charm are hardly the point, at Chaumont's astonishing annual festival of gardens. Indeed, keen gardeners may be horrified by what they see here. The Chaumont festival, held in the château's former farm, is more of an outdoor art exhibition, and treats the garden as a medium in which a full range of ideas and messages can be creatively conveyed. Most of the 'gardens' on display resemble modern art installations and may consist of ground-up tyres, smashed bricks, broken glass or rusted metal… as well as plants. Each year, artists around the world apply to be allocated one of the 27 festival plots – all are exactly 250sq m and identically shaped – on which to deal imaginatively with the season's theme. A new theme is announced each year. At the end of the summer the gardens are destroyed.

CHENONCEAUX

ⓘ Chenonceaux Tourist Office *l r. Bretonneau; tel: 02 47 23 94 45; www.chenonceaux-blere-tourisme.com. Open May–Sept daily.*

Dramatic, romantic, beautiful – **Château de Chenonceau** is arguably the greatest of the Loire châteaux. It is also the most popular, and the pretty village of Chenonceaux (the village has an x in its name, the château does not) is often uncomfortably overcrowded during the day. The château stands in the waters of the River Cher, a magnificent display of Renaissance architecture, with one long gallery spanning the river from bank to bank, stepping through the water on arches. The château was built in 1521 and, for almost all of its history, has been owned or managed by women. Two of its proprietresses brought great festivity and society to

Right
Gardens at Chenonceau

Château de Chenonceau €€

Off D176 about 1km E of Chenonceaux; tel: 02 47 23 90 07; fax: 02 47 23 80 88; email: welcome@ chenonceau.com; www.chenonceau.com. Open all year round daily from 0900. Closing time depends on the month as follows: mid-Mar–mid-Sept 1900, second half Sept 1830, first half Oct and first half Mar 1800, second half Oct and second half Feb 1730, first half Nov and first half Feb 1700, mid-Nov–end Jan 1600. Guided tour available if required.

Waxworks Museum €€
At the château, same tel and entry times.

Below
Gallery at Chenonceau

Chenonceau: in the early 16th century Catherine de Medici held extravagant and ostentatious parties here, with naked nymphs, mock river battles and fireworks, for Europe's aristocracy; and 200 years later, at Madame Dupin's huge parties for the most distinguished people of the day, Chenonceau's guests included Voltaire, Bolingbroke and Montesquieu, while Rousseau was hired as a live-in tutor.

The château is reached by an avenue of trees, or on an enjoyable meandering route through the wooded park. There are lovely gardens each side of the keep (Diane de Poitiers' garden upstream, Catherine de Medici's downstream). The park, gardens, riverside paths and maze also make good places to relax after touring the château. To the right of the entrance, in the Orangerie and Bâtiment des Dômes, are places to eat and a **Waxworks Museum**. A drawbridge crosses to a terrace with the circular keep in the far corner. Called the Tour des Marques, this is a last remnant of a fortified manor house that originally occupied this part of the site: it bears the logo TBK (Thomas Bohier and Katherine), and Bohier's amusing motto – *S'il vient à point me souviendra* ('If it works out right I'll be remembered'), in memory of the Bohiers who originally constructed Chenonceau.

A bridge crosses to the main, square body of the château with corner turrets and corbels, standing on the underwater remnants of a watermill that once stood here. Inside, on both floors, four rooms open on to a central hall with curiously offset ribbed vaulting. On the ground floor the Salle des Gardes (Guardroom) has a painted wooden ceiling and large Flemish tapestries. The chapel has windows created by Max Ingrand in 1954 to replace those destroyed during the war. English inscriptions date from the time of Mary Stuart's stay here, when Scottish Guards accompanied her. Diane de Poitiers' room also has good 16th-century tapestries, as well as a distinctive fireplace. The modern portrait above is of Catherine de Medici, not Diane. Among the decorations in the Cabinet Vert (Green Room), Catherine de Medici's study, is a painting by Jordaens and a 16th-century tapestry in honour of the recent discovery of the Americas. It depicts flora and fauna previously unknown to the rest of the world. Off the study is Catherine's small library, with a coffered ceiling dating from 1521, and a view on to the river. François I's room has some beautiful 16th-century furniture, a Renaissance fireplace, Van Loo's *Three Graces* and other paintings, and a cabinet with autographs of Diane de Poitiers,

The Ladies of Chenonceau

One of the most unusual features of Chenonceau is the pre-eminent role played by women in its construction, design and decoration. Although the château was built from 1513 to 1521 by Thomas Bohier, chief tax collector for Charles VIII, Louis XII and François I, he was away in Italy while the work was in progress and left his wife, **Katherine Briçonnet**, to oversee the plans and construction. The basic design, style and positioning are thought to be due to her. In 1535 Chenonceau was taken by the crown in settlement of Bohier's debts and, in 1547, Henri II gave it to his mistress, **Diane de Poitiers**. She added the gardens and a bridge. When Henri died in 1559, his widow, **Catherine de Medici**, avenged herself on the mistress who had shamed her, forcing Diane to move out of Chenonceau (she gave her Chaumont in exchange). Catherine made a second garden, laid out the extensive château park, added the stables and other outbuildings, and turned the bridge into an elegant two-storey gallery. The next two owners were both women – Catherine de Medici left the château to her daughter-in-law, **Louise de Lorraine**, and she in turn bequeathed it to her niece, **Françoise de Lorraine**. The next proprietor was the tax collector Dupin, but the château and estate were managed by his wife. **Madame Dupin** was so popular locally that Chenonceau remained uniquely unharmed during the Revolution. After the Revolution the château was bought by a **Madame Pelouze**, who made several changes, removing some of Catherine de Medici's constructions, and redecorating the interior.

At the château

- free parking

- waiter-service restaurant in the Orangerie

- cafeteria in the Bâtiment des Dômes, former stables

- crèche

- play and games area

- boat rides on the Cher

Overleaf
Château de Chenonceau

who we discover wrote her name as Dianne de Poytié. Several interesting paintings hang in the Grand Salon (or Louis XIV room), including a Rubens and a portrait of Madame Dupin. The upholstery on the chairs is Aubusson tapestry. That the two flights of Italianate stairs to the first floor are straight was considered an innovation when first installed by Madame Bohier. The landing between the two flights has a balustrade with a good river view. The first-floor hall and the beautifully restored rooms on that floor are hung with remarkable 16th- and 17th-century tapestries.

The 60m-long gallery across the Cher, so beautiful when seen from outside, is less remarkable inside. Its bow windows look out on to the water, and at each end is a fine Renaissance fireplace. Stairs lead down to the interesting Renaissance kitchens. The upper floor of the gallery serves as a modern art showplace and opens on to the south bank with a drawbridge. During World War I the gallery became a hospital. In World War II it played a vital secret role for the Resistance because its main entrance on the north bank was in the occupied, German-ruled zone, while on the south bank it was in the so-called Free Zone ruled by the collaborationist Vichy government.

The Château de Chenonceau remains privately owned, property since 1913 of the Menier family, famous chocolate manufacturers.

Accommodation and food in and around Chenonceaux

Hôtel-restaurant Le Cheval Blanc €€ *pl. de l'Eglise, Bléré; tel: 02 47 30 30 14; fax: 02 47 23 52 80; www.lechevalblancblere.com.* Much less touristy than Chenonceaux, yet only 8km away, Bléré is a civilised little town by the Cher. This delightful family-run small hotel offers a friendly welcome and comfortable rooms with beamed ceilings. The restaurant is stylish and serves superb Michelin-rosetted food. Prices are very reasonable.

Hôtel-restaurant Le Bon Laboureur €€–€€€ *6 r. du Bretonneau; tel: 02 47 23 90 02; www.bonlaboureur.com.* 'The Good Workman' may sound plain and simple, but here is an outstanding and long-established restaurant (in the same family for three generations) dedicated to skilful preparation of refined dishes using the best local products. The hotel, a former coaching inn, is exquisite with flowers and greenery. Book well ahead.

MONTLOUIS-SUR-LOIRE

❶ Montlouis Tourist Office *pl. F Mitterrand; tel: 02 47 45 00 16; fax: 02 47 45 87 10; www.ville-montlouis-loire.fr. Open Mon–Sat 0900–1230 and 1400–1830, Sun 1000–1300.*

⬤ Wine producers co-operative *Cave des Producteurs, 2 route de St-Aignan; tel: 02 47 50 80 98; fax: 02 47 50 81 34. Opening times vary seasonally; phone for details. Free tastings.*

⓫ La Maison de la Loire € *60 quai Albert Baillet; tel: 02 47 50 97 52; fax: 02 47 50 81 93; email: maison.loire@wanadoo.fr. Open Mon–Sat 1400–1800.*

Château de la Bourdaisière €€ *Open May or Jun–Sept daily 1000–1900; Oct–mid-Nov 1000–1200 and 1400–1800; rest of year may be closed.*

This unremarkable but pleasant little town climbs the south bank of the Loire, facing Vouvray on the other side. It gives its name to one of the region's highly reputed white wines. The Montlouis *appellation* covers just 350ha extending from the Loire to the Cher, and only one grape variety is grown, Chenin blanc (known locally as Pineau de la Loire). The wines can be sampled in and around town at the **Cave des Producteurs** or a number of private wineries. Several have cellars cut into the tufa cliff along the main road. **La Maison de la Loire** has permanent and temporary exhibitions on the region's wildlife and vegetation. Montlouis was built by the influential Babou family, whose home was **Château de la Bourdaisière**, a short journey away. An imposing, restored Renaissance mansion in 55ha of parkland, it was constructed in 1520 for Philibert Babou, royal silversmith, and his wife, a royal mistress, the first of several to reside at the château. As well as the extensive park, it has a famous 19th-century 2ha vegetable garden where some 500 varieties of tomatoes are grown, with an amazing range of shapes and colours, among many other historic vegetable varieties. Tastings may be possible as part of the visit, according to the season.

Accommodation and food around Montlouis-sur-Loire

Château de la Bourdaisière €€€ *Follow signs from Montlouis-sur-Loire; tel: 02 47 45 16 31; fax: 02 47 45 09 11; email: contact@chateau labourdaisiere.com; www.chateaulabourdaisiere.com.* The charming Renaissance château in its own parkland offers several remarkable, luxurious rooms done out in grand, quasi-aristocratic style reminiscent of former residents. Good breakfasts.

MONTRICHARD

ℹ Montrichard Tourist Office *1 r. du Pont; tel: 02 54 32 05 10; fax: 02 54 32 28 80; email: info@montrichard.fr, www.montrichard.fr, www.officetourisme-montrichard.com. Open Apr Mon–Sat 0900–1200 and 1430–1800, Sun 1000–1200; May–Sept daily 0900–1900; Oct–Mar Mon–Fri 0930–1200 and 1430–1800.*

🏰 Donjon (castle keep) and museums €€ *tel: 02 54 32 05 10. Open Apr 1000–1200 and 1400–1800; May–Sept 1000–1900.*

⚫ Spectacles Médiévaux *In summer daily at 1430, 1600 & 1715.*

🍄 Bourré caves €€ *40 route des Roches, Bourré; tel: 02 54 32 95 33; fax: 02 54 32 42 99; www.le-champignon.com. Open Mar–Nov. The Caves Champignonnières and Ville Souterraine each have a 50-min guided tour. Tours depart at 1000, 1100, 1400, 1500, 1600, 1700, 1800 (the 1000, 1700 & 1800 tours do not run in Oct or Nov). Combined tickets available for the two tours, or to include Caves Monmousseau. Rare mushrooms for sale before or after tour, including some new varieties being developed here.*

This lively, picturesque little town rises from the Cher riverside up steep steps and narrow lanes lined with tiny white tufa houses. At the top of the town the imposing ruins of its massive square **donjon (castle keep)** are still enclosed by remnants of once-daunting fortifications. As well as giving a wonderful view along the Cher, the keep houses archaeological, ethnographic and historical museums and a bird of prey centre, which puts on impressive flight demonstrations. The *donjon* is also the setting for **'Spectacles Médiévaux'** on summer afternoons. Just below stands the Romanesque castle chapel, now the local parish church, where Jeanne de France, the disabled 12-year-old daughter of Louis XI, was married to an unwilling Louis d'Orléans. He abandoned her later to marry Anne of Brittany and be crowned Louis XII. Fine 15th- and 16th-century Gothic and Renaissance houses cluster near the church, and in r. Porte-au-Roi and other streets. Take the stairway called Petits-Degrés Ste-Croix to reach cave dwellings carved into the tufa cliff. The **Caves Monmousseau** wine cellars, making a traditional local sparkling wine, have 15km of underground storage tunnels in the cliff. Tufa, or *tuffeau*, the stone used for constructing the Loire châteaux, used also to be called Pierre de Bourré, because so much of it was quarried around Bourré, 3km east of Montrichard. The roadside cliff between the two villages is riddled with dwellings, a silk farm and storage areas carved out of the soft rock (some can be visited – ask at the tourist office). Impressive tours can be made in the darkness of the **Bourré caves**, labyrinthine underground tufa quarries now used for growing various varieties of mushrooms (*Caves Champignonnières*), with another section (called the *Ville Souterraine*, or 'Underground City') where cut and carved quarry walls eerily resemble real châteaux.

Right
Donjon, Montrichard

Caves Monmousseau €€ *tel: 02 54 71 66 66; fax: 02 54 71 66 64; email: monmousseau@monmousseau. com; www.monmousseau.com. Open Apr–Nov daily 1000– 1900 (last tour 1800); rest of year 1000–1200 and 1400–1700.*

Accommodation and food in Montrichard

Hôtel de la Tête Noire €€ *24 r. de Tours; tel: 02 54 32 05 55; fax: 02 54 32 78 37; www.latetenoire.com.* Unpretentious family-run hotel with simple, comfortable rooms. Ask for a room away from the road; it is prettier and quieter at the back, with a shaded terrace facing the Cher. Pleasant, reliable restaurant with modestly priced set menus.

PAGODE DE CHANTELOUP

Pagode de Chanteloup €€ *On the outskirts of Amboise on the Bléré road (D31); tel: 02 47 57 20 97; email: info@ pagode-chanteloup.com; www.pagode-chanteloup. com. Open daily Apr 1000– 1200 and 1400–1800; May & Sept 1000–1830; Jun 1000–1900; Jul–Aug 0930– 1930; Oct–Nov 1000–1700. Other months closed.*

Festival Easter Egg Festival at the Pagoda on Easter Monday.

The Château de Chanteloup was demolished in 1830, but its curious pagoda remains. Built in 1778, inspired by the similar structure at Kew Gardens in London, the exquisitely elegant 44m-tall tower stands in a lovely lakeside setting close to the Forêt d'Amboise woodland. There is a superb view from the top. Picnic baskets are available on the site, as well as a variety of traditional games and boat rides.

Right
Pagode de Chanteloup

Above
Vouvray produce

VOUVRAY

ℹ️ **Vouvray Tourist Office** *12 route Rabelais; tel: 02 47 52 68 73. Open approx Apr–Oct 0900–1300 and 1400–1830 (on Sun, am only); rest of year Tue, Wed, Fri & Sat 0900–1300 (on Fri, also 1400–1700). Times may vary. When closed, tel: 02 47 52 70 48 (Mairie).*

🛒 **Markets** *Tue and Fri am.*

🎭 **Festivals** *Wine Fairs are held at Whitsun, in mid-Aug, mid-Nov and at the end of Jan.*

🏛️ **Ecomusée du Pays de Vouvray** *€ 30 r. Victor Hérault; tel: 02 47 52 68 69. Open Wed–Mon 1030–1800.*

The small, rustic village lies off the busy main road beside the north bank of the Loire, hugged by its famous vineyards. On the edges are several cave dwellings or wine cellars cut out of tufa escarpments. Among the most highly regarded of French wines, with great character and finesse, the Vouvray appellations are all produced from Chenin blanc (called Pineau de la Loire locally). Nevertheless, Vouvray comes in several different styles, from crisply dry to richly sweet wines, still or sparkling. All should be drunk chilled. They are made by small growers in and around the village; several offer tastings. The **Ecomusée du Pays de Vouvray** explores local history, folk culture and winemaking.

Accommodation and food in Vouvray

Le Grand Vatel €–€€ *8 av. Brûlé; tel: 02 47 52 70 32; fax: 02 47 52 74 52.* This modest but comfortable family-run hotel has a popular restaurant with excellent set menus at moderate prices. River fish is the speciality, though meat is expertly prepared, too, and wines, of course, are Vouvray – the wine list features about 200 of them. Dine indoors, or on an attractive terrace with pink and white tables and chairs.

Suggested tour

W *www.tourism-
touraine.com* (Indre-et-
Loire *département*);
www.chambordcountry.com
(Loir-et-Cher
département). Both in
English and French.

Z *Autoroute* A10
(Paris–Bordeaux) and
the N152 on the north
bank, and the quieter
D951 on the south bank,
go to Tours and Blois.
TGVs run direct to Tours
from Paris and Lille (with
Eurostar connection to
London). There is a
frequent rail service along
the Loire Valley between
Tours and Blois.

Total distance: 95km, or 100km with the detour.

Time: The driving takes only 2hrs, but allow 2 days to visit the sights.

Links: At Tours (*see page 42*) this route connects with the Grands Chateaux: Tours–Chinon tour (*see page 68*), while at Blois (*see page 202*) it links up with that of the Cher and the Sologne (*see page 212*).

Route: From **Tours**, leave town on the D952, the main road (direction Orléans) on the north bank of the Loire. The road passes **Lulu Parc**, a 3ha family leisure park with play areas, a *guinguette*-style café and masses of entertainment (*daily 1000–2200*). It takes just a few minutes to reach **VOUVRAY** **①**.

Right
Vineyards at Vouvray

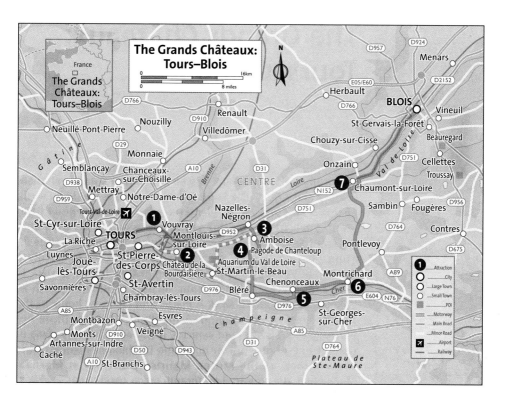

Detour: Cross the Loire here and follow signs carefully on complicated road junctions to reach **MONTLOUIS-SUR-LOIRE ❷**. Leave the village centre, again following signs carefully, to **Château de la Bourdaisière**. Using either the D751 along the Loire's south bank via Lussault-sur-Loire, or taking the cross-country route via St-Martin-le-Beau, continue towards Amboise. The **Aquarium du Val de Loire** lies just off the D283, the road between Lussault-sur-Loire and St-Martin-le-Beau. Continue into Amboise (*end of detour*).

From Vouvray, continue on the Loire's north bank road into **AMBOISE ❸**. When leaving the town, the **Parc Mini-Châteaux** and **PAGODE DE CHANTELOUP ❹** are both easily reached from the D31 as it circles Amboise on the south side. From the Pagoda, take the D31 to the attractive and appealing old market town of **Bléré**, turning there for **CHENONCEAUX ❺** (or travel straight from Amboise to Chenonceaux on the D81 through the Amboise Forest).

Follow either bank of the River Cher upriver to **MONTRICHARD ❻**. Take the D764 out of Montrichard (direction Blois) and turn off on to the D62 for **CHAUMONT-SUR-LOIRE ❼**. From Chaumont, take the Loire's south bank riverside road into Blois.

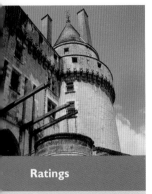

The Grands Châteaux: Tours–Chinon

Ratings

Châteaux	●●●●●
Architecture	●●●●○
Gardens	●●●○○
Food and drink	●●○○○
Museums	●●○○○
Villages	●●○○○
Children	●○○○○
Geology	●○○○○

This route, west of Tours, takes in a further selection of distinguished châteaux as well as offering a good variety of scenery and sights. The Loire is never far away, and vineyards, pear orchards and willow plantations flourish on its great flood plain. Each of the castles along the way has its own very different speciality – the great medieval fortress at Langeais, atmospheric *son-et-lumière* at Azay-le-Rideau, immaculate gardens at Villandry and the 'Sleeping Beauty' legend at Ussé. In between, there are fascinating villages to discover, such as Villaines, where wickerwork is made, and Quinçay, home of the ancient craft of pear-drying. A highlight, even for those not normally interested in old vehicles, is the extraordinary array of them, from a horse-drawn guillotine to children's scooters and fire engines, at the Musée Maurice Dufresne at Marnay. Meanwhile, the countryside, though never spectacular, is always pleasantly rural and quiet.

AZAY-LE-RIDEAU

ℹ️ **Azay-le-Rideau Tourist Office** *4 r. du Château; tel: 02 47 45 44 40; email: tourisme@ot-paysazaylerideau.fr; www.ot-paysazaylerideau.com. Open daily (except Sun Oct–Apr).*

🛒 **Market** *Wed*

This pleasant little town is worth a visit in its own right, though the attraction for most visitors is its charming **château**. It has an 11th-century church, a small toy museum, the **Musée du Jouet**, which displays the lifetime collection, particularly trains, of Michel Le Tenaff, a speciality delicatessen and a *salon de thé*.

The elegant Renaissance château, built by Gilles Berthelot, Treasurer to François I, is one of the Loire's most visited, thanks in part to its beautiful riverside setting and extensive park. Work on it started in 1518, but after nine years, before it was completed, the king confiscated it, accusing Berthelot of embezzlement.

Slender turrets crown each corner, while the centre has an ornately carved square staircase. This is unusual because most grand buildings up to that time had spiral ones. The fine rooms have impressive stone

The Grands Châteaux:
Tours–Chinon

France

Attraction
City
Large Town
Small Town
POI
Motorway
Main Road
Minor Road
Airport
Railway

The Grands Châteaux:
Tours–Chinon

0   12km
0   6 miles

Château €€ *tel: 02 47 45 42 04; fax: 02 47 45 26 61; http://azay-le-rideau.monuments-nationaux.fr. Open summer 0930–1800 (1900 in Jul–Aug); winter 1000–1230 and 1400–1730. Son-et-Lumière Les Imaginaires d'Azay in the grounds daily mid-May–Sept, usually from 2230.*

Right
Château, Azay-le-Rideau

Musée du Jouet €
*31 r. Nationale; tel: 02
47 45 97 65; www.
jouetsdautrefois.com. Open
Jun–Sept pm, then by
arrangement.*

J P Esclasse *22 r.
Nationale; www.
traiteur-esclasse.com.
Specialises in home-made
conserves.*

or marble fireplaces but are only sparsely furnished with portraits and tapestries. The kitchen is impressive, with rib vaulting and a huge fireplace. The château's *son-et-lumière* show is outstanding. Spectators wander around the grounds, to the accompaniment of music and lighting effects that evoke the château's heyday during the Renaissance.

Accommodation and food in Azay-le-Rideau

Le Grand Monarque €€ *3 pl. de la République, Azay-le-Rideau; tel: 02 47 45 40 08; www.legrandmonarque.com.* This 200-year-old coaching inn (with later additions) has an inner courtyard shaded by trees where guests can dine during the summer months. Menus are limited but inventive.

LA CHATONNIÈRE

La Chatonnière €
*tel: 02 47 45 40 29;
fax: 02 47 45 91 40;
www.lachatonniere.com.
Open daily Apr–Nov.*

When the owner of this small castle decided in 1992 to replace the orchards around it with a themed garden, he enlisted the help of a gardener who had been working in the famous château grounds at Villandry. Already it is fascinating to see how the garden, now divided into six themes, is gradually maturing. The *Jardin des Romances* has bowers of white roses, the *Jardin de l'Exubérance* is full of colour and the *Jardin de l'Abondance* grows many varieties of vegetable and fruit. The *Jardin des Sciences* was created in 2003. The *Jardin de l'Invraisemblance* was added in 2007, and the rose-filled *Jardin de la Luxuriance* was unveiled in 2008.

CINQ-MARS-LA-PILE

Tourist office *At the
Mairie; tel: 02 47 96
20 30; fax: 02 47 96 38 52.*

**Château de Cinq-
Mars €** *tel: 02 47 96
40 49; fax: 02 47 96 36 60;
email: chateau-cinq-mars@
wanadoo.fr. Open Apr–Jun &
mid-Sept–Oct weekends
1100–1800 or 1900;
Jul–mid-Sept daily except
Tue 0900–2000.*

This small village, now virtually a continuation of Langeais, owes the last part of its curious name to the square red-brick tower, over 30m high and dating back to Gallo-Roman times in the 2nd century, which stands on a wooded ridge above its eastern approach. No one knows why it was built. All that remains of the **Château de Cinq-Mars**, originally a classic feudal castle with a moat, is two fine round towers, each with beautifully vaulted rooms and superb views over the Loire. The rest of it was demolished in the 1640s by Louis XIII's ruthless minister, Cardinal Richelieu (*see page 99*), after its flamboyant owner, the 22-year-old Marquis de Cinq-Mars, made the mistake of plotting against him. The Marquis' exploits subsequently become well known when local writer Alfred de Vigny made them into a heroic story. The gardens are informally romantic, with sweet-smelling bushes, topiary and many trees.

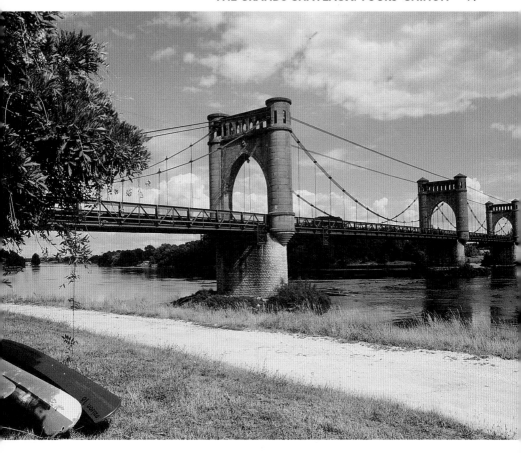

Above
Bridge at Langeais

LANGEAIS

🛈 **Langeais and Castelvalérie Tourist Office** *pl. du 14 Juillet; tel: 02 47 96 58 22; www.tourisme-langeais.com. Open daily except Sun pm.*

🏛 **Château de Langeais** *€€ tel: 02 47 96 72 60; fax: 02 47 96 54 44; email: contact@ chateau-de-langeais.com; www.chateau-de-langeais.com. Open May–mid-Sept daily.*

This pleasant little riverside town is dominated by its castle-like château, built by King Louis XI in the 1460s to establish his authority on the north bank of the Loire. Looking extremely forbidding, with high, sturdy walls, three round towers and a heavily machicolated drawbridge that still works, it broods over the short main street. However, viewed from the interior courtyard, the mullioned windows and delicately pointed dormers make it seem much more like a manor house. Originally four wings were planned, but only two were built. They form a right angle and, remarkably, have been altered very little since. In 1491 Anne of Brittany and Charles VIII of France married here in secret. A tableau of lavishly costumed figures in the room where the ceremony took place depicts the event, and Anne's wedding chest is among the items on show. At the end of the 19th century the

Market *Sun am.*
Good selection of
small shops selling local
food specialities and crafts.

château was owned by Jacques Siegfried, a rich businessman and art lover, who devoted many years to refurnishing it in the authentic style of the 15th century, complete with fine French and Flemish tapestries. The terraced gardens lead up to the ruins of a keep. The oldest still extant in France, it was built in the 11th century by Foulques Nerra, Count of Anjou. The suspension bridge over the Loire at Langeais, opened in 1849, has had a rather chequered history, having had to be closed three times for repairs totalling nine years.

Accommodation and food in Langeais

Hotel-Restaurant Errard €€ *2 r. Gambetta; tel: 02 47 96 82 12; www.errard.com.* Only 200m from the castle, this small, ivy-clad inn is family run. The owner-chef, Yannick Errard, specialises in seasonal country produce and local wines.

LUYNES

Château de Luynes
€€ *tel/fax: 02 47 55
67 55. Open Apr–Sept daily.*

The sturdy grey stone towers of **Château de Luynes**, high on the hillside above the little terraced town, make it look like a real fortress. In fact, it was transformed from a castle to a home 600 years ago and is now occupied by the 12th Duke. The main rooms, overlooking a charming courtyard, are sumptuously furnished with antiques and tapestries. Neatly laid-out gardens spread down the hillside. Over the years it has hosted many royal visitors, from King Louis XI of France in the 15th century to Britain's Prince Charles in the 20th.

A little way northeast of the village stand 44 arches of a Gallo-Roman aqueduct.

MUSÉE MAURICE DUFRESNE

**Musée Maurice
Dufresne** €€€ *Off
D120 in Marnay; tel: 02 47
45 36 18; fax: 02 47 45 28
62; email: info@musee-
dufresne.com; www.musee-
dufresne.com. Open low
season daily 0915–1800;
high season daily
0915–1900. Closed
Dec–Jan.*

This wide-ranging and still growing collection of over 3,000 vehicles, engines and machines has been gathered over a lifetime by Maurice Dufresne, a local businessman who built up a thriving business repairing and renovating second-hand machinery. He opened the museum in **Marnay** to the public in 1992, having rebuilt an old mill to house it. Everything on show has been lovingly restored and smartly painted. The variety is amazing, ranging from a macabre horse-drawn guillotine to a British double-decker bus. There are children's scooters, a 150-year-old hearse, a 1930s fire engine, traction engines, a World War II American tank, a 1959 shiny grey Buick and antique farm vehicles galore. Something for everyone, in fact! Adding to their interest, a notice by each exhibit says where it was found – often abandoned and rusting in a barn.

QUINÇAY

Poires Tapées à l'Ancienne *Quinçay, near Rivarennes; tel: 02 47 95 45 19; www.poiretapees. com. Open daily.* Pears also on sale as jam or pâtés, or in pots with wine.

The traditional way of preserving the pears grown in this area for centuries was to dry and crush them, producing *la poire tapée*. Christine and Yves Herin still use this *ancienne* method in a troglodyte cave at their home, where visitors are welcome to watch them at work. The whole pears are first dried very slowly in a wood-fired oven. Then they are squashed flat in a simple wooden press that expels any remaining air. The result is a delicious speciality for eating on its own or with a variety of dishes.

SACHÉ

Château de Saché *€ In Saché village; tel/fax: 02 47 28 86 50; www.musee-balzac.fr. Open Apr–Jun and Sept daily 1000–1800; Jul–Aug daily 1000–1900; Oct–Mar Wed–Mon 1400–1700 (closed Tue).*

This is a place of pilgrimage for devotees of the 19th-century writer, Honoré de Balzac. He was a frequent visitor to the **château**, as it was owned by one of his friends, and he wrote many of his famous novels while staying here. It is a large country house rather than a castle, surrounded by open parkland running down to the River Indre. Now impressively restored and furnished as Balzac would have known it in the 1830s, including reproduction wallpaper, it contains many of his personal possessions. Most of his manuscripts show his detailed corrections – he was a consummate perfectionist. One room is devoted to caricatures of some of the contemporaries featured in his books; another contains the old printing presses and equipment he used while trying to earn a living in publishing.

Accommodation and food in Saché

Auberge du XIIème Siècle €€ *tel: 02 47 26 88 77.* Balzac liked to frequent this ancient hostelry close to the château. To dine under its 900-year-old beams today, you need to book well ahead; its gourmet menus have a high reputation.

Balzac

Born and educated in Tours, Honoré de Balzac (1799–1850) spent most of his working life in Paris. However, he was a frequent visitor to the Loire Valley and often set his novels here. His first attempts at writing were unsuccessful so he went into publishing instead, but fared no better. At the age of 30 he tried again, spurred on by the need to pay off his debts, and went on to produce over 90 books. They reflected contemporary society in extraordinary detail through a wide variety of vividly portrayed characters.

RIGNY-USSÉ

ⓘ Château d'Ussé €€ *for guided (obligatory) visits of the interior; € for grounds, chapel and 'Sleeping Beauty' tower only. Tel: 02 47 95 54 05; www.chateaudusse.fr. Open mid-Feb–mid-Nov daily 1000–1800 (Apr–Aug daily 1000–1900); last tickets 1hr before closing. A Boutique Gastronomique next to the castle has a selection of local specialities, including wines, jams, biscuits and sweets.*

Set against a wooded hillside overlooking the River Indre, **Château d'Ussé** looks as much like Sleeping Beauty's castle as one could wish. Covered with pointed turrets and mysterious little windows, it inspired the French writer Charles Perrault to use it as the setting for his version of the famous fairy tale, after he was invited to stay there by his friend, the Count of Blacas, an ancestor of the present owner who is an international lawyer. Today's visitors can climb 84 steps up a spiral staircase in one of the towers to see life-size tableaux depicting the story. Occupying the site of a medieval fortress, the building dates from 1642 but was extended over the following two centuries to create an elegant family home to which formal gardens and an orangery were added. The main part of the castle is furnished with original pieces and many of the walls are covered in Flemish tapestries. The grounds also contain a 16th-century chapel in pure Renaissance style with fine stone carving and wood panelling.

Accommodation and food in Rigny-Ussé

Le Clos d'Ussé € *7 r. Principale; Rigny-Ussé; tel: 02 47 95 55 47.* An intimate eight-room hotel with a terrace restaurant in the long street below Ussé castle.

Below
Château d'Ussé

SAVONNIÈRES

Grottes Pétrifiantes de Savonnières € *Situated left of D7 just west of Savonnières; tel: 02 47 50 00 09; www.grottes-savonnieres.com; 60min guided tours of the caves Feb–Dec daily. Small museum, shop and wine on sale.*

Above
Fishing on the Indre

The main reason to head for this riverside village is the **Grottes Pétrifiantes de Savonnières**, two extraordinary caves, where *tuffeau* stone was quarried out of the hillside as early as Gallo-Roman times. One was discovered around 500 years ago but the other remained hidden until 1947. Over the centuries water has seeped into them from springs, creating shallow pools and forming stalactites and other curious patterns in their extensive galleries. Both can now be visited and are exciting for all ages, although children will particularly like the models of dinosaurs and other animals displayed in alcoves. Everything has been petrified by the dripping water, leaving it coated in creamy white calcium. The museum shop at the entrance sells a range of small items such as vases, dishes and carvings that have been petrified through being left in the caves for at least six months. Visits end with a glass of local wine served in a large grotto that has been transformed into a bar, at the far end of one of the caves.

VILLAINES-LES-ROCHERS

🅗 **Co-opérative Vannerie de Villaines** I r. de la Cheneillère, Villaines-les-Rochers; www.vannerie.com. Large shop open Apr–mid-Oct daily 0900–1200 and 1400–1900 (except Sun) and hols 1000–1200 and 1400–1900; mid-Oct–Mar daily 1400–1900. Admission free.

Museé de la Vannerie 22 r. des Caves Fortes. Open May–Sept Tue–Sun pm.

Over 150 years ago, one of France's earliest co-operatives was set up in this straggling village where wickerwork has been the main source of income since the Middle Ages. Baskets and furniture made by local craftspeople – who grow and gather the canes from the riverside willows – are on sale in workshops throughout the village and also at the workers' **co-operative**, where visitors can watch the different products being made. In the village's small **Musée de la Vannerie**, old basket-making implements are on show, together with a variety of antique wickerwork items.

Right
Basket-maker, Villaines-les-Rochers

VILLANDRY

Château de Villandry €€
tel: 02 47 50 02 09; www.
chateauvillandry.com. Open
daily 0900 until sunset or
1930 at latest. Details of all
the plants are displayed on
boards.

The **Château de Villandry**'s chief attraction is its outstanding gardens, but it would be a mistake to underrate the building itself, which has elegant classical façades and an ornamental moat. When Joachim de Carvallo, a Spanish doctor, bought the estate in 1906, he and his family devoted themselves to restoring the extensive gardens to their original formal Renaissance style. The best way to appreciate their scale and precise detail is to look down on them from the top of the château's keep. There are three large terraces to walk around, as well as a maze. The top terrace has a small lake and water garden, the middle one is a flower garden where neat box hedges form geometric shapes, and the bottom level has seasonal fruit and vegetables, including melons (a speciality of the area), artichokes and asparagus, growing in precise patterns bordered by box and yew hedges.

Accommodation and food in and around Villandry

Auberge Le Colombien € *2 r. de la Mairie, Villandry; tel: 02 47 50 07 27.* A short walk from Villandry castle, this charming family-run hotel and restaurant in the centre of the village occupies three converted cottages set around a small courtyard.

L'Etape Gourmande € *Domaine de la Giraudière, ask in Villandry for directions; tel: 02 47 50 08 60; www.letapegourmande.com.* This lovely farmhouse restaurant a few kilometres from Villandry is well worth seeking out for the delicious and simple meals featuring their own goat's cheese, complemented by excellent local wines. Visit the dairy and buy more cheeses if you like.

Right
Château and gardens, Villandry

Suggested tour

Total distance: 104km. The detour to Crissay-sur-Manse adds 22km.

Time: 2 hours' driving time, but allow 2 days for the full route. Those with limited time should concentrate on Villandry, Azay-le-Rideau and Ussé.

Links: At Tours the route links with the Grands Châteaux: Tours–Blois tour (*see page 52*) and the two routes could easily be combined into one longer tour, starting from Blois and driving the first tour in reverse order. Likewise, at Chinon, the route links with the circular South Touraine tour (*see page 90*), and these (or indeed all three) could be linked into a major tour of this part of the region.

Route: Leave **Tours** (*see page 42*) along the north bank of the Loire on the N152 to see **LUYNES** ❶ and its magnificent castle. Then, after a further 10km, turn right to **CINQ-MARS-LA-PILE** ❷ and then **LANGEAIS** ❸. Leave Langeais across its handsome suspension bridge over the Loire, turning immediately left on to the D16, which goes northeast, following the river closely to **VILLANDRY** ❹. On this pleasant country road, just before **SAVONNIERES** ❺, you see the **Grottes Pétrifiantes** beside the road at the foot of the wooded hillside. Then, passing through the village itself, animal lovers should look out for the unusual doorway of the church on the left as it is carved with doves and other animals, though now eroded by time. After the church, turn right past the *Mairie* and shortly fork right following the signs to **Druye**. Here, the road climbs up to large expanses of open fields, crossing the railway and the new A85 motorway to continue along the D751 to **SACHÉ** ❻. From here, it is about 12km to **Château de Candé**, a fascinating short detour. Leave Saché on the D17 signed for Azay-le-Rideau, turning left on to the D217 to go to **VILLAINES-LES-ROCHERS** ❼.

Detour: Continue on the D217 for a detour to **Crissay-sur-Manse**. Crissay has been designated one of France's *Plus Beaux Villages* (Most Beautiful Villages). Nestling below the ruins of its medieval castle are

---

◐ **Château de Candé**
€ *Near Saché; tel: 02 47 26 10 85 or 02 47 26 78 30. Open daily all year.* It is worth making a detour to this extraordinary and impressive château where, on 3 June 1937, Edward VIII (renouncing the British throne to become the Duke of Windsor) married the American Wallis Simpson. Originally 16th-century, the building was refurbished as a private home in the 1930s to the highest standard of luxury and taste of the time. The exterior is neo-Gothic and Renaissance, while the opulent interior includes a superb Art Deco bathroom.

Right
Crissay-sur-Manse village

France

The Grands
Châteaux:
Tours–Chinon

D749

Gizeaux

1 ....Attraction
O ....City
O ....Large Town
O ....Small Town
........POI
........Motorway
........Main Road
........Minor Road
........Airport
........Railway

N

D959   D938   A28   Chanceaux-
sur-Choisille   A10

D34   Ambillou   Mettray   Notre-Dame-d'Oé

Tours-Val-de-Loire ✈

Cléré-
les-Pins   St-Cyr-sur-Loire   Vouvray   D952

TOURS   Montlouis-
Luynes   La Riche   sur-Loire
1   St-Pierre-
2   Joué-   des-Corps   Château de la
Cinq-Mars-la-Pile   lès-Tours   Bourdaisière
Langeais   **4** **5**   St-Avertin   D976
3   Villandry   Savonnières   Chambray-lès-Tours
Val de Touraine   D943

Marnay   La Chatonnière   A85   Esvres
9   Montbazon   Veigné
Quinçay   CENTRE   Monts   D943
A85   **10**
Rigny-   **11**   **8**   Azay-le-Rideau   Artannes-
Ussé   sur-Indre   D910
Huismes   D751   Saché
12   **7**   **6**   St-Branchs
Avoine   120   D132   Villaines-les-   A10
Beaumont-en-Véron   ▲   Roches   D757   D50
Touraine

Chinon   Avon-les-   D138   Neuil
D21   Roches   St-Epain
Crissay-   D21
Musée de la Devinière   Vienne   Tavant   sur-Manse
Château du Rivau
D759   D760   L'Ile-Bouchard

**The Grands Châteaux:
Tours–Chinon**

0   12km
0   6 miles

an old church with a spire, a handful of 15th-century houses with
small turrets, and two tiny shops. One sells antiquarian books, the
other delicious home-made honey. Leaving the D21 shortly after
Crissay, a narrow country road leads past cornfields to another tiny
village, **Avon-les-Roches**. Its small, 12th-century church is one of the
route's real gems, particularly the porch, which has delicately carved
pillars and arches. Visitors who want to see inside can borrow the key
from the *Mairie* round the corner. Next, turn right on to the long,
straight D132, which leads directly to Azay-le-Rideau. On the way it
crosses a military training area where you pass a small memorial on
the right to members of the French Resistance who were executed at
the nearby Ruchard barracks in 1944 (*end of detour*).

From Villaines, take the D57 for 6km to **AZAY-LE-RIDEAU** **8**. Leave
Azay-le-Rideau on the D57 to visit **LA CHATONNIERE** **9** gardens and
then return to the junction with the D120, which leads to **MUSÉE
MAURICE DUFRESNE** **10** at **Marnay**. From there, the D7 continues to
QUINCAY **11** and on to **RIGNY-USSE** **12**. Leave the village on the D7
beside the Chinon forest, turning left on to the D16 at **Huismes** to
continue to Chinon (*see page 80*).

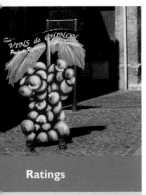

Chinon

Ratings

Restaurants	●●●●●
Wine tasting	●●●●●
Châteaux	●●●●○
History	●●●●○
Architecture	●●●○○
Historical sights	●●●○○
Walking	●●●○○
Museums	●●○○○

Wine is Chinon's primary concern, which may explain why this small, pretty town has never become swamped with visitors, despite its attractive riverside setting and 2,000 years of history. You sense that its inhabitants are too deeply steeped in the trade to want to get involved in anything as frivolous as tourism. And yet Chinon has much to offer the interested visitor – after all, it was here that Joan of Arc first stepped into the pages of history and Richard the Lionheart lay in state – without the trappings of tourist exploitation that sometimes accompany such an illustrious heritage. Built in creamy *tuffeau* stone with grey rooftops, Chinon nestles between a wooded ridge, topped by the ruins of its once-formidable castle, and the serene River Vienne. All the sights are easily manageable on foot and could be covered in a single day, although this would prevent you from doing justice to the outstanding choice of restaurants. From their calibre it's clear that the people of Chinon take their food as seriously as they do their wine.

Getting there and getting around

ⓘ Chinon Tourist Office *pl. d'Hofheim; tel: 02 47 93 17 85; www.chinon.com; also at the castle, av. François Mitterrand, Jul–Aug.*

◑ Market *Thur, pl. Jeanne d'Arc; produce am only, clothes etc all day. A recent Chinon speciality is wine jam.*

By road
Leaving the A85 at exit 5 (where it currently ends), the town centre is a 14km journey south along the D749. From Tours, the shortest route is on the D751.

By rail
Trains operate between Chinon and Tours. There are also steam excursions in summer departing from Richelieu (35km southeast).

Parking
In the town centre, parking is allowed beside the River Vienne and on other streets, except in the old town. Meters operate 0900–1200 and 1400–1800 on the central streets (maximum 1hr 20min), or you can stay in the town's car parks for up to 3hrs. Free parking Sunday and Monday can be found near the castle or streets further afield. Several

Chinon

Attraction
Important Building
Park
Main Road
Other Road
Information

Chinon
0 .... 100 metres
0 .... 100 yards

Marché à l'Ancienne *Third Sun in Aug* when Chinon turns the clock back to the 1900s, celebrating with costumed stallholders, local products and folk music.

central streets are pedestrianised: r. Voltaire and its continuations (r. Haute St-Maurice and r. Jean-Jacques Rousseau) and also r. du Commerce/r. Rabelais.

Getting around

Bicycles, including children's cycles and tandems, can be hired from the Hôtel Agnès Sorel, *4 quai Pasteur; tel: 02 47 93 04 37.*

Guided walking tours of the old town are run *Jun–Sept*. A 45min 'road train' tour with English commentary runs *Easter–Sept weekends, Jul–Aug daily*.

Sights

Caves de Pierre Plouzeau *94 r. Haute St-Maurice; tel: 02 47 93 32 11; www.plouzeau. com. Open Apr–Sept Tue–Sat 1000–1230 and 1500–1830.*

Caves de Pierre Plouzeau

This network of tunnels beneath Chinon castle are wide enough for a car to drive through. They result from the quarrying carried out in the 12th century for stone to build the castle above. The shaft through which it was hauled up can still be seen. Today, they make perfect wine cellars, being at a constant 12°C. However, the 150,000 bottles stored here take up only a fraction of the space available and the caves are a sight in themselves, whether or not you intend to invest in a bottle or two of the excellent wine.

Château de Chinon

Chinon's castle has seen 2,000 years of history, though its most glorious time was the second half of the 12th century when it was the favourite residence of the Plantagenet kings. Henry II (Count of Anjou and King of England) built most of it, intending to make it the hub of his vast empire. After he died of a fever there in 1189, it was completed by his son, Richard the Lionheart.

Spread along a hillside above the town, the massive fortress is now largely in ruins. Nevertheless, its three main sections, separated by dry moats, can still be detected. Fort St-Georges, built by Henry II to protect the eastern end, is now a complete ruin. From the fort, you cross a bridge over a dry moat leading into the unusually shaped Tour de l'Horloge (Clock Tower), which is tall and thin. This houses a small exhibition about Joan of Arc, the Musée Jeanne d'Arc. The sturdy ramparts around the main part, called the Château du Milieu, now enclose lawns and the remains of various towers whose slit holes and steep interior steps, leading down as well as up, make them intriguing to explore and particular fun for children. From the walls, you get good views down to the river over the rooftops of the town. Inside the Royal Apartments, now a stone shell, a large model shows the castle as it was 500 years ago, and a 10-minute audiovisual presentation in their Guardroom provides a useful introduction to its history. Next

Below
View of Château de Chinon and bridge

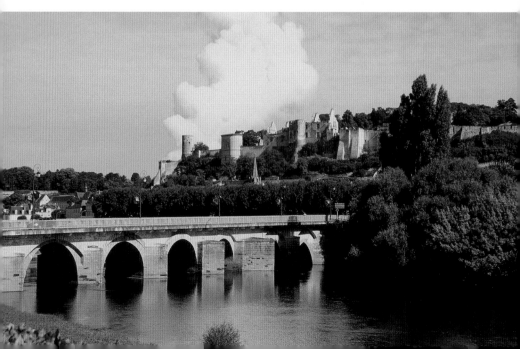

comes the Great Hall, empty except for a huge fireplace, where Joan of Arc was received by the Dauphin, Charles VII. In an anteroom, a life-size tableau depicts the famous meeting at which the king hid in the crowd but was immediately recognised by Joan, convincing him that she was a divine messenger. Across another dry moat, the round Fort du Coudray keep is where four Templar knights were imprisoned in 1308 on their way to be tried. Their names, which they carved on the north wall, can still be seen.

Maison de la Rivière 2 quai Pasteur; tel: 02 47 93 21 34. Open Apr–Nov Tue–Sun.

Maison de la Rivière

A unique collection of scale models of the boats that once plied up and down the Loire is gathered in this airy 150-year-old building, formerly an abattoir. The collection shows how the river's trade reached its height in the 18th century when cargo boats sailed up and down it for 400km, until the arrival of railways largely superseded them. Other models illustrate the role that ferries played until they were replaced by bridges. Altogether, the displays illustrate a fascinating variety of stories about the Loire's history. The museum's workshop shows how boats were built.

Water jousting

Until World War I water jousting was a popular feature of the river festivals held each summer along the Loire and other rivers in the area. The last surviving example of one of the dunking horses used is on show in the Maison de la Rivière at Chinon. Attached to a rope, the 'horse' – hinged in the middle – was rolled down a sloping 8m plank overhanging the river. When the rope abruptly stopped it, the rear half shot upwards, catapulting the rider into the water. As he flew through the air he had to try to grab a flag placed alongside. The few who succeeded were acclaimed, but rewarded only with a few coins.

Chapelle Ste-Radegonde

This tiny 11th-century frescoed chapel is built into a cave in the hillside, where a 6th-century hermit had his cell and was buried.

Musée du Vin et de la Tonnellerie € 12 r. Voltaire; tel: 02 47 93 25 63. Open Apr–Sept daily.

Musée du Vin et de la Tonnellerie

Having descended into an ancient wine cellar, visitors pass a series of tableaux with full-size animated models illustrating how the commentator's 'grandfather' used to transform his grapes into wine in the days before mechanisation took over. The 19th-century equipment on show includes casks, grape-pickers and a huge wooden winepress. Halfway round comes a welcome touch: you are invited to sample a glass of Chinon wine produced by today's methods. A selection is on sale in a small shop at the end of the tour.

Overleaf
View from the château

Musée de la Devinière € 2km SW of Chinon in the village of Seuilly; tel: 02 47 31 43 27; www.musee-rabelais.fr. Open daily.

Musée de la Devinière (Musée Rabelais)

La Devinière, the farmhouse where the writer François Rabelais was born in 1494, is a simple rectangular building. Its upper storey now houses some of his books and other memorabilia. A network of cellars runs under the house – you can go in one side and out the other.

Rabelais

Menus, streets and even restaurants are named after one of Chinon's best-known sons. François Rabelais, son of a local lawyer, was born here in 1494, became a monk, studied Ancient Greek and also became a doctor before making his name as a writer. His racy but erudite *Pantagruel*, published in 1532, and *Gargantua*, three years later, established his literary reputation throughout Europe. These two books tell the story of a father, Gargantua, and his son, Pantagruel, and their adventures, written in an amusing, extravagant and satirical vein. Even though most chapters are humorous, wildly fantastic and sometimes absurd, a few relatively serious passages have become famous for descriptions of humanistic ideals of the time. The author is believed to have written a one-line will: 'I have nothing, I owe a great deal, and the rest I leave to the poor.'

Musée des Amis du Vieux Chinon et de la Batellerie € 44 r. Haute St-Maurice; tel: 02 47 93 18 12; www.chinon-histoire.org. Open Easter–Oct daily.

Musée des Amis du Vieux Chinon et de la Batellerie

The Dauphin, Charles VII, summoned his supporters to a parliament in 1428 in this then newly built mansion, the Maison des Etats-Généraux, in order to raise support and funds to rid the country of the English. Today, a fine collection of porcelain, furniture, paintings and other local treasures is on display in its beamed rooms.

Shopping

The town centre lacks any large stores, but there is a Leclerc hypermarket, *open daily 0900–2000*, just beyond the castle on the D751. Most of the small shops are gathered around pl. Victoire and the pedestrianised r. du Commerce that runs off it. Local specialities include wine jam and goat's cheese.

Accommodation and food in and around Chinon

Agnès Sorel € *4 quai Pasteur; tel: 02 47 93 04 37; www.agnes-sorel.com.* This small, charming hotel, with ten smartly decorated rooms, is well placed on the edge of the old town overlooking the River Vienne – though some rooms face a rear terrace. No restaurant, but picnic lunches are available; also bike hire.

Camping Municipal € *quai Danton;* *tel: 02 47 93 08 35. Open mid-Mar–mid-Oct.* Facing Chinon castle and close to the River Vienne, the site has 275 pitches set among trees and gardens.

Crêperie du Grand Carroi € *30 r. du Grand Carroi; tel: 02 47 93 18 94.* A small, informal restaurant with a friendly style, serving an array of savoury and sweet pancakes and wholemeal Brittany *galettes*, along with huge salads to make them into a meal.

Le Manoir de la Giraudière € *15 r. Giraudière, Beaumont-en-Véron; tel: 02 47 58 40 36; www.giraudiere.com.* In peaceful countryside a short drive northwest from the town (follow the Savigny sign off the D749), this 17th-century farmhouse spreads around a courtyard shaded by lime trees. The 25 bedrooms are atmospherically furnished with antiques and period décor, but have

modern bathrooms. After dining in the restaurant (**€€**), guests can retire for a drink to the unusual square *pigeonnier* (dovecote), which has 901 holes in its white stone walls for the birds.

Les Années 30 €€ *78 r. Haute St-Maurice; tel: 02 47 93 37 18.* Though located in the heart of old Chinon, and with a 1930s theme, the menus are definitely not old-fashioned. Instead, they feature inventive modern cuisine with striking flavour combinations, such as a tagine of wild boar with lemon.

Hôtel de France €€ *47–49 pl. du Général de Gaulle; tel: 02 47 93 33 91.* Chinon's oldest hotel occupies a 16th-century residence in the centre of town. Some of its 30 rooms, each individually furnished, have views of the castle.

Restaurant l'Océanic €€ *13 r. Rabelais; tel: 02 47 93 44 55.* Chef Patrick Descoubes, owner of this highly regarded restaurant, specialises in seafood – huge plates of oysters and choose-your-own lobsters from a tank – served by his wife, Marie-Paule, and a team of nimble waitresses. There are three small indoor sections and a terrace outside.

Suggested walk

Total distance: 2km; the detour to the Chapelle Ste-Radegonde adds 1km.

Time: 1 hour, but allow a day to see all the sights.

Start your walk at the town's highest spot – the **CHATEAU DE CHINON ❶**. Its ramparts provide a splendid panorama over the town – a tightly packed jumble of cream buildings under steep grey roofs – down to the tree-lined River Vienne and its red sandbanks. Turn right outside the castle, where a rough stone path leads sharply downhill. The 5-minute walk over large cobbles brings you to the old **r. Voltaire**, a narrow street that runs straight through the medieval part of the town. You join it at the **Grand Carroi**, the crossroads where Joan of Arc arrived in the town on 6 March 1649 and took her horse to drink at the well. It is said that this was the moment when she was transformed from mere peasant girl to the famous warrior who was to lead the French against the English. The Maison Bleue, now a craft shop, and the Maison Rouge restaurant both occupy carefully restored medieval houses there. Many other buildings along r. Voltaire date back to the 15th century, including the **Maison des Etats-Généraux**, now the **MUSEE DES AMIS DU VIEUX CHINON ET DE LA BATELLERIE ❷**, where in 1428 the Dauphin summoned his supporters. It stands on the spot where Richard the Lionheart died on 6 April 1199 from wounds he had received in Châlus. A map on the nearby wall indicates which buildings date from the Middle Ages and which from the Renaissance. Quiet courtyards, interesting gables, miniature towers, white shutters and colourful window boxes all add to the interest of a stroll along this attractive old street. The Gargantua Hotel at No 48 occupies the 15th-century **Palace du Baillage**.

On reaching **Eglise St-Maurice**, which was rebuilt by Henry II and has a fine square tower and spire, you leave the cobbles – thankfully – and soon come to the end of the street. There, the subterranean **CAVES DE PIERRE PLOUZEAU ❸** wine cellar deep under the castle provides a welcome opportunity to sample and buy some of the excellent local vintages. On **Quai Pasteur** beside the river, a memorial to 271 prisoners massacred in the

Below
Statue of Rabelais

Chinon

- **1** Attraction
- Important Building
- Park
- Main Road
- Other Road
- **i** Information

0 — 100 metres
0 — 100 yards

Ile de Tours

Vendéen War in 1793 is a reminder of the town's often troubled past. The **MAISON DE LA RIVIERE** ❹ is a little further along the riverside promenade. After visiting it, turn back and continue under the neat row of plane trees beside the river, past the arched bridge to the bronze **statue of François Rabelais**. He sits, book in hand, with his back to the water looking thoughtfully towards the busy **pl. du Général de Gaulle**.

The pedestrianised **r. Rabelais** (to the right off the square) has interesting shops and restaurants. A left turn along **r. de la Lamproie**, past its timbered houses, leads to the tourist information office on pl. d'Hofheim. Then it is a short way back across pl. du Général de Gaulle to the **MUSEE DU VIN ET DE LA TONNELLERIE** ❺ for another glass or two of wine.

Detour: Before succumbing to the temptations in the wine museum, it is worth continuing along r. Jean-Jacques Rousseau to the **Collégiale St-Mexme**, an impressive white-towered church. The road continues uphill to **r. du Côteau Ste-Radegonde**, a quiet lane along a leafy ridge above the outskirts of the town which leads past troglodyte dwellings to the ruins of the **CHAPELLE STE-RADEGONDE** ❻, a delightfully peaceful spot.

South Touraine

Ratings

Churches	●●●●
Châteaux	●●●
History	●●●
Archaeology	●●●
Wines	●●●
Forests	●●●
Gardens	●●
Children	●●

South Touraine is one of the most battle-scarred parts of France. Long before written accounts recorded a succession of conquests, the area was inhabited by primitive tribes who have left us their Neolithic tools and dolmens. When the Romans came they ousted the Celtic tribes; later, the Moors tried to take the area but were turned back at Poitiers, and then the powerful counts of Anjou expanded their domain and built fortresses to protect it. Under the Plantagenets the English made much of the area their own, ultimately to lose it to the French crown at the end of the Hundred Years War. With growing stability, the gentle hills of South Touraine were to enjoy some prosperity and peace, while their geographical position – between Anjou and Bourges, Poitiers and Paris – ensured the constant passage of travellers and a continuing royal presence. Today, the fortified castles surmounting many towns are part of the area's great attraction, while its good wines and varied cuisine are an undeniable lure to the gourmet traveller.

AZAY-LE-FERRON

ⓘ Azay-le-Ferron Tourist Office 35 r. Hersent Luzarche; tel: 02 54 39 29 08; fax: 02 54 39 25 12; email: tourisme-azayleferron@wanadoo.fr. Open Jun–Aug 0915–1200 and 1400–1715.

ⓗ Château d'Azay-le-Ferron € tel: 02 54 39 20 06; www.chateau-azay-le-ferron.com. Open May–Sept 1000–1800 except Tue.

Like so many small towns in rural France, Azay-le-Ferron grew around its **château**. This stately 15th- to 18th-century building has four principal sections: the 15th-century tower Frottier, the 16th-century François I Pavilion, the 17th-century Brateuil Pavilion and 17th-century buildings for the domestic staff. Managed by the Musée des Beaux-Arts de Tours, it has been renovated and its 20-odd rooms redecorated with period furniture and paintings (including the well-known and rather risqué depiction of the beautiful Agnès Sorel, slightly underdressed to reveal a naked breast) re-creating the opulence of its original reception rooms. It was often used as a hunting lodge, and its 18th-century park is also open (*free of charge*) and boasts a neatly trimmed garden of geometric box hedges and an amusing topiary garden. Azay also boasts an interesting church dating from Romanesque times: the **Eglise St-Nazaire**. Of particular note in this church (hiding behind a 19th-century façade) is its nave, which

The map shows South Touraine region with the following locations:

Quinçay, Monts, Veigné, Champeigne, A85, Azay-le-Rideau, Artannes-sur-Indre, Rigny-Ussé, Caché, Villaines, D910, St-Branchs, D764, D751, 120, D757, D132, A10, D31, Avon-les-Roches, Touraine, Neuil, D50, D943, Forêt des Loches, Chinon, D21, Crissay-sur-Manse, Chartreuse du Liget, Montrésor, Tavant, D760, St-Epain, Manthelan, Loches, Beaulieu-lès-Loches, Nouans-les-Fontaines, Château du Rivau, L'Ile-Bouchard, D760, Plateau de Ste-Maure, Loché, Champigny-sur-Veude, Pouzay, Ste-Maure-de-Touraine, E05, D31, D43, D749, Ligueil, CENTRE, Richelieu, La Celle-St-Avant, Bridoré, D61, D20, Port-de-Piles, D31, Châtillon-sur-Indre, Attraction, Large Town, Les Ormes, Descartes, D50, St-Flovier, D943, Small Town, D749, D58, Abilly, POI, Dangé-St-Romain, Le Grand-Pressigny, D975, Clion, Motorway, St-Gervais-les-Trois-Clochers, La Guerche, Espace Animalier, Main Road, A10, Ingrandes, Preuilly-sur-Claise, Azay-le-Ferron, Minor Road, D750, D725, D925, Railway, Thuré, 171, D725, Coussay-les-Bois, D41, Martizay, D926, Scorbé-Clairvaux, Chatellerault, D14, Mézières-en-Brenne, D925, La Roche-Posay, Yzeures-sur-Creuse, South Touraine, Naintré, POITOU-CHARENTES, Tournon-St-Martin, France, Beaumont, Pleumartin, D6, South Touraine, Vouneuil-sur-Vienne, Angles-sur-l'Anglin, D950, Bonneuil-Matours, St-Pierre-de-Maillé, Fontgombault, 12km, 6 miles, N, A85

Eglise St-Nazaire €
*Open daily, in summer
0830–1800, in winter
0900–1700.*

drew on the cathedral of Angers for its inspiration, and the various heads carved in the form of capitals and as keystones on the vaulting. The Romanesque portal on the south side of the church is also in a good state of repair.

BRIDORÉ

Château de
Bridoré €–€€
*tel: 02 47 94 72 63;
www.chateau-bridore.com.
Open Jun–Sept 1300–1900.*

On the southern limits of this village, amid fertile agricultural country, rises the fortified **Château de Bridoré** with, between the servants' quarters and those of the seigneur, an impressive dungeon. Records mention it in the 7th century but most of what can be seen today is 13th- to 15th-century. Among its guests were Joan of Arc, Charles VII and VIII, and François I. Imbert de Bastarnay was responsible for remodelling it in the 1400s. One of its curiosities is the steam bath on the ground floor, believed to have been brought back from the Crusades. The small and unfinished **Eglise St-Roch** contains,

Opposite
Château d'Azay-le-Ferron

in its crypt, the tomb of the family of Boursault de Vintais, one-time owners of the château. There's a fine 15th-century statue of St Roch sporting an interesting floppy hat.

Accommodation and food around Bridoré

Le Relais du Berry € *2 route Tours, Fléré-la-Rivière; tel: 02 54 39 32 57.* There are inexpensive eating places and bars at the neighbouring village of Fléré, including this charming and homely restaurant offering good traditional menus and excellent value for money.

CHÂTEAU DU RIVAU

Château du Rivau
€ *tel: 02 47 95 77 47; email: info@chateaudurivau. com; www.chateaudurivau. com. Open May & Oct weekends and hols 1400–1900; Jun & Sept daily except Tue 1300–1900; Jul–Aug daily 1300–1900. Closed at all other times except by appointment.*

The impressive **château** sits amid arable land just near the small town of **Le Coudray-Lémeré**. Although not particularly fancy in style, it has all the ingredients of a fairy-tale castle and has been almost totally restored. With drawbridge, moat and a 13th-century feudal exterior (Joan of Arc passed through its portals), the castle has a Renaissance core built by the Beauvau family, who knew considerable fame some 500 years ago. In front of the residential building, the castle's stables, granary and domestic wings form an important part of the complex. Rabelais immortalised this mansion in his famous story of *Gargantua*. Gargantua's grandfather gave Le Rivau to Captain Tolmère, captain of the footsoldiers, as a reward for his victories in the Pirocholine War. The gardens are one of its highlights: a more recent addition, there are some 12 different themed plantings (including wild flowers, rose garden and secret garden) laid out to old documents and using paintings and tapestries as inspiration.

Accommodation and food near Château du Rivau

Auberge du Val de Vienne €€ *30 route de Chinon, Sazilly (4.5km from Le Rivau); tel: 02 47 95 26 49; fax: 02 47 95 25 97; www.aubergeduvaldevienne. com. Closed Sun and Mon.* A simple inn with a rustic ambience and a good restaurant with an excellent regional menu and large choice of wines.

CHÂTILLON-SUR-INDRE

Châtillon Tourist
Office *pl. du Champ-de-Foire; tel: 02 54 38 74 19; email: otsi-chatillonsurindre@ wanadoo.fr; www.chatillon-sur-indre.fr. Open summer*

The profile of this walled, hilltop town promises more than it offers. Its history dates back over a millennium but visitors have to content themselves with vestiges. The narrow lanes and flights of stairs in the old town, past its castle (built originally by Philippe III between 1274 and 1278 as a royal residence but not open to the public), are not

only Tue–Sat 0900–1900,
Mon 1000–1900, Sun
1000–1300. Winter, info
from the Mairie.

🅟 Market pl. du
Marché, Fri am.

🄝 Tour de César €
Open daily
1030–1230 and 1430–
1830. Guided tour available.
May be closed for
restoration. Check with
tourist office before
visiting.

Eglise Notre-Dame €
Open daily 0800–2000.

often trodden by tourists who prefer to visit the **Tour de César**, the town's dungeon, or spend time in the **Eglise Notre-Dame**, the former collegiate church of Ste-Outrille. The church began its life under the influence of Romanesque art and was finished in Gothic style, and the visitor can see the gradual progression of its construction in moving from the earlier apse towards the later façade. Probably the most impressive element in this building is the fine work on its individual 11th-century carved capitals (one of which in the nave is, unusually, signed by its sculptor, Petrus Janitoris). The sculpture on the western portal is also remarkable and narrates events from the Old Testament starting with the *Temptation of Adam and Eve*.

Accommodation and food in Châtillon-sur-Indre

Auberge de la Tour €–€€ *2 route du Blanc; tel: 02 54 38 44 20*. A friendly, small hotel just on the edge of town. It also has a noted restaurant. The old town is within an easy walk.

Below
Château de La Guerche

LA GUERCHE

Château de La Guerche € *tel: 02 47 91 02 39; www. chateaudelaguerche.com. Open Jul–mid-Sept daily 1000–1300 and 1400– 1900, Sun pm only.*

Today, La Guerche looks like a peaceful backwater, along the slow-moving Creuse Valley, but in the Middle Ages it was a veritable hotspot. By the time the Renaissance took hold in France, La Guerche was a staunch Catholic settlement, and during the Wars of Religion sheltered, among others, Catherine de Medici. The most impressive views of the **Château de La Guerche** are from the bridge crossing the River Creuse. The fortified town was surrounded by massive walls rising, in parts, 35m above its moats and the river. There is still a handful of ancient houses in its crooked streets that date from the Middle Ages, while the good-looking Romanesque church of **St-Marcellin** was built in the 11th century and was under the control of the Benedictine Abbey at Preuilly-sur-Claise. Later restoration has unfortunately dealt a blow to its originality.

LE GRAND-PRESSIGNY

Le Grand-Pressigny Tourist Office *pl. Savoie-Villars; tel: 02 47 94 96 82; www.le-grand-pressigny.net. Open May–Sept 0930–1200 and 1400–1800; Oct–Apr 0930–1200 and 1400–1630.*

Market *Thur am.*

Château du Grand-Pressigny (and Musée de la Préhistoire) €€ *tel: 02 47 94 90 20; www.musee-prehistoire.fr. Open Feb–Mar & Oct–Dec 0930–1230 and 1400–1700; rest of year 0930–1900. Closed 25 Dec & Jan.*

Far from the main roads that dissect France, Le Grand-Pressigny retains much of its old-world atmosphere. It was a strategic point between the battling Plantagenets and Capetians, so Guillaume de Pressigny, seigneur of Le Grand-Pressigny and a Philippe-Auguste faithful, decided to fortify his hilltop domain at the end of the 12th century. Ancient stone houses border the steep streets that mount the rocky hill on which the town's once-magnificent **château** perches. Its most interesting features are the Renaissance gallery, which was added in the mid-1500s by Honorat de Savoie, the 12th-century dungeon and the **Musée de la Préhistoire**. This area of South Touraine has high-quality flint, which, millennia ago, was the ideal stone for fashioning tools. The deposits of flint attracted primitive man, who inevitably left his mark, and archaeologists are still discovering a rich heritage that charts the development of man between the Palaeolithic era and the Bronze Age. The museum groups some of the finds and outlines the history of these early settlers. If you are coming to Le Grand-Pressigny in summer, check out the dates for the town's summer festivities, held in the château.

Accommodation and food in Le Grand-Pressigny

Chez Grand'Ma € *10–12 Grande Rue; tel: 02 47 91 09 09. Closed Mon evening and Tue.* Good traditional cooking at remarkably low prices at this unpretentious restaurant with a large shaded terrace.

Auberge Savoie-Villars €–€€ *pl. Savoie-Villars; tel: 02 47 94 96 86; fax: 02 47 91 07 81. Restaurant open year-round except Mon and Tue Sept–Jun.* An attractive and very central hotel with a pleasant garden. Restaurant with local dishes and traditional French cuisine.

LOCHES

ℹ️ **Loches Tourist Office** *pl. de Marne;* tel: 02 47 91 82 82; fax: 02 47 91 61 50; *www.loches-touraine cotesud.com. Open summer Mon–Sat 0930–1900, Sun 1000–1300 and 1400– 1800; winter daily 0930– 1230 and 1400–1730.*

How pleasant it is that Loches is a grossly under-publicised tourist destination, for it helps preserve the charm of this exceptional medieval town located on the banks of the Indre. Once through the 15th-century entrance gates, the **Porte des Cordeliers** or the **Porte Picois**, you'll soon decide that Loches merits a stay rather than a quick visit. Impregnable walls, impressive city gates and narrow cobblestone streets lead through the fortified walls to its **Cité Médiévale** crowned by the fine residence, **Le Logis Royal**. This Renaissance palace

Above
Château du Rivau

Right
Rooftops of Loches

The human cage

It was in Loches that the infamous human cage was used to house prisoners. Made from wood covered in metal, it was, at its most spacious, 2m on each side enabling a prisoner to stand, though there was a reduced version that forced him to crouch. Stories tell how prisoners spent their sentences incarcerated in these cages, but documents suggest that they were for temporary, rather than permanent, use.

Markets Wed 0700–1500, Sat 0700–1300; monthly market first Wed of the month.

Le Logis Royal and Dungeon €€ pl. Charles VII; tel: 02 47 59 01 32; fax: 02 47 59 27 45. Open Oct–Mar 0930–1230 and 1400–1700; Apr–Sept 0900–1900. Closed 25 Dec & 1 Jan.

Le Maison Lansyer € r. Lansyer; tel/fax: 02 47 59 05 45. Open Apr–Sept daily except Tue 1000–1230 and 1430–1900; Oct–Mar 1000–1300 and 1400–1700, closed Sun.

During the summer months the city of Loches mounts a number of interesting spectacles that include son-et-lumière performances, concerts, theatre and evening markets. It is also known for its Christmas market mid-December.

dominates Loches and was one of the favourite royal residences from the mid-13th century onwards. It is particularly associated with the beautiful Agnès Sorel, favourite mistress of Charles VII and mother to four of his children. On her death, she was brought back to Loches and her tomb is now in the Logis Royal. It features the 11th- to 13th-century **Eglise St-Ours** (named after the 5th-century Lochois saint), an imposing rectangular **dungeon** and towers built by Foulques Nerra. Logis residents, temporary or long term, also included Anne of Brittany and Ludovic Sforza. Of humbler proportions than the Logis, the nearby **Maison Lansyer** was the home of noted landscape painter Emmanuel Lansyer (1835–93), who was arguably as good as, if not better than, his well-known friend, Gustave Courbet. On display in his house are some hundred or so of his fine works, an interesting collection of Japanese art and another of original engravings by notable 19th-century artists such as Corot, Canaletto and Gustave Doré.

Foulques Nerra

Foulques Nerra, nicknamed the Black Falcon, crops up all over this area of France. It would seem he was responsible for the construction of almost all the Middle Age fortresses – and in many cases he actually was. But watch out: there were three Foulques. Our man is Foulques Nerra III (970–1040), Count of Anjou from 987 until his death. The great expansion of the house of Anjou at the beginning of the second millennium was due to Nerra. As expected of such a powerful character, he is said to have had an extreme character, given to periods of piety (including four trips to Jerusalem) and then of cruelty. He married three times and, with each marriage, increased his sphere of power.

Accommodation and food in Loches

Hôtel de France €–€€ 6 r. Picois; tel: 02 47 59 00 32; fax: 02 47 59 28 66; www.hoteldefranceloches.com. Open daily in season, restaurant closed Sun pm and Mon Sept–Jun. A pretty, smallish hotel right in the centre of the old town with a good restaurant featuring both traditional and modern cuisine.

Luccotel €€ 12 r. des Lézards; tel: 02 47 91 30 30; fax: 02 47 91 30 35. Restaurant closed Sat lunch and from mid-Dec–mid-Jan. A modern hotel, slightly away from the centre, with some rooms looking out over Loches. Comfortable rooms and a noteworthy restaurant.

MONTRÉSOR

Montrésor Tourist Office *43 Grande Rue; tel: 02 47 92 70 71; www.tourisme-valdindrois-montresor.com. Open 1000–1200 and 1400–1800.*

Château de Montrésor *€€ tel: 02 47 92 60 04. Open Apr–Oct daily 1000–1200 and 1400–1800, except Jul–Aug 1000–1900. Guided tours of the interior and free exploration of the garden.*

Market *Sat am.*

Montrésor justly earns its sobriquet as one of the most beautiful villages in France. This tiny medieval settlement, clustered on the hill around its **château**, sits above the shallow waters of the River Indroise. With its ancient stone houses, half-hidden gardens and profusion of flowering plants, it is picture-postcard perfect and invites leisurely exploration. Foulques Nerra, Count of Anjou, built the original feudal fortress but it was Imbert de Bastarnay who improved the town's silhouette by constructing a Renaissance château. He also commissioned a collegiate church, consecrated in 1532, to shelter the mortal remains of his family, and within its walls hangs a superb 17th-century *Annonciation* by Philippe de Champaigne. The family tombs are particularly moving, but it's a pity that the Revolution removed the heads of all the saints, mutilating otherwise fine statues. Interestingly, the château has been, and still is, owned by Polish nobility – Count Branicki – whose antecedents served with Napoleon III. Montrésor owes its medieval and Renaissance prosperity to the lucrative wool trade: in the 18th-century wooden building, the Halles des Cardeux, local wool was carded and woven for export.

Accommodation and food in and around Montrésor

Auberge des Charmettes € *Beaumont Village, 3km from Montrésor; tel: 02 47 92 75 81.* A small, family-run hotel and restaurant near Montrésor. Attractive old inn with the usual regional fare.

Montrésor Café € *29 Grande Rue; tel: 02 47 92 75 31; www.cafedelaville. fr.st. Open Tue–Sun.* This family-run restaurant offers snacks and a full menu with local dishes. Although it's the only choice in Montrésor, it is a pleasant, friendly place.

RICHELIEU

Richelieu Tourist Office *7 pl. Louis XIII; tel: 02 47 58 13 62; fax: 02 47 58 29 86; http://office.tourisme-richelieu.fr. Open Apr–mid-May & Oct Mon–Sat 0900–1230 and 1400–1730; mid-May–Sept Mon–Sat 0900–1230 and 1400–1800; Nov–Mar Mon, Tue, Thur, Fri & Sat 0900–1230.*

Forerunner of our grid-plan towns, Richelieu was commissioned by Cardinal Richelieu (Armand du Plessis, Bishop of Luçon) and designed by Jacques Lemercier, who gave the execution of the work to his two brothers, Nicolas and Pierre. Overseen with interest by the cardinal, and with the aid of 2,000 workmen, it took some 11 years to complete and was largely finished on Richelieu's death in 1642. The wooden Halles, assembled out of chestnut and oak, were erected in 1638 and house exhibitions and markets. The rather dingy, Baroque Eglise de Notre-Dame-de-l'Assomption wasn't completed before the death of its architect, Pierre Lemercier, but the broad, 12m-wide Grande Rue, flanked by its 28 distinctive mansions – the town's central axis – was, and has lost little of its original dignity and elegance. The gracious

Markets *Mon and Fri am, and second & fourth Mon pm.*

Hôtel de Ville € *I pl. du Marché; tel: 02 47 58 10 13; fax: 02 47 58 16 42. Open Wed–Fri & Mon 1000–1200 and 1400–1600, or to 1800 in Jul & Aug. Guided 15min visits.*

Parc du Château € *Open Apr–Oct 1000–1900; Nov–Mar 1000–1800. Closed 1 Jan & 1 May.*

Right
Richelieu riverside

buildings either side are all designed to a similar plan, with an interior courtyard and a small garden. However, they obviously didn't appeal to many purchasers for it is related that the illustrious cardinal had to pressurise his wealthy friends and associates into buying these and, after his death, there was a scramble to sell them, with the result that few were ever actually finished on the inside. Either end of the Grande Rue, the pl. du Marché and the pl. des Religieuses bring space into the plan and function as social gathering points. The **Hôtel de Ville** now houses a museum relating to the cardinal. The nearby **Parc du Château** is also open and can be visited, in tandem with the town, by a *petit train touristique.*

Accommodation and food in Richelieu

Hôtel Restaurant Le Puits Doré € *Pl. du Marché; tel: 02 47 58 16 02; fax: 02 47 58 24 39; www.lepuitsdore.fr; restaurant closed Sun pm and Mon, Oct–Mar.* An attractive small hotel on the main square with a good restaurant offering traditional cuisine.

Train rides

For train buffs, a restored steam train runs along the Veude Valley between Richelieu and Ligré (some 12km each way) *during the weekends in Jul and Aug.* Tickets €€ and information from *La Gare, Richelieu; tel: 02 47 58 12 97; fax: 02 47 58 28 72.*

Cardinal Richelieu

Armand du Plessis, better known as Cardinal Richelieu, was born in Richelieu in 1585, his father being the seigneur of Richelieu. Forsaking a military career, he entered the Church and politics, became a cardinal in 1622 and, under King Louis XIII, rose to become his chief minister. To thank him for his services, the cardinal was given the title of duke and, amassing a number of properties around Richelieu, created a duchy. He decided to abandon the family mansion and commission the building of a noble château (no longer extant) for himself and a town to house his followers. He died as the new town neared completion.

TAVANT

Eglise de Tavant € *tel: 02 47 58 58 06. Guided visits Wed–Sat & first Sun each month 1000–1230 and 1330–1700.*

In the middle of this hamlet is a small **Romanesque church** dedicated to St Nicolas, with fine 12th-century frescoes in its low-ceilinged crypt and somewhat restored paintings in the small apse. As you enter, the mesmerising image of Christ in a mandorla gazes down at you from behind the raised altar. The realism of the figure is uncommon among similar, contemporary works. The church was once part of the Abbey of Tavant.

Suggested tour

i **Comité Départemental du Tourisme de Touraine** *9 r. Bouffon; tel: 02 47 31 47 48; fax: 02 47 31 42 76; www.tourisme-touraine.com. Open Mon–Fri 0900–1800.*

La Sainte-Chapelle *€ Champigny-sur-Veude. Open 1500–1800. Closed Tue.*

Musée René Descartes *€ 19 r. René Descartes, Descartes; tel: 02 47 59 79 19. Open Jun–Sept 1400–1800. Closed Tue.*

Espace Animatier de la Haute-Touche *€ tel: 02 54 02 20 40. Open daily Easter–1 Nov 1000–1800, Jul–Aug 0900–1800.*

Corroirie *€ route de Loches à Montrésor, Chemillé-sur-Indrois; tel: 02 47 92 64 23. Open daily 1000–1800.*

Chartreuse du Liget *€ tel: 02 47 92 60 02. Open daily 0900–1200 and 1400–1800.*

Total distance: About 230km.

Time: Anything from 2 to 3 days.

Links: Chinon (*see page 80*), our starting point, also features as the starting point of the Chinon–Saumur tour (*see page 102*), and the end point of the Grands Châteaux: Tours–Chinon tour (*see page 68*). The N143 from Châtillon-sur-Indre leads to Buzançais, part of the tour of the Berry (*see page 268*).

Route: Leaving **Chinon** to the south, join the D751E and head eastwards in the direction of Loches. You'll drive around 4.5km before you see the D749 turning, on the right, towards Richelieu and Châtellerault. Don't miss the left turning in **Le Coudray-Lémeré** which leads off to the château, **LE RIVAU ❶**. To continue the route, backtrack to Le Coudray and pick up the same road again, to **Champigny-sur-Veude**, and stop here to admire the impressive glass windows in the 16th-century **La Sainte-Chapelle**, founded by the Bourbon Montpensier family, and once part of the château. The latter was destroyed by a jealous Cardinal Richelieu. This old village still has a number of 16th-century houses. It is only 6km along the wooded D749 till you reach **RICHELIEU ❷**.

Leave by the D757 that leads to the D20 in the direction of Marigny-Marmande, then **Les Ormes**, on the banks of the River Vienne. Dog-leg through Les Ormes on to a well marked road, via Alleux, to **Descartes**, named since 1967 after its most famous resident, philosopher René Descartes (1596–1650). His home is now a **museum** where, among other memorabilia, there is an original edition of his opus magnum, *Principia Philosophiae*. The D42 southwards splits after 3km and you'll take the right fork, the D750, before you take a right turn and reach the largely medieval village of **LA GUERCHE ❸**, fanning out around its 15th-century fortified château. Backtrack on to the D750 and continue for 3km to Barrou. Here, you turn left on to the D60, which comes in on the south side (stop to take in the views) of **LE GRAND-PRESSIGNY ❹**. The D42 leading out of Le Grand-Pressigny follows the Claise Valley and enters the attractive town of **Preuilly-sur-Claise**, noted for its Benedictine

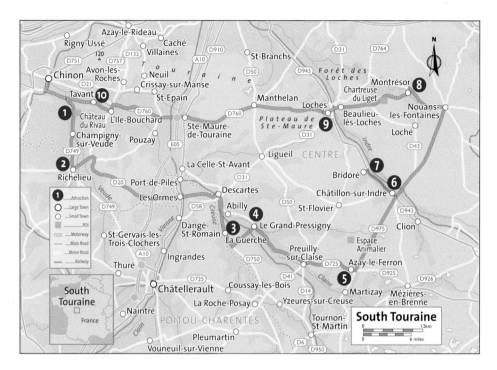

abbey. It's just 12km from here to **AZAY-LE-FERRON** ❺. Taking the D975 northeast, you'll pass a sign on the left to the breeding zoo, **Espace Animalier de la Haute-Touche.** This is a good place to spend an hour or so if you have children with you.

Another 14km and you'll see the citadel at **CHATILLON-SUR-INDRE** ❻. Leaving the town, follow the Indre Valley northwest and, just after the village of Fléré-la-Rivière, turn left on the D241 to **BRIDORE** ❼. The easiest way to continue on the tour is to retrace your steps to Châtillon and pick up the D975 to Blois, which passes by the little town of **Nouans-les-Fontaines,** known for a beautiful rendition of the *Pietà* by 15th-century painter Jean Fouquet. The pretty D760 follows the Indre Valley to **MONTRESOR** ❽. The same road continues and enters the important **Forêt de Loches** (there are plenty of pleasant places to walk or cycle here). On the right, there's the ancient Corroirie, a fortified refuge for the Carthusian monks from the nearby 12th-century **Chartreuse du Liget.** Founded by Henry II, King of England, this *chartreuse* was a grandiose charterhouse. The cloisters and remains of the church are open to visitors. The D760 continues, to meet the Indre and the city of **LOCHES** ❾, from where it continues through **L'Ile-Bouchard** westwards passing through **TAVANT** ❿, a tiny hamlet. The old church is just off to the left. It is a few minutes' run from here back to Chinon.

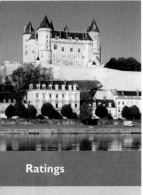

Chinon–Saumur

Ratings

Caves	●●●●●
Châteaux	●●●●●
Architecture	●●●●○
Churches	●●●●○
Food and wine	●●●○○
Historical sights	●●●○○
Museums	●●●○○
Villages	●●●○○

Though not as well known as many of the Loire's grands châteaux, each of the castles dotted around the *tuffeau* (tufa) plain south of Saumur is a little gem. This region also offers a journey of discovery, as many other outstanding sights lie hidden underground in galleries left by centuries of quarrying the soft *tuffeau* stone to build the area's castles, towns and villages. At Brézé an underground stronghold is open to visitors, and at Rochemenier you can go round a *village troglodyte*. A quarry at Doué-la-Fontaine has been imaginatively transformed into a top-class zoo. Good use is being made of many of the other quarried-out caves, too, as homes or for storing wine or growing mushrooms. While the scenery along the route is less spectacular than elsewhere in the region, an exception is the section where it runs beside the Loire – a glorious stretch!

BOURGUEIL

ⓘ Bourgueil Tourist Office *16 pl. de l'Eglise; tel: 02 47 97 91 39; www.ot-bourgueil.fr. Open daily except Sun pm and Mon am.*

ⓘ Cave Touristique du Pays de Bourgueil *tel: 02 47 58 58 40; www.cavesbourgueil. com. Open Apr–Sept Tue–Sun.*

Abbaye de St-Pierre *tel: 02 47 97 72 04. Guided tours Apr–Oct.*

It can be hard to stay sober in this pleasant little white-stone town, 19km north of Chinon, because of the constant opportunities to sample and buy its famous full-bodied red wine, produced from the Cabernet Franc vines grown in the area. The Maison des Vins de Bourgueil, in pl. de l'Eglise, features a different producer's wines each week, and the **Cave Touristique du Pays de Bourgueil**, a cellar hollowed out of the rock, has a collection of old presses on show. Two more wineries occupy the cloisters of the **Abbaye de St-Pierre**, a large group of buildings dating back to the 10th century when it was one of the richest abbeys in Anjou and had vineyards stretching for kilometres around. Today, only about 20 nuns live there. Its vaulted hall and staircase, built in 1730, are open to the public and a small folk museum occupies former monks' cells.

Markets Stalls with local produce, clothing and bric-a-brac take over the streets and market hall on *Tue am*; food only in the market hall on *Sat am*. Evening markets featuring local wines and specialities like wine jams and *rillettes* (potted meat) *Jul–Aug*.

La galette bourgueilloise

This *brioche* (sweet bread), filled with creamy vanilla custard, is the town's speciality. The recipe – top secret! – was created in the 1970s by Monsieur Ancelin, owner of the Bourgueilloise *pâtisserie* (beside the market hall), the only place where it can be bought.

Accommodation and food in and around Bourgueil

L'Ecu de France € *r. de Tours; tel: 02 47 97 70 18.* A small, family-run hotel and restaurant in the centre of town, handy for the market and the abbey.

Auberge La Lande €–€€ *D35, 24 r. la Lande; tel: 02 47 97 92 41. Closed Mon and Tue.* In fine weather you can dine on the terrace of this charming restaurant. Good, regional cooking uses local produce, complemented by excellent Bourgueil wine.

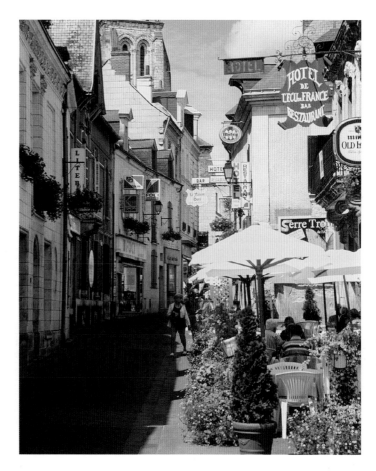

Right
A picturesque street in
Bourgueil

CANDES-ST-MARTIN

This attractive riverside village, spread along the south bank of the Vienne at its confluence with the Loire, is named partly after St Martin, Bishop of Tours, who died here in 397. The splendid white 12th-century church, notable for its soaring pillars and rib vaulting, was erected to mark the spot. Three hundred years later a lavishly carved defensive porch supported by a central pillar was added. A series of steep cobbled paths, starting beside the church, climb to a hillside that provides a magnificent panoramic view of the two rivers (10min walk). Opposite the church a short alley off the main street leads down to the river and its former slipways. These are a reminder that the Loire was once a busy waterway for transporting coal, slate, stone and grapes. An old notice lists the distances to the river's various ports.

CHÂTEAU DE BRÉZÉ

Château de Brézé
€€ *tel: 02 41 51 60 15;*
www.chateaudebreze.com.
Open Apr–Sept daily
1000–1830 for guided
tours: castle (1hr),
underground (90min). Free
admission to grounds.

Though little known compared with many of the Loire's châteaux, Brézé's is nevertheless one of the most extraordinary of all. On arrival you see a typical fortified *tuffeau* castle with two round towers surrounded by lawns from which there are wide views over the Loire Valley. The first surprise comes as you cross the moat, since it is 15m deep – the deepest in Europe – and has never been filled with water. The present building, consisting of three wings around a courtyard, dates from the 16th and 19th centuries and is elegantly furnished with antiques. One wing is occupied by the Count and Countess of Colbert, descendants of the family who built the original château in the 11th century. However, the visible building is merely the 'modern' part of the castle. There is almost as much to see below ground, where an extensive network of chambers, linked by low zigzagging passages, has only recently been discovered. They

were hollowed out of the soft white *tuffeau* stone, probably around the 9th century, to provide a safe refuge. The torch-lit tour through them includes large kitchens, which were added later, complete with two big bread ovens, and wine cellars that had a direct shaft from the vineyards so that grapes could be dropped straight down for pressing. Today's vintages are on sale to visitors in the grounds near another remarkable feature, a tall, circular *pigeonnier* (dovecote).

Right
Moat at Château de Brézé

CUNAULT

Cunault Music Festival *May.*

Beneath a delicate stone figure of the Virgin, framed by semicircular recessed arches, massive double doors lead into the village's huge cathedral-like abbey church, one of the most remarkable buildings in the whole of the Loire area. Built in the local creamy white *tuffeau* stone and dating back partly to the 11th century, it is a masterpiece of Romanesque art, pure in design yet richly decorated. Soaring pillars line its single nave, each with elaborately carved capitals at the top. The original bell tower is topped by a spire added in the 15th century. Only fragments of the frescoes that decorated the interior at that time have survived, but other notable features include a rare carved and painted shrine and a 16th-century statue of the Virgin. The 3,074-pipe organ is in excellent condition thanks to President Georges Pompidou, who personally authorised its restoration after he visited the church in 1968.

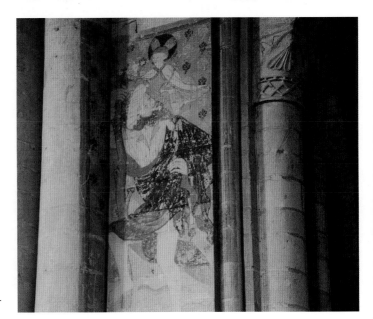

Right
Fresco at Cunault

Opposite
Les Chemins de la Rose, Doué-la-Fontaine

Accommodation and food near Cunault

Le Prieuré €€€ *Chênehutte-les-Tuffeaux, near Cunault; tel: 02 41 67 90 14; www.prieure.com.* Looking down across the Loire from its commanding position on a wooded hillside, this gracious former priory is easily the most distinguished and luxurious place to stay in the area. The view at the front extends for 48km. All 20 bedrooms in the main building are a good size and furnished with antiques. Fifteen more are in modern villas in large wooded grounds that also include a heated outdoor pool and mini-golf; these rooms provide a less expensive option but lack the view across the river. The hotel's restaurant has large picture windows facing the river and serves gourmet dishes, notably local fish. Its waiters combine formality with friendliness and are particularly helpful over choosing wine. Breakfast and drinks can be taken on the terrace.

DOUÉ-LA-FONTAINE

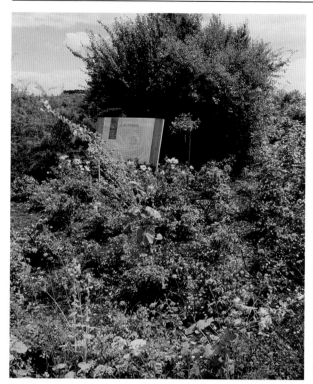

Though seemingly unremarkable when you drive into it, the town has three attractions which are definitely worth seeking out. Its **zoo** is unusual because it occupies former quarries and caves. Now overgrown with trees and foliage, they have been ingeniously converted into attractive enclosures with streams, waterfalls and grottoes where the animals and birds can largely roam free. There is even a large aviary in which visitors can mingle with 20 vultures, although, even with keepers on hand for reassurance, this can be a rather unnerving experience! Other areas are home to a wide range of animals, including lions, tigers, pigmy hippopotamuses and several kinds of monkey. Visitors observe them from a network of pathways that lead on two different levels through the almost jungle-like surroundings. Altogether, the zoo has about 500 animals representing 65 different species. At least half are involved in international breeding programmes for the conservation of endangered species, a major concern of the zoo's founder, Louis Gay, since he opened it in 1961. Subsequently he created **Les Chemins de la Rose**, a 6ha rose garden a short walk away. Planted with over 6,000 bushes, it is truly a rose-lover's paradise. As you stroll around the beds, information boards provide a history lesson on the 950 varieties, ranging from the very latest to antique ones now rarely seen elsewhere. Every conceivable rose product is on sale in the shop, plus a small selection of plants. Nearby is the **Musée des Commerces Anciens** where two 'streets' of old shops have been re-created inside the former stable block of a manor house. Although the French will be more familiar than foreign visitors with the old brand names, the objects on show, dating from 1850 to 1950, are highly nostalgic for all nationalities. The shops, each realistically laid out and fully stocked, include a grocer, ironmonger, clockmaker, seed supplier, parasol maker and a pharmacy whose shelves are lined with large jars of potions and powders.

ⓘ Doué-la-Fontaine Tourist Office *pl. Fontaine; tel: 02 41 59 20 49; email: tourisme. doue.la.fontaine@wanadoo.fr; www.ot-douelafontaine.fr*

ⓖ Zoo de Doué €€ *route de Cholet; tel: 02 41 59 18 58; www.zoodoue.fr. Open daily Feb–mid-Nov: winter and autumn 1000–1830, spring 0900–1900, summer 0900–1930.*

Les Chemins de la Rose €€ *www.cheminsdelarose.fr. Open May–Sept daily.*

Musée des Commerces Anciens € *Les Ecuries du Baron Foullon; tel: 02 41 59 28 23. Open Feb–Dec daily.*

FONTEVRAUD-L'ABBAYE

Fontevraud-l'Abbaye Tourist Office *pl. St-Michel; tel: 02 41 51 79 45; fax: 02 41 51 79 01; email: officetourisme.fontevraud@libertysurf.fr; http://perso.wanadoo.fr/tc.fontevraud. Open Easter–end Sept.*

Abbaye Royale € *www.abbaye-fontevraud.com. Open daily.*

Right
Tombs at Fontevraud-l'Abbaye

The village grew up beside the **Abbaye Royale**, the largest group of monastic buildings in Europe and now the Centre Culturel de l'Ouest, a venue for concerts, exhibitions and conferences. Four recumbent effigies, lying in state in the abbey's huge 12th-century church, provide a vivid reminder that this part of France was under the same rule as England for many years. They are Henry II (King of England and Plantagenet Count of Anjou), his wife, Eleanor of Aquitaine, their crusader son, King Richard the Lionheart, and Isabelle, wife of Richard's brother, King John. The church itself has impressive stonework and is roofed with domes, a feature usually only found in southwest France. The abbey also has four 16th-century cloisters – including both the smallest and largest in France – together with its original refectory and chapterhouse. Particularly remarkable is the huge octagonal Romanesque kitchen and smokeroom that rises to a high pointed hood – the only surviving example from the period in France. It has several fireplaces so that, depending on the direction of the wind, the cooking could be done on whichever would work best. The original monastery, founded in 1099, consisted of four separate priories, all under the rule of an abbess. Each had a different vocation, such as caring for the sick or poor. Three priories were for nuns and one, prudently sited outside the main walls, for priests and brothers. During the Wars of Religion the buildings suffered considerable damage. More occurred in Napoleon's time when the abbey became a prison, which it remained until 1963. Fortunately, much survived in excellent condition and, thanks to the largest restoration programme in France outside Paris, its impressive white *tuffeau* buildings will continue to be improved.

Accommodation and food at Fontevraud-l'Abbaye

Hostellerie de la Croix Blanche € *7 pl. Plantagenets; tel: 02 41 51 71 11; fax: 02 41 38 15 38.* For simple dishes – salads, pancakes and ice-cream sundaes – drop in at the *crêperie* of the family-run Croix Blanche hotel, a 400-year-old *auberge* with 21 rooms. It also has a more formal restaurant (€€).

Prieuré Saint-Lazare €€ *Abbaye Royale de Fontevraud, Fontevraud-l'Abbaye; tel: 02 41 51 73 16; www.hotelfp-fontevraud.com. Open Apr–Oct.* Fifty-two smart modern bedrooms now occupy a section of the abbey buildings that was transformed into a hotel in the early 1990s, creating a very special place to stay. The restaurant (€€) is located in serene white cloisters, now enclosed for comfort by large windows. Its various menus – des Moines, Abbesses or Plantagenêts – feature local fish and other Anjou specialities. Afterwards, guests can retire to the lofty former refectory for drinks.

GENNES

ⓘ Gennes Tourist Office *Square de l'Europe; tel: 02 41 51 84 14; email: ot-gennois@wanadoo.fr. Open Mon–Sat and Jul–Aug Sun.*

ⓗ Amphithéâtre Gallo-Romain € *tel: 02 41 51 55 04. Open Apr–Sept Sun pm; Jul–Aug daily.*

Gallo-Roman remains have been discovered around this small riverside town that was on a major trading route between Tours and Rennes in the 2nd century. The most important is an **amphitheatre** that could have held up to 5,000 spectators, sitting on the grassy bowl of the hillside as there were no stone tiers.

MONTREUIL-BELLAY

ⓘ Montreuil-Bellay Tourist Office *pl. du Concorde; tel: 02 41 52 32 39; www.ville-montreuil-bellay.com. Open Mar–Jun Tue–Sat 0930–1300, 1430–1800, Sun 1000–1300; Jun–Aug Mon–Sat 0930–1300, 1400–1900, Sun 1000–1300, 1400–1700; Aug & Sept Mon–Sat 0930–1300, 1430–1800, Sun 1000–1300, 1400–1700; Sept & Oct Tue–Fri 0930–1300, 1430–1800.*

ⓜ Markets *Tue, also Sun am mid-May–mid-Sept.*

ⓗ Château de Montreuil-Bellay *€€ tel: 02 41 52 33 06; fax: 02 41 52 37 70. Open Apr–Oct Wed–Mon (guided tours); € gardens only.*

This lively little town, attractively situated beside the River Thouet, is the only one in Anjou still to have ancient ramparts dating back 1,000 years. Its impressive 15th-century **château**, itself largely surrounded by sturdy walls, stands guard over the river in terraced grounds that slope down towards the water. Entered over a moat and through a formidable gateway, it certainly looks like a fortress with its battlements and turrets. In fact, much of it was built as a family residence, which it remains today. Seven beautifully furnished rooms and a medieval kitchen can be visited, together with the colourful terraced gardens. A stroll around the old part of the town takes you past several grand 15th- and 16th-century houses, each with a pretty courtyard, which have recently been refurbished. The grounds of a former convent, the Petits Augustins, have been made into a small botanic garden.

Food in Montreuil-Bellay

Auberge des Isles €€ *312 r. Boëlle/pl. des Vieux Ponts, Montreuil-Bellay; tel: 02 41 50 37 37; fax: 02 41 50 92 40.* Sandwiched between the castle and river, this looks like a snack bar but is actually an excellent restaurant with a reliable range of well-prepared and attractively presented classic French dishes, but especially good for fish.

MONTSOREAU

Château de Montsoreau €€
tel: 02 41 67 12 60;
www.chateau-montsoreau.
com. Open mid-Feb–mid-Nov
daily.

The impressive 15th-century **Château de Montsoreau** – the only one whose grounds extend to the banks of the Loire – has recently undergone extensive renovations. Originally the home of the Chambes family, it was the setting of the Alexandre Dumas story, *La Dame de Montsoreau*, which he based on a true saga of infidelity and murder. Though the interior is unfurnished, it is brought to life by an innovative *son-et-lumière*-style presentation as you pass through the rooms. This explains the story of *La Dame de Montsoreau* and also covers the Anjou countryside, its traditions and people.

Accommodation and food in and around Montsoreau

Hôtel le Bussy € *4 r. Jehanne d'Arc; tel: 02 41 38 11 11.* A small, family-run hotel with Louis-Philippe-style furnishings and views of the castle and river.

Troglo Resto €€ *W of château, on the D751; tel: 02 41 51 70 30; www.troglo-sautauxloups.com. Open Mar–mid-Nov.* This amazing restaurant, specialising, of course, in mushrooms, is inside the 2km-long Le Saut aux Loup mushroom caves, quarried out in the 15th century. Before eating, take the cave tour. Mushrooms have been cultivated here for around 100 years. Visitors see how they are grown in bags, and how new varieties are developed. A tasty speciality is *galipettes* (huge mushrooms up to 15cm across, baked with a variety of toppings).

Below
Château de Montsoreau

ROCHEMENIER

 Village Troglodyte
€ *Open Apr–Nov daily.*

Occupied until the 1930s by two farming families, Rochemenier's tiny **Village Troglodyte** consists of their homes, animal pens and a chapel, all built inside the caves of a medieval quarry around a central courtyard area. The method of construction was certainly very practical. When a family grew, they simply hollowed out the wall to make room for an extra bed! Photographs of the families and ancient farm tools are on display, too. One dwelling is relatively modern, with electric light and simple furniture, as it was lived in by a caretaker until 1984. The tower of the underground chapel is visible above ground next to a tiny 13th-century chapel, **Ste-Emérance**, which has a beautiful apse and carved wooden ceiling. Elsewhere in the village, and around the area, there are modern troglodyte houses, as this style of accommodation has become rather fashionable.

Right
Troglodyte houses,
Rochemenier

ST-HILAIRE-ST-FLORENT

Bouvet-Ladubay Wine Cellars
www.bouvet-ladubay.fr. Open daily but no production to watch at weekends or in Aug.

St-Hilaire-St-Florent, now very much a suburb of Saumur, is synonymous with wine. Several of the Loire's most famous wineries are to be found here, situated on both sides of the main street. This runs between the River Thouet, just as it joins the Loire, and the foot of the tufa cliffs. The most interesting to visit is the **Bouvet-Ladubay Wine Cellars**, one of the great names for Saumur Mousseux (sparkling wine). Founded in 1851, their cellars occupy kilometres of galleries in ancient *tuffeau* quarries. Visitors can see production in full swing, starting with the wine being piped from huge metal vats into bottles, which after fermentation in the bottle are placed in special cubes of racks. These tilt and shake automatically every three months to force the sediment up into the neck so it can be removed by freezing. The bottles eventually emerge to be corked, wired and labelled. Visits end – of course – with a tasting of three wines, including Saumur's unusual sparkling red.

Centre d'Art Bouvet-Ladubay
Open daily.

Musée du Masque *r. de l'Abbaye; tel: 02 41 50 75 26. Open Easter–mid-Oct daily.*

Musée du Champignon
€ route de Gennes; tel: 02 41 50 31 55; www.musee-du-champignon.com. Open Feb–Nov daily.

Pierre et Lumière *€ Near St-Hilaire-St-Florent, route de Gennes; tel: 02 41 50 70 04; fax: 02 41 50 61 94; www. pierre-et-lumiere.com. Open Feb–Nov daily.*

Mushroom growing

For over 300 years mushrooms have been cultivated in the *tuffeau* caves that seam the hillsides along the Loire west of Saumur. Today, production is on a massive scale, accounting for around 70 per cent of France's total output. Most are *champignons de Paris* (button mushrooms). The caves provide perfect conditions for them to develop – darkness, unvarying 90 per cent humidity and a constant temperature of 15°C. The process begins with *mycelium* (seeds) being planted in trays or bags of compost. After six weeks these are transferred to the caves. Five weeks later a 'burst' of mushrooms appears over three days, followed at two-weekly intervals by four lesser ones. Picking is done early in the morning, and a skilled operator can collect up to 60kg a day.

Opposite the winery is the **Centre d'Art Bouvet-Ladubay**. The gallery's nine exhibition halls are each devoted to the work of a different contemporary artist. There is also an architectural centre and a cinema where documentary films are premiered.

Also in St-Hilaire-St-Florent is the **Musée du Masque**. The César company, manufacturers of masks for a century, has set up an imaginative grotto-like museum to display some of its most famous creations, as well as others gathered from around the world. The exhibits show how the materials used have developed over the years, from the *papier-mâché* used for characters like Punch and Judy in the 19th century to synthetic materials like latex in which contemporary models are fashioned for television. There are tableaux in fairy-tale settings, as well as realistic scenes such as a baccarat table where political figures, from Winston Churchill to Fidel Castro, are laying their bets. Some 2,000 masks, many inexpensive, are on sale in the shop and even more are available by mail order.

Just west of St-Hilaire-St-Florent are two more fascinating places to visit. The **Musée du Champignon** explains all you ever wanted to know about mushrooms, in underground galleries created by quarrying for *tuffeau* stone. It shows how growing techniques have developed over the years, and you can see examples being cultivated in bags and trays of compost. Wild varieties are on show, too, together with fossils found during the quarrying. At the end of the tour *galipettes* (large mushrooms grilled or stuffed) can be sampled in a small restaurant.

Pierre et Lumière (Stone and Light) is an appropriate name for this unusual *parc miniature* inside the caves of an old quarry hewn into the hillside west of St-Hilaire-St-Florent. It contains 17 large models of famous places in the area, each meticulously carved into the walls by sculptor Philippe Cormand and skilfully lit to show off the details. They include Fontevraud Abbey and the intricately decorated churches of Cunault and Candes. Most impressive of all is a large panorama of Saumur, complete with the Loire depicted by water flowing from a natural spring.

Suggested tour

Total distance: 86km. The detour to the **Abbaye d'Asnières** adds 2km, the detour to **Les Rosiers** adds 3km, and the one to **Bourgueil** adds 14km.

Time: 2 hours' driving time, but allow at least 2 days for the full route. Those with limited time should concentrate on Fontevraud l'Abbaye and Brézé.

Links: At Chinon (*see page 80*) this tour links with the South Touraine tour (*see page 90*). From Gennes, it is a 10km scenic drive along the river to link up with the Western Châteaux tour (*see page 126*).

Route: From **Chinon**, set off west along the north bank of the **Vienne** on the D749. The road swings north to **Avoine** past the nuclear power station whose untidy mixture of enormous ugly buildings appears on the right, heralded by power lines sweeping over the road.

Detour: To visit **BOURGUEIL** ❶ continue on the D749 across the river and over the start of the A85 autoroute, straight into the town, before retracing your route (*end of detour*).

Immediately before the river (or immediately after, if you have visited Bourgueil), turn left on to the D7 to **CANDES-ST-MARTIN** ❷. This provides some good views of the lake-like river, though it is mostly just out of sight behind trees. Immediately after crossing the Vienne, turn right into Candes where you pass its church on the left.

Getting out of the car: In Candes a short walk opposite the church leads down to the wide river and its old slipways. Better still, take the steeper series of paths (well signposted) behind the church up to a hillside vantage point, to enjoy a superb view of the confluence of the Loire and Vienne rivers.

Continue to **MONTSOREAU** ❸. The château is on the left beside a paved section of road along the riverbank. Originally, this was the château's private terrace and all traffic had to go instead through the pretty but narrow village street at the back. Shortly beyond the château, **FONTEVRAUD-L'ABBAYE** ❹ is signed to the left.

After visiting it, take the D162 signed St-Cyr-en-Bourg from the roundabout on its west side. On reaching the crossroads with the D93, turn left to Brézé. The **CHATEAU DE BREZE** ❺ is 2km further on the left (but unsigned until you reach the turning to it). Next, continue on the same road to the village church, turn right beside it and follow signs to **MONTREUIL-BELLAY** ❻ and its château along the D178 and then D166.

Getting out of the car: A stroll around Montreuil-Bellay's 1,000-year-old ramparts provides excellent views of the oldest part of the town and the surrounding countryside. The ramparts skirt the castle beside the **River Thouet** and pass three of the town's old fortified gateways. Leaving Montreuil-Bellay, follow the signs for Angers. After 5km on the D761, the **Abbaye d'Asnières ❼** is signed off to the right.

Detour to the Abbaye d'Asnières: A short drive towards Cizay-la-Madeleine takes you to this ancient abbey (*open Jul–Aug Wed–Mon pm*), which, except for the nave, has survived remarkably intact since the 13th century, including decorative glazed tiling (*end of detour*).

The D761 continues to **DOUE-LA-FONTAINE ❽**, a somewhat confusing town to find your way around due to poor signing. The **Zoo de Doué** is on its southwest side on the main D960 leading towards Cholet; **Les Chemins de la Rose** are a little further along it. If you approach the D960 along the blvd du D Lionel, watch out for the **Maison Carolingienne** on the left. This fortified house, dating from the 9th century but still in good condition, looks like a castle keep. To visit the **Musée des Commerces Anciens**, return along the D960 to the Soulanger suburb where it is signposted to the left. The extraordinary troglodyte village of **ROCHEMENIER ❾** is shortly signed to the right, off the busy D761 to Angers. Next, head north on the D69 through woods to **GENNES ❿**. Just before Gennes, the ancient **Dolmen de la Madeleine** stands in splendid isolation in a field to the right, a few paces from the road. It is the most impressive of the many megaliths, dating from around 4000–2000 BC, to be found in this area south of the Loire. Stepping inside, you realise how colossal the stones are – how did they get here, and why?

Detour: In Gennes take a brief trip north across the pretty suspension bridge over the Loire to **Les Rosiers** to savour its serene views of the broad, gently flowing water (*end of detour*).

From Gennes, the D751 keeps close to the river as it passes through **CUNAULT** ⑪ and then the little hamlet of Trèves. There, just off the road, lurks a gleaming white crenellated tower, all that remains of a 15th-century castle, and a delightful little church. Then you pass another small Romanesque chapel with a handsome doorway beside the road in the village of Chênehutte-les-Truffeaux, which nestles at the foot of a wooded hillside. Just before arriving at **ST-HILAIRE-ST-FLORENT** ⑫, home of Saumur's sparkling wine, both the **Pierre et Lumière** sculpture cave and the **Musée du Champignon** are beside the road. Then a short run takes you into **Saumur** itself, though the journey could take a long time if you succumb to the temptation of lingering at any of St-Hilaire-St-Florent's wineries.

Saumur

Ratings

Castles	●●●●●
Wine tasting	●●●●●
Gastronomy	●●●●○
Entertainment	●●○○○
Historical sights	●●○○○
Museums	●●○○○
Shopping	●●○○○
Outdoor activities	●○○○○

Saumur is the 'white city' of Anjou, built in the creamy local *tuffeau* stone from the limestone plain south of the Loire. People say it is a particularly agreeable place to live, and you soon realise why. Attractively situated beside a broad, dreamy stretch of the river, it is large enough to have an interesting selection of shops, restaurants and leisure facilities, yet also feels very laid-back. No doubt the fact that it is the home of some of France's best sparkling wines helps, too! Most of the wineries are in the St-Hilaire-St-Florent suburb (*see page 111*), west of the town centre beside the River Thouet. The town's heyday was 400 years ago when it became a centre of Protestant scholarship. It was renowned for its tolerance, rather than getting involved in feudal power struggles. The huge castle – dating back to earlier times but still in good condition – is by far the most distinctive feature.

Getting there and getting around

ⓘ Saumur Tourist Office *pl. de la Bilange; tel: 02 41 40 20 60; www.saumur-tourisme. com*

◔ Markets *Thur and Sat.*

◭ Summer Festival *Mid-Jul, with two weeks of concerts, street parades and fireworks. Mostly free.*

By road
Saumur is on the N147, 9km south of exit 3 on the A85.

By rail
There are frequent services from Angers (20min), Nantes (1hr) and Tours (40min). The railway station is on the right (north) bank of the Loire, av. David d'Angers. For train enquiries, *tel: 08 36 35 35 35.*

Parking
Parking is free 1200–1400, 1900–0900 and all day Sunday. Meters operate in the town centre but many of the streets are no-parking zones. The most central car parks are the riverside pl. de la République, handy for the **tourist office**, and pl. St-Pierre. Elsewhere, car parks are free, including one next to the castle. A leaflet showing parking is available from the tourist office.

⏱ **Equestrian events** throughout the year include the *Carrousel de Saumur*, a grand tattoo in *Jul*, featuring cavalry demonstrations by the horsemen of the Cadre Noir; *tel: 02 41 67 36 37*.

Getting around

The central area is easily manageable on foot. To go further afield there are local buses, including the B line to St-Hilaire. Bus station: *r. St Nicolas; tel: 02 41 51 11 87*. There are tours of the town by tourist train and horse-drawn carriages *Apr–Sept*. Boat trips run from quai Lucien Gautier *Jun–Sept Tue–Sun*. Cycle hire: *Cycles Peugeot, 19 av. du Général de Gaulle; tel: 02 41 67 36 86*. Canoeing and sailing on the Loire from *Base de Loisirs de Millocheau, 1 r. des Tennis; tel: 02 41 51 17 65*.

Sights

🏛 **Château de Saumur** € *tel: 02 41 40 24 40. Castle/museums open Oct–May Wed–Mon, Jun–Sept daily. Floodlit tours Jul–Aug Wed & Sat 2030–2230.*

Musée de la Figurine-Jouet € *r. des Moulins. Open mid-Jun–mid-Sept Wed–Mon pm.*

Dolmen de Bagneux € *56 r. du Dolmen, Bagneux. Open daily.*

Ecole Nationale d'Equitation *In suburb of Terrefort; tel: 02 41 53 50 60; www.cadrenoir.fr. Open Mar–Nov for 45min demonstrations, mostly Sat. Bookings tel: 02 41 53 50 60.* Visitors can also have a guided tour of the stables and watch any classes taking place at the time €€ *Apr–Jul & Sept Mon–Sat.* Showjumping in *May* and *Sept*.

Château de Saumur

Saumur's castle, topped by a forest of 'pencil' turrets, dominates the town from a mound once occupied by windmills. The views over the town and river from both the interior and the grassy ramparts are superb. Built in the 14th century as a residence for Louis I, Duke of Anjou, with spacious rooms and several spiral staircases, it became a Protestant stronghold 200 years later when a mighty outside wall was added to fortify it. Subsequently, it was used as a prison and, later, as an army barracks. Now, still in a good state of repair, it houses two museums. The **Musée des Arts Décoratifs** displays a fine collection of tapestries, furniture and ceramics from the 13th to the 19th century. The **Musée du Cheval** traces the history of the horse and the development of riding from prehistoric times to the present. An elaborately carved sleigh from Russia and a large collection of horseshoes and saddles from around the world are among the highlights. The castle's powdermill houses a third museum, **Musée de la Figurine-Jouet**. This displays a collection of lead soldiers and models of the kings of France, together with 19th-century toys made from flour and plaster.

Dolmen de Bagneux

The dolmen, tucked away in the garden of a bar, is one of the biggest and most impressive Neolithic burial chambers in Europe. At 21m long and 7m wide, it is made of massive sandstone slabs standing 3m high. Astonishingly, they were transported, lifted and wedged together 5,000 years ago. It's a shame that access to such an atmospheric place is through an uninteresting modern bar, although it does afford the opportunity to enjoy a drink in the garden as you contemplate this feat of ancient construction.

Ecole Nationale d'Equitation

Saumur is home to France's prestigious riding academy, l'Ecole Nationale d'Equitation, which has 400 horses, an Olympic-size indoor riding school, 50km of specially laid-out tracks and its own veterinary hospital. Leading riders come here from all over the world to be taught by its famous instructors, the Cadres Noirs, some of whom have a military background.

Opposite
Château de Saumur and Saumur vines

Eglise St-Pierre *pl. St-Pierre.* Concerts on the superb 18th-century organ on *Sat pm.*

Eglise St-Pierre

This fine old Plantagenet church, which, in its time, has been used as a barn and gunpowder factory, is an architectural mixture of Romanesque, Gothic and Renaissance styles. The original façade was severely damaged when it was struck by lightning in 1674. Inside, there is an outstanding set of intricately carved oak choir stalls depicting an entertaining array of characters. Unusually, they are arranged in a horseshoe around the altar. Some of the stained glass is medieval, and the walls are hung with a particularly fine collection of 16th-century tapestries illustrating the lives of St Florent, a locally venerated hero, and St Peter.

Musée des Blindés € *1043 route de Fontevraud; tel: 02 41 83 69 95; http://musee-des-blindes.asso.fr. Open daily.*

Musée des Blindés

This is the largest collection of tanks in Europe. All 200 are in working order, so they are much in demand as props for films. Now run by France's ministry of defence, the collection was started by Michel Aubry, an army officer, in 1964. Housed in a former cigarette factory, it ranges from examples of the earliest tanks, used in World War I, to modern tanks that saw action in the Gulf. Sprucely painted and clearly labelled, they are grouped according to nationality in separate halls, and put into context by pictures and newspaper reports displayed around the walls. A small cinema shows archive film.

Notre-Dame de Nantilly *Pl. Nantilly.*

Notre-Dame de Nantilly

Saumur's oldest church, dating back to the 12th century, is an austere-looking building with few windows, a small neat spire and interesting tapestries. A pillar on the nave's south side bears an epitaph that the 15th-century King René, the last Duke of Anjou and a scholar and poet, wrote to his nurse.

Right
Place St-Pierre

Shopping

Saumur is not a major shopping centre, though it has a branch of the **Printemps** department store in r. Franklin Roosevelt as well as a number of specialist shops. These include small shops selling the traditional local lace, or lace dresses, bonnets, parasols and other whimsical-looking lace items. **Girardeau**, *53 r. St-Nicolas*, stocks everything for the gourmet, particularly regional products such as mustards and *foie gras*; **La Boîte à Pêche**, *7 pl. de la République*, stocks everything for the angler from rods to bait. For fashionwear, r. St-Jean has several small boutiques. For antiques, r. St-Nicolas is the place to look. **La Maison des Vins de Saumur**, next to the tourist office, offers advice about wines. You can sample and buy there, too. Or head for one of the cellars – **Les Caves de Grenelle**, r. Marceau, are the most central.

Above
Château de Saumur

Entertainment

Live music comes on to the streets in July and August, particularly at pl. St-Pierre and pl. de la République, where groups play outside the bars and restaurants. Nightclubs with live music include **Blues Rock**, r. de la Petite Bilange, and **La Loco** on the north bank of the river on route de Rouen. Or head out to the suburb of St-Hilaire-St-Florent (*see page 111*), where several bars in *tuffeau* caves have music and dancing.

Boule de Fort

La Boule de Fort, a centuries-old game played indoors throughout Anjou, is bowls with a difference. The balls, 126cm in diameter, weigh 1.3–1.5kg and are made of wood or plastic with a metal strip around them. They are also weighted, making them *fort* – strong – on one side, giving the game its name. This makes them wobble when bowled towards the *maître*, or jack. The course is between 21m and 24m in length, 6m across, and slopes up on both sides like a boat. Indeed, one theory on the origins of the game is that it was devised by boatmen or prisoners on voyages along the Loire. To avoid damaging the plastic surface of the course, players wear slippers. Today, there are about 400 *Boule de Fort* clubs, playing in the special halls devoted to it, so visitors should be able to find a game to watch. Women were not allowed to play until the mid-1980s, but many are now as addicted to it as their menfolk.

Accommodation and food in and around Saumur

Les Caves de Marson € *1 r. Henri Fricotelle, Rou Marson, 5km W of Saumur; tel: 02 41 50 50 05; www.cavesdemarson.com. Open lunchtime Sept–Jun weekends and Jul–Aug Tue–Sun.* Booking recommended. The restaurant occupies a series of large caves where you are served a meal of *fouace* – rounds of soft pitta-like bread baked in a troglodyte oven – which you spread with butter and fill with *rillettes* (potted meat), goat's cheese and white beans. Baked mixed fruit completes the unusual menu, which is best accompanied by a bottle of Saumur Rouge.

Hôtel de Londres € *48 r. d'Orléans; tel: 02 41 51 23 98; fax: 02 41 51 12 63; www.lelondres.com.* There's a fresh, light feel, with wooden floors and uncluttered attractive décor, at this inexpensive, well-placed town-centre hotel.

L'Orangeraie € *cour du Château; tel: 02 41 67 12 88.* In the castle grounds, this is a handy spot for a pre- or post-visit meal or snack, though it also offers menus and local dishes in the evenings.

Anne d'Anjou €€ *32–33 quai Mayaud; tel: 02 41 67 30 30; www.hotel-anneanjou.com.* Overlooking the Loire, this grand 18th-century building is an ideal place to stay for those with a sense of history. Some of the rooms are furnished in Louis XVI style and the façade and staircase are listed.

Auberge St-Pierre €€ *6 pl. St-Pierre; tel: 02 41 51 26 25; www.auberge-saintpierre.net.* Fifty metres from the Hotel Saint-Pierre, but a completely separate establishment, this is definitely the most interesting restaurant in the square at the front of the St-Pierre church, even if you get no further than admiring its distinctive 15th- to 17th-century façade of diagonal beams and red-brick panels. The interior is spacious and heavily beamed. Excellent for snails and oysters as well as more homely fare like *coq-au-vin grandmère*.

Cristal Hôtel €€ *10–12 pl. de la République; tel: 02 41 51 09 54; www.cristal-hotel.fr.* This 300-year-old hotel, well positioned facing the main square, bridge and river, has 23 rooms. Those at the front can be somewhat noisy but provide a good vantage point. No restaurant, but the ground floor is occupied by a lively bistro.

Le Grand Bleu €€ *6 r. Marché; tel: 02 41 67 41 83.* Despite this restaurant's name, its décor is pale green, though the tables outside in summer are certainly blue. Big choice of fish, including a *Spécial Grand Bleu* for two that includes 16 oysters, 10 crayfish, 2 crabs and lots more.

Hôtel Saint-Pierre €€ *31 r. Haute-St-Pierre; tel: 02 41 50 33 00; www.saintpierresaumur.com.* A smart 15-room hotel tucked away handily in a narrow side street beside the St-Pierre church. Part of it dates back to the 15th century but the décor is modern and stylish throughout. Tiny bar and garden. Breakfast only.

La Mascotte €€ *60 r. St-Nicolas; tel: 02 41 51 12 01.* One of several small restaurants in this street, it has pretty green décor and a conservatory-style extension jutting out on to the pavement. Plenty of interesting fish dishes such as salmon roasted in port and cream.

Les Ménestrels €€€ *11 r. Raspail; tel: 02 41 67 71 10; www.restaurant-les-menestrels.com.* Generally regarded as one of the best restaurants in town, it features regional cuisine that changes with the seasons. Distinguished list of Loire wines.

Suggested walk

Total distance: 2km.

Below
Hôtel de Ville

Time: 1 hour, but allow a day to see all the sights.

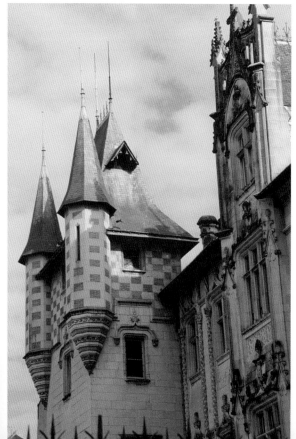

Route: After a stroll along the riverbank and admiring the impressive **Hôtel de Ville**, parts of which date back to the 1500, in **pl. de la République**, take **r. Corneille** beside it to the pedestrianised **r. St-Jean**. A neglected-looking apartment above one of the shops, **Les Fleurs se Font Belles**, is where the fashion icon Coco Chanel (real name Gabrielle Bonheur) was born. **R. St-Jean** leads to **pl. St-Pierre**, the scenic heart of the old quarter where three half-timbered houses with gables and decorative red brick have survived since medieval times beside **EGLISE ST-PIERRE ❶**. Always a lively place, thanks to its pavement cafés, the square is at its busiest during the summer festival when street entertainers perform there. The narrow **r. de la Tonnelle** running off it was once a main road leading down to a wooden bridge across to the **Ile d'Offard** in the middle of the Loire.

As you begin to climb towards the castle along the short but steep

Monté du Fort, you pass a house that fans of the 19th-century writer Honoré de Balzac will recognise from the novel *Eugenie Grandet*, which is set in Saumur. Steps then lead up to the grassy grounds of the CHATEAU DE SAUMUR ❷, from which there are fine views over the red chimneys, grey slate roofs and white stone walls of the town and the river. The **Maison des Compagnons**, just below, is a school for apprentice stonemasons who can often be seen hewing lumps of white *tuffeau* in the courtyard. Considering the amount of restoration going on in and around Saumur, their skills are sure to be much in demand.

After leaving the ramparts, turn left into **r. Duruy**, which leads to the NOTRE-DAME DE NANTILLY ❸ church. Return along r. Duruy to **Grande Rue**, which was the town's main street in the 17th century, when it had 25 bookshops and printers. At the time, Saumur was a centre of learning and tolerance, welcoming both Protestants and Catholics to its university, including William Penn who went on to found the city of Pennsylvania in the USA. A 15th-century mansion with red gables and a delightful courtyard off **r. des Païens** was a favourite hideaway with the poet-king Roi René – he preferred it to the castle. Later, it was also used by Mary Queen of Scots for a two-night stay on her way to marry François II. The imposing **Maison des Abbesses** on the corner of **Ancienne Messagerie**, which leads back to r. St-Jean, is where abbey visitors once stayed; now it is the residence of the director of the **Ecole Nationale d'Equitation**.

Tuffeau quarries

The limestone hillsides around Saumur are seamed with caves and tunnels left over from the quarrying, which has been going since Gallo-Roman times. Almost all the châteaux, as well as many other buildings in the area, are built in the chalky beige stone – called *tuffeau* or tufa – deposited here when the sea covered the area millions of years ago. Around 1,500km are now used commercially, mostly for cultivating mushrooms. Others are occupied by wine cellars, restaurants and other businesses. Today, *tuffeau* is extracted from only one quarry, in St Cyr-en-Bourg, and is used exclusively for restoration work.

Ecole Nationale
d'Equitation

N

AVENUE FOCH R BEAUREPAIRE

RUE ST-NICOLAS

QUAI CARNOT

AVENUE DU GÉNÉRAL
DE GAULLE

RUE PAUL BERT

QUAI MARINE

Loire

RUE DES AULNES

PLACE DE LA
BILANGE

i

RUE ST-JEAN

QUAI LUCIEN GAUTIER

PLACE
DE LA
RÉPUBLIQUE

PLACE
ST-MICHEL

RUE D'ALSACE

RUE D'ORLEANS

RUE DU PORTAIL-LOUIS

ANCIENNE
MESSAGERIE

RUE PERRONELLE

PLACE
ST-PIERRE

❶

RUE DACIER

Eglise
St-Pierre

QUAI MAYAUD

RUE RASPAIL

PLACE
MAUPASSANT

RUE BODIN

RUE DES DRAPIERS

RUE DU TEMPLE

GRANDE RUE

RUE DU MARÉCHAL LECLERC

RUE DU DOCTEUR BOUCHARD

AVENUE DU DOCTEUR PETON

RUE DUPEV

❷

Château de
Saumur

RUE DES MOULINS

RUE LAMARTINE

RUE SEIGNEUR

Jardin des
Plantes

RUE MARCHE

RUE HOCHE

RUE DE NANTILLY

PLACE DE
NANTILLY

❸

Notre-Dame
de Nantilly

BOULEVARD LOUIS RENAULT

Dolmen de Bagneux

RUE DU MOUTON

RUE MARCEAU

BOULEVARD DE LA MARNE

RUE LOUCHEUR

RUE CHEMIN VERT

RUE ROBERT AMY

AVENUE VICTOR BORET

RUE FRICOTELLE

RUE DE FONTEVRAUD

Musée
des Blindés

❶ .... Attraction
.... Important Building
.... Park
.... Main Road
.... Other Road
.... Path
i .... Information

Saumur

0   100 metres
0   100 yards

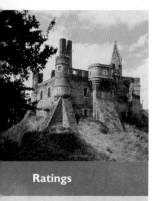

The Western Châteaux

Ratings

History	●●●●●
Activities	●●●○○
Châteaux	●●●○○
Museums	●●●○○
Restaurants	●●●○○
Scenery	●●●○○
Wine tasting	●●●○○
Children	●●○○○

As the Loire nears Angers, there's a change in tone. This is the very heart of Anjou, land of the Plantagenets. For generations, Plantagenet counts sat on the English throne and spoke not English, nor French, but Angevin. That led to the Hundred Years War, and eventually Anjou and the other Plantagenet possessions in France came under the control of the French king. Here, the Loire expands on its right bank into a great watery plain, and several rivers converge from the north. The Loir, the Sarthe and the Mayenne join to become the Maine, which passes grandly through the city of Angers to reach the Loire. In every direction, Anjou's history, art and architecture, culture and civilisation enrich a gentle landscape. As well as its châteaux, the area has abundant fruit orchards, productive vegetable farms and famous vineyards.

BAUGÉ

ℹ Baugé Tourist Office In the château; tel: 02 41 89 18 07; fax: 02 41 89 04 43; www.ville-bauge.fr. Open mid-Sept–mid-Jun Mon–Sat 1130–1230 and 1330–1800, rest of year Mon–Sat 1000–1230 and 1330–1830.

⊖ Markets Mon pm and Sat am.

⊞ Apothecary r. Dr Zamenhof. Open Wed–Mon, Jul–Aug daily (check with tourist office).

This appealing little market town on the River Couasnon, close to the extensive Chandelais forest, became illustrious as a medieval residence of the Anjou nobility, and was the preferred home of Good King René, Duke of Anjou, Count of Provence and King of Naples. That accounts for the many fine mansions along its old streets. René lived in the old **château**, which he greatly enlarged and improved, turning it into a handsome castle. A lovely tower staircase is its finest feature. Today, the château houses the **tourist office** and the town's modest Musée d'Art et d'Histoire.

One of the town's almshouses, Hospice St-Joseph, retains a 17th-century **apothecary**, with panelled walls, beautiful wooden flooring and 16th-century faience containers. In another former almshouse chapel, the Chapelle des Filles-du-Coeur-de-Marie, is a venerated religious treasure, the **Croix d'Anjou (Cross of Anjou)**. A striking double-armed cross brought back from Palestine in 1241 by a

The Western Châteaux

Château de Baugé €€ *tel: 02 41 84 00 74; www.chateau-bauge.com. Open Easter–Sept 1000–1230 and 1330–1730 (no midday closing Jul–Sept); other months 1330–1730. Closed mid-Nov–Christmas.*

Croix d'Anjou (Cross of Anjou) *Chapelle des Filles-du-Coeur-de-Marie, r. de la Girouardière; tel: 02 41 89 12 20. Open for guided visits Wed–Mon 1430–1630. Closed Pentecost weekend and preceding three days, first Sun in Jul, 24–26 Jul, 11–12 Dec & 25 Dec.*

Crusader, it has been worshipped by some as Christ's cross. It was reconstructed and exquisitely decorated with jewels and gold in the 14th century, and was especially revered by King René. Christ is depicted on both sides. Just out of town is another remarkable – and more ancient – religious relic, the Dolmen de la Pierre Couverte. It stands off the road in a forest clearing.

Accommodation and food in Baugé

La Boule d'Or €€ *4 r. Cygne; tel: 02 41 89 82 12; fax: 02 41 89 06 07.* An appealing, family-run little hotel-restaurant offering decent board and lodging at a moderate price.

BÉHUARD

Béhuard Tourist Office *9 r. Chevalier Buhard; tel: 02 41 72 84 11; fax: 02 41 72 84 11.*

The long, narrow Loire island of Béhuard was formed millennia ago – and is still being formed – by the gradual build-up of river silt around a strange dark pinnacle of rock in mid-river. If you find something magical about this curious, serene place, you are not the only one: the island and its rock have been a place of worship and spirituality since time immemorial. Before the Christian era, a river goddess was venerated here. Her shrine became a sailor's chapel in the 5th century. In the 15th century Louis XI constructed the present unusual church on the site, dedicated to Our Lady of Béhuard. The narrow, concentric lanes of the island's attractive village keep many of their 15th- and 16th-century houses. Periodic floods, reaching about 7m, add to the island's unique character. There's a beach and picnic area, and a waterside footpath around the island.

Accommodation and food in Béhuard

Les Tonnelles €€ *12 r. Chevalier; tel: 02 41 72 21 50. Closed Sun pm, Mon (except lunchtime in summer), Tue in winter, and Wed.* For a true taste of the Loire in mid-stream, this excellent restaurant brings perfectly prepared fish or game dishes together with the best of local wines.

Above
Béhuard village

BRISSAC-QUINCÉ

ⓘ Brissac-Quincé Tourist Office *8 pl. de la République; tel: 02 41 91 21 50; fax: 02 41 91 28 12; email: accueil@ot-brissac-loire-aubance.fr; www.ot-brissac-loire-aubance.fr. Open daily May–Sept, rest of year Wed & Thur am only, but phone messages may be left on other days.*

The tourist office organises free walking tours in summer with English-speaking guides.

Market *Thur am.*

Surrounded by vineyards, the sleepy little commune of Brissac-Quincé was, until 1964, two separate villages, Brissac and Quincé, divided by the narrow River Aubance. Though the castle is its main attraction, a recently discovered curiosity exists under the market square. It's an **underground chapel** with secret passages. No one knows why or when it was built, but possibly it was a hiding place.

Seat of the dukes of Brissac for 500 years, the massive **Château de Brissac** towers grandly up for nine storeys in its leafy park beside the River Aubance. Guided tours of a handful of its 203 rooms include Louis XIII's plush red bedroom and its large bathroom, a small 17th-century-style theatre (still occasionally used for performances), a chapel with fine woodcarvings, and the opulent *Salles des Gardes* where Aubusson tapestries hang beneath a gilded ceiling. All the rooms have intricately painted ceilings and are lavishly furnished with Renaissance pieces. The current duke's son now administers the castle, and recent family photographs stand on the grand piano in the Grand Salon. Visits end with a wine tasting in the 900-year-old cellars – and an opportunity to buy.

Underground chapel € *To visit, and for information, call at the tourist office.*

Château de Brissac €€€ *tel: 02 41 91 22 21; www.chateau-brissac.fr. Open Apr–Oct, several guided visits daily 1000–1715 (closed Tue, except Jun–mid-Sept). Nov–Mar some guided tours during school holidays.*

Accommodation and food in Brissac-Quincé

Le Clémenceau **€** *21 r. de la Marne; tel: 02 41 91 22 01.* A simple restaurant in a beamed room behind a bar. Menus feature country fare like rabbit and perch. Popular with locals.

Hôtel Le Castel **€€** *1 r. Louis Moron; tel: 02 41 91 24 74; www.hotel-lecastel.com.* Handily placed opposite the castle, and all the rooms have recently been refurbished to a high standard, including a spa bath in the 'honeymoon suite'. No restaurant.

CHÂTEAU DE LA LORIE

Segré Tourist Office *(2km) 5 r. David d'Angers; tel: 02 41 92 86 83; fax: 02 41 61 05 73; email: OTSI.SEGRE@ wanadoo.fr. Open Mon–Fri 0900–1230 and 1430–1800, Sat 1000–1200 and 1500–1700. Guided tours are available.*

Market *Wed am.*

Château de la Lorie € *2km from Segré off D863; tel: 02 41 92 10 04. Open for guided tours at weekends.*

The château stands just outside **Segré**, a striking and attractive little country town of dark houses stepping down a hillside to an old bridge and river quays on the bank of the Oudon. Built in the 17th century, altered in the 18th, La Lorie represents a last fling of aristocratic extravagance before the Revolution. Its glittering ballroom in particular, the highlight of the visit, has an unabashed opulence and was the last of its kind to be built. It forms part of the two wings added in the 1770s. It has a musicians' gallery in a rotunda, and fine marble-work created by Italian craftsmen brought here specially. The whole château has a light, elegant, almost frivolous formality, with French-style gardens, and pale tufa window surrounds and corners contrasting with the rest of the stonework.

CHÂTEAU DE MONTGEOFFROY

Château de Montgeoffroy €€€ *Just outside Mazé on D74; tel: 02 41 80 60 02; fax: 02 41 80 62 66; email: montgeoffroy@wanadoo.fr. Open for 1hr guided tours mid-Jun–mid-Sept 0930–1830, rest of year 0930–1200 and 1430–1830. Closed Nov–mid-Mar.*

Standing with elegant dignity within its spacious parkland, Montgeoffroy is one of the best examples in this area of the later style of château, more stately home than castle. It was built for the Maréchal de Contades, governor of Strasbourg, during the 1770s and has been treasured and well maintained by his descendants. Everything is still in place, nothing modernised. Furniture and tapestries specially made for the house remain in the rooms, which are light and airy thanks to rows of tall windows, while the kitchen has kept its impressive collection of copperware and pewter. The house has its own chapel (part of an earlier structure on the site), stables displaying antique carriages, and elegant 18th-century gardens.

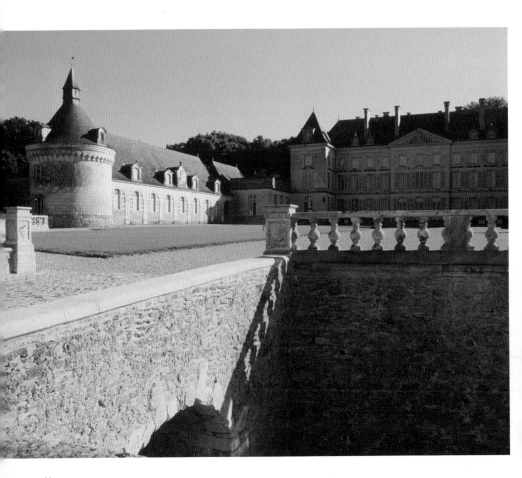

Above
Château de Montgeoffroy

Château de Pignerolle

🅘 **Château de Pignerolle, Musée Européen de la Communication** €€ *5km E of Angers on D61; tel/fax: 02 41 93 38 38; www. musee-communication.com. Open daily 1000–1230 and 1430–1800.*

A delightful 18th-century château, built as an exact copy of the Petit Trianon at Versailles, Pignerolle finds itself only just beyond the expanding suburbs of Angers, and its 70ha of grounds have become a public park. In World War II the château was, in turn, the seat of the exiled Polish government, a German HQ, and then an American base under General Patton. Today, the château houses the imaginative **Musée Européen de la Communication**, popular with families, with fascinating displays illustrating the development of human communications from the cry of the newborn baby, via tom-tom drums and the invention of printing, right up to satellite broadcasting.

CHÂTEAU DU PLESSIS-BOURRÉ

Château du Plessis-Bourré €€€
Ecuillé; tel/fax: 02 41 32 06 01; www.plessis-bourre.com. Open for 1hr guided visits Jul–Aug daily 1000–1800; Apr, May, Jun & Sept daily except Wed & Thur am 1000–1200 and 1400–1800; Feb, Mar, Oct & Nov Thur–Tue 1400–1800; rest of year closed.

Le Plessis-Bourré is a splendid white château, rising dream-like from a wide moat crossed by a long low bridge of many arches. Four graceful towers stand guard to protect this palatial country house where kings and queens have stayed. It's lavish inside – and the slightly vulgar and sometimes amusing scenes painted on the wooden ceiling of the *Salles des Gardes* (guardrooms) have been raising eyebrows for centuries! The castle's two drawbridges, still in good working order since it was completed in 1473, are shut every evening by the château's owner. The state rooms around the arcaded inner courtyard are airy, and decorated with finely carved stonework. Apart from Revolutionary graffiti on the library fireplace, the building has survived the centuries remarkably undamaged. The château was originally the home of its architect, Jean Bourré, royal adviser and treasurer, who went on to design Langeais and Jarzé, which similarly mark the transformation of Loire castles from military fortresses into palatial homes.

Accommodation and food around Le Plessis-Bourré

Château de Noirieux €€€ *26 route du Moulin, Briollay; tel: 02 41 42 50 05; fax: 02 41 37 91 00; www.chateaudenoirieux.com.* Between Le Plessis-Bourré and Angers, this beautifully located, exceptional 15th- to 17th-century château-hotel is tranquil, well equipped and each bedroom has its own style. The restaurant – with a charming terrace – is outstanding, offering interesting seafood and fish dishes prepared with skill, imagination and flair, and a connoisseur's wine list.

Below
Château du Plessis-Bourré

CHÂTEAU DU PLESSIS-MACÉ

Château du Plessis-Macé €€
13km NW of Angers on N162; tel: 02 41 32 67 93; www.chateauplessismace.fr. Open for 1hr guided tours end Mar–end Jun & Sept–mid-Nov 1330–1800; Jul–Aug 1030–1900 (ticket price on Thur includes Baroque music concert at 1530). Closed rest of year.

Built as a dark, powerful fortress in the 11th and 12th centuries, Le Plessis-Macé was reconstructed as a luxurious palace 400 years later, after gradually falling into ruin. As part of the transformation, white tufa was added to decorate and lighten its appearance, and the building's fine Flamboyant Gothic stonework also dates from that period. Yet the château still has an impressively defensive character, with its battlements and broad moat. It's famous for the kings of France that stayed here, from Louis XI to François I. Le Plessis-Macé fell into ruin for a second time in the 19th century, and served a spell as a farmhouse before being bought and fully restored by the shipbuilding Walsh family from Nantes. Among several rooms visited on the tour of the house, one is the bedroom reserved for royalty. There's a private chapel with interesting Gothic panelling forming balconies. Around the courtyard are delightful balconies – one a hanging balcony built on a corner – where the household could safely watch jousting contests.

CHÂTEAU DE SERRANT

At the *Mairie*, St-Georges-sur-Loire
tel: 02 41 72 14 80, fax: 02 41 72 14 99.

 Market Thur.

Carré Cointreau €€
Carrefour Molière, Saint Barthélémy d'Anjou; tel: 02 41 31 50 50; www.cointreau.com

Château de Serrant €€€
Just outside St-Georges-sur-Loire on N23, W of Angers; tel: 02 41 39 13 01; fax: 02 41 39 18 22; email: contactserrant@wanadoo.fr; www.chateau-serrant.net. Open for guided tours (English/French) 0945–1715 (1745 in peak season).

Said to be the most westerly of the châteaux of the Loire, this elegant rural palace, cream-coloured under a black roof, keeps plenty of its former defences – solid walls, domed towers and a moat. A beautiful Renaissance covered stairway, known as the Escalier d'Honneur, with intricately carved balustrades under an elaborately painted ceiling, is the highlight of the interior. Such staircases would have led to the owner's private suites, guest bedrooms and the banqueting rooms used on special occasions. Built in 1546 but sympathetically extended over the next three centuries, it is still owned by the descendants of the Duc de la Trémoille who bought it in 1830. Before that, another owner had been the prosperous Nantes shipbuilder of Irish descent, Antoine Walsh. The splendid marble tomb of a previous owner, the Marquis de Vaubrun, can be found in the chapel. The rooms have kept their original exquisite furniture and decorations, including much priceless art, a fine collection of Flemish tapestries and a library of 12,000 books.

ST-FLORENT-LE-VIEIL

A tranquil place nowadays, St-Florent was the scene of a bloody insurrection by Royalists in 1793: the fighting spread throughout the Vendée *département* to the south, and became known as the Vendéen

ℹ **St-Florent-le-Vieil Tourist Office**
Pavillon de la Mairie; tel: 02 41 72 62 32; fax: 02 41 72 62 95; email: off.tour.florentlevieil@ wanadoo.fr; www.ville-saintflorentlevieil.fr. Open May–Aug 0930–1230 and 1430–1830; Sept–Apr 0900–1230 and 1400–1730.

📞 Contact the tourist office for guided tours.

🍴 **Market** *Fri pm.*

🎵 **Musical festival** *Les Orientales – end Jun.*

ℹ **Angers Tourist Office** *7–9 pl. Kennedy; tel: 02 41 23 50 00; www.angersloiretourisme.com. Open May–Sept Mon–Sat 0900–1900, Sun 1000–1800; Oct–Apr Tue–Sat 0900–1800, Mon pm only, Sun am only.* The area's main tourist office in Angers offers hotel reservations, currency exchange, booking for local events, and riverboat hire. Some villages in the region also have a small tourist office.

🌐 *www.angersloire tourisme.com* (the tourism site of the greater Angers area); *www.anjou-tourisme.com* (site of the départemental tourist office); *www.loire-france.com* (regional tourism site, French site); *www.ville-angers.fr* (the official site for residents of the region's capital).

War. On a high point overlooking the town, Republican citizens took refuge in the church – one of them the father of sculptor David d'Angers. Royalists locked them in and planned to massacre them, but Royalist leader Bonchamps insisted that the plan be abandoned. The sculptor showed his thanks by carving the marble bust of Bonchamps that forms his tomb inside the church. The esplanade by the church gives a broad view over town and river. On the little quayside by the Loire, a former salt-tax customs house has become a hotel.

Accommodation and food in St-Florent-le-Vieil

Hostellerie de la Gabelle €–€€ *quai de la Loire; tel: 02 41 72 50 19; fax: 02 41 72 54 38.* The salt tax was called the *gabelle*, hence the name of this pleasant little waterside hotel-restaurant in a former salt-tax collector's office. Family-run, charming and unpretentious, it offers comfortable accommodation and good cooking.

Suggested tour

Total distance: 146km, or 220km including the detours.

Time: Allow 1 to 2 days.

Route: Start from **Angers** *(see page 136)*. Leave the centre of town on r. Lise, by the Jardin des Plantes, continuing in the same direction (east) on av. Montaigne to join the N147, in the direction of Saumur. After 3km a right turn leads to **CHATEAU DE PIGNEROLLE ①**, with its Communications Museum. A little further along the same road is the village of Saint Barthélémy d'Anjou, where the **Distillerie Cointreau** produces 28 million litres per annum of the region's famous orange liqueur. Visitors are taken around the distillery, and can wander in its museum. Continue on the N147 to **CHATEAU DE MONTGEOFFROY ②**.

Detour: It's a pleasant 17km along the D61 to **BAUGE ③**. Return along the same road to rejoin the route *(end of detour)*.

From Montgeoffroy, return to the N147 and cross over on to the D55 – you pass through Mazé – heading to **St-Mathurin-sur-Loire**, where you cross the river. Follow the D55 as it makes its way across the countryside to **Château de Brissac** on the far side of the village of **BRISSAC-QUINCE ④**. The D130 continues west, reaching the N160. Cross the main road and carry on to the village of Denée. Turn left there to follow the Loire downstream. At **Rochefort-sur-Loire** you can take the bridge that crosses the Loire via the island of **BEHUARD ⑤**.

Autoroute A11 (Paris-Nantes) passes through the centre of the region. It can also be reached from east or west on the A85 or the N147, and from the south on the A87 or the N160.

Anjou Festival, *from mid-Jun–mid-Jul,* is one of France's principal cultural and arts festivals. The emphasis is on theatre. Events take place throughout Anjou. *www.festivaldanjou.com*

It is possible to drive the short distance straight from here to St-Georges-sur-Loire and the Château de Serrant, but our route returns to the pretty south bank of the Loire. The river is much broken up here by islands and tributaries, as can be seen when the road climbs on to slightly higher ground following the **Corniche Angevine**, winding along the cliff face between Rochefort-sur-Loire and the appealing riverside village of **Chalonnes-sur-Loire**, with a cobblestone quay and waterside church. The Loire is crossed here by a series of bridges that step from island to island – it's just 7km to St-Georges-sur-Loire and Château de Serrant.

Detour: Before you take that route it's worth continuing further downstream for a few kilometres. Even after Chalonnes, the villages and road give excellent views; for example, at **Montjean-sur-Loire**. Follow the south bank road as far as **ST-FLORENT-LE-VIEIL** ❻. Instead of heading back on the same road, cross the Loire and take the N23 on the north side of the river direct to **CHATEAU DE SERRANT** ❼ (*end of detour*).

Drive to **CHATEAU DU PLESSIS-MACE** ❽. The fastest way to do this is to return on the N23 to the Angers ring road (D106), join the N162, and turn off left to the château after 6km. However, it is more enjoyable to drive north from St-Georges on the D961, turning right at **Bécon-les-Granits** and taking the little D105 to Le Plessis-Macé. Follow the N162 up to **Le Lion-d'Angers**, a small picturesque town on the Oudon, a tributary of the nearby Mayenne. Its Eglise St-Martin is largely Romanesque, with 16th-century murals, and there's an 18th-century château. Take the road (D863) to the **CHATEAU DE LA LORIE** ❾ and Segré.

Return to Le Lion-d'Angers, and leave the little town on the road that goes to Châteauneuf-sur-Sarthe, but after just 2km turn right for **CHATEAU DU PLESSIS-BOURRE** ❿. The little D107 returns to Angers.

The Wines of Anjou

The area around Angers is noted for abundant and popular light wines, delicate and fruity whites and rosés, and some easy-drinking reds. The inexpensive, slightly sweet Rosé d'Anjou is one of Europe's favourites as a summer aperitif, or for outdoor parties and picnics. East of Angers, white wine vineyards grow close to the waterside on the Loire's right bank. South of Angers, vineyards massed along the pretty slopes above the Layon Valley are famous for their sweet, golden wine.

Opposite
Château du Plessis-Macé

The Western Châteaux

0   20km

0   10 miles

France

The Western Châteaux

N162

Segré ⑨ Oudon

Château de la Lorie

D863

D961

Champigné

D770

D768

La Flèche

D859

Durtal

N

Le Lion-
d'Angers

Loir

Vern-d'Anjou

D923   D770

Angrie   Château du Plessis-Macé
Pouëze

Château du
Plessis-Bourré

Tiercee

D323

A n j o u   D938

Candé

A n j o u

⑧

D963

PAYS DE LA-LOIRE

Feneu

Seiches-
sur-le-Loir

⑩

Montreuil-
Juigné

D107

Ecouflant

E501

Jarzé   D976

Baugé

③

Le Louroux-
Béconnais

D57

Bécon-les-Granits

D105

Avrillé

Beaucouzé

ANGERS

A11

Château de
Pignerolle   D347

Corné

E60

A85

B a u g e o i s   D61

Château de Montgeoffroy

Mazé

②

D10

E60

D723

St-Georges-
sur-Loire

Bouchemaine

A11

Varades

Ingrandes

Château de
Serrant

Montjean-
sur-Loire

Loire

⑦

Mûrs-Erigné

Béhuard

Trélazé

①

Les Ponts-de-Cé

D748

Beaufort-
en-Vallée

D55

D952

Val d'Anjou

St-Florent-
le-Vieil

⑥

La Pommeraye

Chalonnes-
sur-Loire

D751

⑤

Layon

A87

D130

D160

Brissac-
Quincé

④

D751

Les Rosiers

Gennes

Cunault

D761

Bourgneuf-
en-Mauges

D752

D961

St-Lambert-du-Lattay

① Attraction
○ City
○ Large Town
○ Small Town
▪ POI
Motorway
Main Road
Minor Road
Railway

Angers

This is the imposing, ancient capital of Anjou, land of the Plantagenets who, in the Middle Ages, became the royal line of England. Angers (pronounce it *Ahnjay*) makes sharp contrasts with the rest of château country. Instead of standing by the bright Loire, it turns towards the Maine, a tributary from the north. Instead of the familiar soft white stone called tufa, with its fairy-tale, sugar-icing look, the old heart of Angers, rising from its riverbank, is dark slate. 'Black Angers', as it was known, still has a proud, resolute bearing, as one imagines the Plantagenets themselves may have had. And, instead of decorative Renaissance, its château is a daunting, dark medieval fortress. Its cathedral and church preserve fine Gothic architecture in the soaring Plantagenet style. Above all, the real treasures of the town are its tapestries, ancient and modern, especially the remarkable Apocalypse Tapestry.

Getting there and getting around

By road
Angers lies a little north of the Loire. *Autoroute* A11 (Paris–Nantes) gives direct access to the town. It can also be reached from east or west on the A85 or N147, and from the south on the A87 or N160. All these main roads create a ring road around the whole town, while another square of boulevards encloses the central old quarter.

By air
Angers-Marcé airport is 20km northeast of the town centre on *autoroute* A11. The airport receives internal flights from Bourges, Clermont-Ferrand, Dijon, Lille, Lyon, Marseille, Montpellier, Mulhouse, Nice, Saint-Etienne, Strasbourg, Toulon and Toulouse. International flights arrive here from Amsterdam, Düsseldorf, Geneva, Milan, Turin and Munich. Airport information *tel: 02 41 33 50 00; reservations tel: 02 41 33 50 20; www.angers.aeroport.fr*

Angers

0 _____ 200 metres
0 _____ 200 yards

- Musée Jean Lurçat et de la Tapisserie Contemporaine
- PLACE DU TERTRE ST-LAURENT
- PONT DE LA HAUTE-CHAINE
- VOIE DES BERGES
- BOULEVARD ARAGO
- QUAI MONGE
- QUAI GAMBETTA
- BOULEVARD AYRAULT
- RUE DE RENNES
- RUE DU MAINE
- AVENUE BESNARDIERE
- Eglise St-Serge
- La Trinité
- RUE THIERS
- Maine
- BOULEVARD H ARNAUD
- RUE MAILLE
- RUE BOISNET
- BOULEVARD CARNOT
- RUE BOREAU
- Jardin des Plantes
- QUAI R BAZIN
- PLACE MOLIERE
- RUE DU COMMERCE
- Centre des Congrès
- QUAI DES CARMES
- PONT DE VERDUN
- PLACE DE LA POISSONNERIE
- RUE PARCHEMINERIE
- RUE DU MAIL
- PLACE LOUIS IMBACH
- Notre-Dame
- RUE DE LA ROE
- RUE PLANTAGENET
- BOULEVARD BESSONEAU
- QUAI LIGNY
- RUE BAUDRIERE
- RUE LENEPVEU
- Hôtel Pincé (Musée Turpin-de-Crissé)
- RUE ST-MAURILLE
- RUE ST-AILLE
- PLACE DU Mal LECLERC
- PROM DU BOUT DU MONDE
- RUE ST-AIGNAN
- PLACE DU RALLIEMENT
- RUE DAVID D'ANGERS
- Jardin du Mail
- Château d'Angers
- PLACE FREPPEL
- Cathédrale St-Maurice
- RUE VOLTAIRE
- RUE ST-JULIEN
- RUE D'ALSACE
- BLVD DU Gal DE GAULLE
- PLACE KENNEDY
- RUE TOUSSAINT
- Tour St-Aubin
- RUE ST-MARTIN
- Galerie David d'Angers
- Musée des Beaux-Arts
- RUE DES LICES
- RUE ST-AUBIN
- RUE HANNELOUP
- BOULEVARD DU ROI RENE
- Hôtel du Département
- BOULEVARD DU Mal FOCH
- RUE HOCHE

Legend:
- O .... Attraction
- .... Important Building
- .... Park
- .... Main Road
- .... Other Road
- i .... Information

local events, and riverboat hire.

www.angers.fr and www. angersloiretourisme.com (the town's official sites).

Markets There's a market in town almost every day of the week. Main town-centre markets are on Thur (square Jeanne d'Arc) and Sat (pl. Leclerc, pl.

By rail

TGVs direct from Paris take 1hr 30min. Other TGVs run direct to Lyon and Lille. There are frequent trains from Nantes, La Baule, Les Sables d'Olonne, Saumur and Tours.

Parking

There is plenty of car parking in the town, including in the squares near the boulevards, pl. Louis Imbach, pl. François Mitterrand, pl. Mendès-France and pl. Maréchal Leclerc. In the town centre try pl. du Ralliement and pl. Freppel. On the other side of the river there is ample parking in pl. de la Rochefoucauld-Liancourt.

Guided tours

In summer the tourist office organises 2hr guided tours of the town and local sights, as well as a 'little tourist train' round the town centre, and taxi tours of the surrounding area.

Sights

Cathédrale St-Maurice

Standing in the centre of historic Angers, the cathedral is a good example of the 12th- and 13th-century Angevin Gothic style, although with unusual proportions and some later additions. The handsome west front is especially tall, and is entered by a 12th-century doorway with a fine tympanum above. The Calvary on the left is by the great sculptor David d'Angers. Rising above the façade are three towers, the middle one being a 16th-century Renaissance addition. Inside, the nave is one of the earliest and best examples of Plantagenet-style Gothic vaulting. There is an imposing organ and carved choir stalls of the 18th century, as well as fine stone carving and statuary, including Ste Cécile in marble by David d'Angers. The 12th- and 13th-century stained-glass windows are magnificent, and there is a superb 15th-century rose window in the transept.

Château d'Angers

The sombre and imposing château that dominates Angers is quite different from the other Loire châteaux. This is decidedly more fortress than palace. Paler bands relieve its dark stone, but the overall impact is powerful and grim. It is one of the finest surviving examples of a French feudal castle.

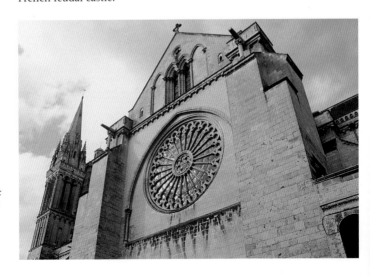

Ste-Geneviève Chapel, Logis Royal, Tapisserie de l'Apocalypse (Apocalypse Tapestry) *included in the château ticket.*

A massive structure, fortified by 17 round towers, the château stands on the site of an earlier wooden fortification. It was constructed in just 10 years, from 1230 to 1240, and was originally far more daunting than today. Its walls and towers stood much taller, and were surrounded by a broad, deep moat. During the Wars of Religion one faction after another – Protestant and Catholic – used the château as a stronghold. In the 16th century Henri III ordered that it be razed to the ground to prevent further use by hostile forces. Henri's order had only been partly carried out when he died, and the destruction of the castle was abandoned. The moat has been filled and planted out with beautiful flower gardens in the neat, geometric French style. The high ramparts walk, on the east side of the château, runs by another pretty garden.

Within the ramparts wall the large **Ste-Geneviève Chapel** was built in the 15th century by Louis II of Anjou and his wife, Yolande of Aragon. Its door is especially notable for the exquisite foliage carvings. From the same period, the **Logis Royal** houses the Royal Apartments, where superb 15th- and 16th-century Flemish tapestries are displayed, including the four that make up the remarkably rich Passion tapestry.

The highlight of the château – and of Angers – is the **Tapisserie de l'Apocalypse (Apocalypse Tapestry)**, displayed in the Grand Gallery, which has been turned into an enclosed area with controlled atmospheric conditions designed to prolong the life of the fabric. It was commissioned by Louis I of Anjou. Based on drawings by Hennequin of Bruges, the manufacture was carried out in Paris by Nicolas Bataille and Robert Poinçon. It took them five years – from 1375 to 1380 – to complete the work.

Today, much of the tapestry is missing, and much is badly faded, but it is remarkable that anything survives of it at all considering that, during the Revolution, the populace of Angers sacked the town's cathedral and renamed it as a Temple of Reason. Local people took the tapestry out and cut it into strips for use as rugs, curtains, bedspreads and furniture covers. Some 50 years later, an effort was made to recover the fragments and re-create the tapestry. Surprisingly, about two-thirds was found and sewn back together. The length on display is about 100m, compared to the original length of 130m.

The Apocalypse Tapestry is in a series of dramatic panels, each depicting an element in the hallucinatory Revelation of St John, the final book in the New Testament. After vivid imaginings of a bloody Armageddon, it culminates in the victory of Christ and the Church over all the earth.

Black Angers

The château's dark stone once echoed the colour of all else in the old town, which became known as 'Black Angers'. It is built mainly from locally quarried slate. Only in recent times have modern building materials lightened the town's colour, especially with the addition of suburbs in white.

Opposite
Façade, Cathédrale St-Maurice

Overleaf
View across the Maine to Château d'Angers

Eglise St-Serge €
av. M Talet; open most days am and pm.

Eglise St-Serge

At the other end of the town centre from the cathedral, Angers has a second exceptional example of the light, intricate Plantagenet Gothic vaulting in the former Benedictine abbey church of St-Serge. The 12th- to 13th-century chancel is particularly beautiful, while the 15th-century nave has stained glass of the 16th century.

⊕ Galerie David d'Angers € *33bis r. Toussaint; tel: 02 41 87 21 03. Open mid-Jun–mid-Sept daily 0900–1830, rest of year 1000–1200 and 1400–1800. Closed Mon & national hols.*

Hôtel Pincé (Musée Turpin-de-Crissé) € *32bis r. Lenepveu; tel: 02 41 88 94 27. Open mid-Jun–mid-Sept daily 0900–1830; rest of year 1000–1200, 1400–1800, closed Mon.*

Musée des Beaux-Arts € *10 r. du Musée; tel: 02 41 05 38 00. Open mid-Jun–mid-Sept daily 1000–1900; rest of year 1000–1200, 1400–1800, closed Mon.*

The Plantagenets

The Plantagenets were a lordly dynasty of Angers who, under Geoffrey V (1131–51), became monarchs of England. The name comes from the sprig of *plante à genêt* – yellow-flowering broom – which Geoffrey liked to wear in his hair. His son, Henri, married the powerful heiress Eleanor of Aquitaine, and so added her vast domain in western France to the other Plantagenet territories. In 1154 he was crowned King Henry II of England, but continued to spend most of his time at the family's castle in Angers, incorporated into the structure of the later château. In 1205 the French captured Anjou and separated it from England. The ensuing war for possession of the Plantagenet territories in France was to last over a hundred years, and was eventually won by the French crown. Under French rule, Anjou became a Duchy. The last of the Angers-born nobility was the scholarly and popular Good King René (1408–80), Duke of Anjou, King of Naples and Count of Provence.

Galerie David d'Angers

One of Angers' most illustrious sons was the sculptor Jean-Pierre David (1788–1856), far better known simply as David of Angers. His greatest works were massive carved statues and portraits. Many on religious themes found their way into French churches, but he also executed busts of a wide variety of personalities such as writers, philosophers and historical characters. Plaster-cast copies of many of his works, and some originals, are displayed in this imaginatively restored, light-filled remnant of a former 11th-century abbey church.

Hôtel Pincé (Musée Turpin-de-Crissé)

Built in 1530, this Renaissance mansion near the main square was donated to the town in 1861. Today, it is occupied by the eclectic Musée Turpin-de-Crissé. Originally privately owned, it consists of collections of the art and artefacts of various cultures, including Etruscan, Egyptian, Greek and Chinese. The highlight of the museum is a remarkable, extensive Japanese collection, with prints, masks, ceramics and all the accoutrements of a tea ceremony.

Below
Galerie David d'Angers

Musée des Beaux-Arts

The town's Fine Arts Museum occupies the Logis Barrault, a grand mansion built in 1487 by Olivier Barrault, who held such posts as Treasurer of Brittany and King's Secretary, as well as being Mayor of Angers. The house was later occupied by Marie de Médicis and the governors of Anjou. The museum's substantial collection of paintings represents most of the French schools from the 13th to the 20th century, and is especially strong on the 17th to 19th centuries. There are also sculptures, and a floor devoted to local archaeology.

Musée Jean Lurçat et de la Tapisserie Contemporaine €€
4 blvd Arago; tel: 02 41 24 18 48. Open mid-Jun–mid-Sept Tue–Sun 0900–1830; rest of year daily 1000–1200 and 1400–1800.

Musée Jean Lurçat et de la Tapisserie Contemporaine

While medieval tapestry is the treasure of Angers, especially the Apocalypse Tapestry in the château, on the other side of the river this museum celebrates modern tapestry. It is named after Jean Lurçat (1892–1966), reviver and master of tapestry design and weaving in modern times. The museum's centrepiece is Lurçat's famous latter-day version of the Apocalypse, in ten tapestries totalling 80m in length, called *Le Chant du Monde* (literally, 'Song of the World'). It comes to a poignantly different conclusion from the original, reflecting the fears of the Cold War era in which it was made.

The museum occupies the former Hôpital St-Jean, or Hôtel-Dieu, the charity hospital founded by Henry II in 1175. Lurçat's tapestries, which have been displayed around the world, hang in the impressive *Salle des Malades*, the hospital ward, which dates back to the origins of the building and has a fine Plantagenet Gothic vaulted ceiling, supported by elegant slender pillars typical of the style. It continued to be used as a hospital until 1854. Note, too, the 17th-century dispensary to one side, with its shelves of earthenware jars. Other parts of the former hospital display modern tapestries by other artists, and it is one of the world's leading sites for temporary exhibitions of modern tapestry. The former hospital also has an attractive Romanesque cloister and garden, and a chapel.

Accommodation and food in Angers

Wine tasting

Just below the château you can learn about, sample and buy local wines at Maison du Vin de l'Anjou, *5bis pl. Kennedy; tel: 02 41 88 81 13; fax: 02 41 86 71 84. Closed Jan–Feb.* The winery can also provide advice and information on wine tasting in the vineyard region around the town.

Hôtel du Mail €€ *8 r. des Ursules; tel: 02 41 25 05 25; fax: 02 41 86 91 20; email: contact@hotel-du-mail.com; www.hotel-du-mail.com.* An appealing and friendly traditional small hotel of character and charm, in a 17th-century former convent, situated in a quiet street in the old quarter.

Hôtel d'Anjou and Restaurant La Salamandre €€–€€€ *1 blvd du Maréchal Foch; tel: 02 41 21 12 11; fax: 02 41 87 22 21; email info@ hoteldanjou.fr; www.hoteldanjou.fr.* One of the best hotels in Angers, and one of the best restaurants, is an imposing building on the boulevard just south of the old centre of town. This long-established local favourite, now a Best Western, has plenty of character, with its stained glass, mosaics and rooms in Art Deco style. The hotel is well equipped and there is free parking, and a garden. The restaurant (in neo-Gothic style) offers well-prepared classic dishes.

Hôtel de France €€–€€€ *8 pl. de la Gare; tel: 02 41 88 49 42; fax: 02 41 86 76 70.* One of the town's grander old hotels, located close to the TGV station, the France has a range of rooms from small and simple to larger and more luxurious. It has a couple of good, moderately priced restaurants – the simple, inexpensive Bistro, and smarter Plantagenêts.

Suggested walk

Total distance: About 2km, or 4km including the detour.

Time: Although the town centre is very compact, the walk could take most of the day if you allow plenty of time to visit the museums, admire façades and step down side turns. Allow at least 2 hours more to include the detour.

Route: Start from the **CHATEAU D'ANGERS ❶**. A peaceful old quarter separates the castle from the cathedral. Take **r. St-Aignan**, passing some picturesque half-timbered houses on the right and the Hôtel du Croissant on the left. This grand 15th-century mansion is named after the knightly Order of the Crescent, which was founded by Good King René, the 15th-century Duke of Anjou. Continue to the end where the street meets Montée St-Maurice, a long flight of steps climbing from the river to the **CATHEDRALE ST-MAURICE ❷**. There's an impressive view of the façade as you turn up the steps.

Behind the cathedral in pl. Ste-Croix, the Maison d'Adam is a striking 15th-century half-timbered house noted for its apple tree supporting the corner turret, and for some remarkable woodcarving. Turn left into r. Chaperonnière to reach **pl. du Ralliement**, vivacious centre of town and bearer of much of its history. Overlooking the square is the imposing theatre, rebuilt in the 19th-century, while on the corner stands the Renaissance mansion **HOTEL PINCE (MUSEE TURPIN-DE-CRISSE) ❸**.

Detour: Continue from the square along r. Lenepveu and r. du Commerce via pl. Louis Imbach, and across blvd Carnot to reach **EGLISE ST-SERGE ❹**. Behind the church is the town's lovely **Jardin des Plantes** (Botanic Garden), with a pool, an aviary and a small Romanesque church, as well as several rare tree species. Walk or take a bus along blvd Ayrault down to the River Maine. Across the water on the north bank is **MUSEE JEAN LURCAT ET DE LA TAPISSERIE CONTEMPORAINE ❺**. Returning to the south side, turn right from

Right
Vieux Angers

blvd Ayrault on r. Thiers and, reaching r. du Mail, turn left to stroll through the old streets of the St-Laud area – r. St-Laud, r. des Poëlliers – back to pl. du Ralliement (*end of detour*).

Leave pl. du Ralliement and walk up r. St-Martin to today's Prefecture, housed in the restored buildings of the former Benedictine abbey of St-Aubin, founded some 1,500 years ago. There is a lovely glass-covered Romanesque arcade to the left of the courtyard. Cross r. des Lices to **Tour St-Aubin**, the abbey's surviving 12th-century belfry. Beside it, in the 500-year-old Logis Barrault, is the **MUSEE DES BEAUX-ARTS ❻**. Skirt the museum to reach the entrance of **GALERIE DAVID D'ANGERS ❼** in r. Toussaint. Prom. du Bout du Monde leads back to the château.

Le Loir: Vendôme–La Flèche

Ratings

Cave dwellings	●●●●●
Architecture	●●●●
History	●●●●
Scenery	●●●●
Children	●●●
Son-et-Lumière	●●●
Activities	●●●
Wine tasting	●●

Just north of the Loire, and parallel to it, out of sight of the grandeur (and busy holiday traffic) of that immense, wide valley, lies a smaller and far less well-known river – and it, too, is called the Loir. While this Loir (with no 'e') is narrower and more homely, it also runs in a wide, fertile valley, and has white cliffs, distinguished vineyards, handsome villages, good restaurants and historic châteaux. Many rich abbeys and churches were built in the Middle Ages, as this was part of the pilgrims' route to Santiago de Compostela in northern Spain. Flowing in leisurely meanders, the river cuts through the chalk, creating peninsulas and peaceful poplar-lined banks. Abundant fish and riverside farms have made this a prosperous place to live since time immemorial. There is horse riding, walking and river sports at several places along the Loir. The troglodyte dwellings hollowed out of the soft white waterside cliffs have been occupied since the Stone Age and are still used today.

CHÂTEAU-DU-LOIR

ⓘ Château-du-Loir Tourist Office *Parc H Goude, 2 av. Jean Jaurès; tel: 02 43 44 56 68; fax: 02 43 44 56 95; email: ot.loir.berce@wanadoo.fr; www.ot-loir-et-berce.org. Open summer daily approx 1000–1300 and 1400–1830; rest of year Mon–Sat 1000–1230 and 1500–1830.*

⊖ Market *Sat am.*

Opposite
Château-du-Loir Hôtel de Ville

An important, bustling local centre, and a good base. However, the town itself offers little to see. And despite the name, it's not on the Loir and there's no château! Ruins of the castle keep, though, complete with dungeons, can be seen in the public park near the florid town hall.

Food and accommodation in and around Château-du-Loir

Grand Hôtel €€ *59 r. Aristide Briand; tel: 02 43 44 00 17; fax: 02 43 44 37 58.* This decent, traditional family-run hotel and restaurant is in the centre, close to the former château site. Rates are very reasonable.

Le Védaquais €€ *pl. de la Liberté, Vaas; tel: 02 43 46 01 41; fax: 02 43 46 37 60.* Located about 8km west of town, in a former village schoolhouse, this is a charming, unusual and comfortable place, though you may be accommodated in the annexe. The excellent restaurant offers local fish and a good selection of local wines.

LA CHARTRE-SUR-LE-LOIR

This appealing old town has an arm of the Loir running through it. Houses eat into the soft cliff face in the backstreets, which climb the hill of the southern edge of town. Some are right inside the cliff except for their front walls. Though the town itself has few attractions, it is a popular base with good facilities, and is the centre for the sweet wines of the Jasnières *appellation*.

Accommodation and food in La Chartre-sur-le-Loir

Hôtel de France €–€€ *pl. de la République; tel: 02 43 44 40 16; email: hoteldefrance@worldonline.fr.* A satisfyingly traditional family-run small hotel in the village square. Its popular restaurant is excellent, with an array of well-prepared local specialities at modest prices.

LA FLÈCHE

Attractively sited on a bend in the Loir, this busy market town and local industrial centre has little to justify a long stay but rewards a passing visit. Its most famous building is the **Prytanée**, a leading military training academy at secondary school level, housed in the Baroque buildings of a former distinguished Jesuit college and chapel founded in 1604 by Henri IV, who spent part of his early years here. The philosopher and mathematician René Descartes ('I think, therefore I am') was among its many well-known former pupils. The school's library of 45,000 books includes priceless volumes, some as much as 500 years old. The ashes of the hearts of both Henri IV and Marie de Medici are kept in a heart-shaped urn in the 17th-century Jesuit-style **Eglise St-Louis** that stands in the 16ha formal gardens. The college played an important role in the colonisation of Quebec, and one of its pupils went on to become its first bishop. The town was the departure point for many who emigrated to the North American province. In the west of town, the Romanesque chapel **Notre-Dame-des-Vertus** has unusual Renaissance woodcarvings. The old **Château des Carmes** (now the town hall) stands handsomely beside the Loir bridge and waterside public gardens.

Out of town 5km, on the south side, is **Le Tertre Rouge**, a large zoo located in a forest with an extensive range of interesting animals, including great white wolves from the Arctic.

Accommodation and food in La Flèche

Le Moulin des Quatre Saisons €–€€ *2 r. du Général Gallieni; tel: 02 43 45 12 12; fax: 02 43 45 10 31; www.moulindesquatresaisons.com.* This old mill beside the Loir is now a cheerful and easy-going restaurant

Les Affranchis – the town's big festival of street entertainment and fun in *early Jul*.

Boule de Fort – the local game *boule de fort (see page 121)* is popular here; watch out for matches and tournaments.

Prytanée € *r. Henri IV; tel: 02 43 48 67 04. Open during school summer holidays: daily 1000–1200 and 1400–1800; rest of year by appointment only. Entry ticket includes* **Eglise St-Louis***.*

Chapelle de Notre-Dame-des-Vertus € *Beside cemetery off av. Rhin-et-Danube. Usually open daily.*

Le Tertre Rouge €€€ *route de Savigné (5km E of town on D104); tel: 02 43 48 19 19; www.zoo-la-fleche.com. Open Apr–Jun daily 0930–1900; Jul–Sept daily 0930–2000; rest of year Mon–Sat 1000–1200 and 1330–1730, Sun 1000–1730.*

offering a wide variety of imaginative dishes beautifully prepared and served. Excellent wine list, and good value.

Le Relais Cicéro €€€ *18 blvd d'Alger; tel: 02 43 94 14 14; fax: 02 43 45 98 96; www.cicero.fr.* This peaceful and comfortable hotel is close to the Prytanée. Furnished with antiques, it occupies a grand 17th-century mansion, originally part of a convent. There's a pretty garden, too.

Right
The Prytanée, La Flèche

LE LUDE

ⓘ Le Lude Tourist Office *pl. F de Nicolay; tel: 02 43 94 62 20; fax: 02 43 94 48 46; email: otbas.ludois@ wanadoo.fr*

Ⓔ Events *Printemps Culturel* (Cultural Springtime) – theatre, concerts, jazz, exhibitions, *Mar–Apr; Week-end des Jardiniers* (Gardeners' weekends) – plant shows and garden workshops at the château, *early Jun; Son-et-Lumière* – at the château every Fri and Sat, mid-Jun–early Sept; *Les Journées Gourmandes* (Gourmet days) – music and gastronomy at the château, weekends mid-Jul–mid-Aug.

Ⓒ Château du Lude *€€ tel: 02 43 94 60 09; fax: 02 43 45 27 53; www.lelude.com. Open daily Apr–Sept only: grounds 1000–1230 and 1400–1800, interior 1430–1800. Closed Wed except mid-Jun–mid-Aug.*

A pleasant and attractive old town on the banks of the Loir, Le Lude's most splendid possession is the lovely **Château du Lude**, a strange, ornate construction, four-square with a massive tower at each corner, and surrounded by a broad, dry moat with a footpath at the bottom. More approachable and less remote than many other such opulent dwellings, the château of Le Lude is one of the most enjoyable to visit in the Loir valley. Its *son-et-lumière* extravaganzas, telling the history of the château, are held in the grounds on the banks of the Loir almost every weekend throughout the season, with spectacular lights, fireworks and 350 local people in period costume. Many other events are held in the house or grounds. Architecturally, the château is a curiosity, an almost amusing mix of conflicting styles, with a Gothic façade on the north wing, a pretty Renaissance south wing and a plain white classical façade on the east side – a similar mix to that seen at the royal château of Blois. Yet the whole building and its gardens and terraces somehow create a majestic unity. Henri IV and Louis XIII were both house guests before the Revolution. For the last 200 years the château has belonged to the same family and, although open to the public, it remains their private residence, very much with an air of being a grand family home. Inside, sumptuous rooms, fine pictures, Flemish tapestries, superbly restored Renaissance decoration, furnishings and period clothing are displayed.

Right
Manoir de la Possonnière

Overleaf
Château de Lude

MANOIR DE LA POSSONNIÈRE

Manoir de la Possonnière €€ *1km S of Couture-sur-Loir; tel: 02 54 72 40 05. Open for guided visits (45min) from about 1500 to 1730 on Sat, Sun & national hols in Apr, May, Jun, Sept & Oct–mid-Nov. Jul & Aug tours from 1500 to 1830 Wed–Sun.*

A grand Renaissance country house in white stone, standing within walled grounds on the edge of green forest, La Possonnière was the birthplace and home of the 16th-century romantic poet Pierre de Ronsard. A prolific and immensely successful writer of sonnets, he was appointed Poet Laureate and travelled to Scotland with Princess Madeleine, James V's future wife. The mansion is sumptuously decorated. On the garden side of the house Latin sayings are inscribed on the walls, while on the courtyard side is an elegant staircase tower.

MONTOIRE-SUR-LE-LOIR

Montoire Tourist Office *16 pl. Clemenceau; tel: 02 54 85 23 30; fax: 02 54 85 23 87; www.otsi-montoire.fr. Open Apr–Sept Mon–Sat 1000–1200 and 1500–1900, Sun & hols 1100–1300; rest of year Tue–Sat 1000–1200 and 1400–1800.*

World Folklore Festival – *mid-Aug; Loir Music Festival – Jul.*

Chapelle de St-Gilles € *33bis r. St-Oustrille. Open according to demand.*

Château de Lavardin €€ *route de Montoire, Lavardin; tel: 02 54 85 07 74. Open Jun–Sept 1100–1630; guided tours on summer afternoons.*

Eglise St-Genest € *Grand Rue, Lavardin. Open according to demand. If closed, enquire at town hall.*

Mairie (Town Hall) rooms € *Grand Rue, Lavardin; tel: 02 54 85 07 74. Open Wed & Fri 1600–1900, Sat 0830–1200.*

Montoire's most infamous moment was on 24 October 1940, when Hitler met Pétain at the station here and urged him to support an invasion of the United Kingdom. Although Pétain enthusiastically ran France's collaborationist government, he refused to agree to the invasion plan. The two men met at Montoire because the collaborationist but independent Government of France, based in Vichy, controlled everything south of the Loire, while France north of the Loire was under direct German rule. Today, Montoire is a peaceful, appealing place, as it may have been then, too. There's a delightful view of the picturesque waterfront from the bridge. The Loir just here is a favourite with fishermen. Near the bridge on the south side stands the **Chapelle de St-Gilles**, with fine murals dating back to the 12th century. On a rocky spur behind rise the evocative ruins of Montoire's castle: for an impression of how the castle used to look, see the model in the town hall.

Take av. du Général de Gaulle out of town and follow the minor road for about 2km upstream to the delightful hamlet of **Lavardin**, with its Gothic bridge and, poised on a rock above, the imposing ruins of the **Château de Lavardin**. Although only the keep and part of the ramparts survive, the castle was vast, and once covered a full four hectares. So daunting were its massive towers and triple walls that in 1188 the forces of Henry II and his son, Richard the Lionheart, were unable to take it, and turned away defeated. Later, Henri IV succeeded in conquering the castle, and ordered it destroyed. In the village, Lavardin's priory church of **St-Genest** is early Romanesque, and has remarkable murals, some of them 12th century. Behind the church the **Town Hall** contains two rooms dating back to the 11th century, partly reconstructed in the 15th century. From the viewpoint at La Rotte aux Biques, a marked footpath leads alongside a succession of inhabited cave dwellings.

Food around Montoire-sur-le-Loir

Le Relais d'Antan €€ *6 pl. Capitaine Vignau, Lavardin; tel: 02 54 86 61 33; fax: 02 54 85 06 46.* Rich and tasty fish and seafood dishes, followed by equally sumptuous desserts, are served at this friendly, highly rated restaurant in the pretty village of Lavardin.

PONCÉ-SUR-LE-LOIR

Château €€ *D305; tel: 02 43 44 45 39. Open Apr–Sept daily 1000–1200 and 1400–1830; rest of year Sun only, same hours; 1hr guided tours available.*

Paillard Mills Craft Centre €€ *D305; tel: 02 43 44 45 31. Open Tue–Sat 0900–1200 and 1400–1830.*

A 16th-century Renaissance **château** on a hillside dominates the village. Badly damaged by fire in the Revolution, much of the building was destroyed. But its great treasure survived – a superb staircase of stone, rising six flights beneath coffered ceilings exquisitely decorated with 130 mythological sculptures. The neatly geometric gardens, with lawns and greenery-covered walks, are beautiful, too. The château's impressive dovecote survives, with its revolving ladders and 1,800 nesting holes. There's a museum of local crafts and folk culture in one of the outbuildings. On the other side of town, in a converted 18th-century paper mill, you can watch glass-blowers and other skilled craftspeople in action at the **Paillard Mills Craft Centre** working in pottery, glass, metal, fabrics and wood. The centre also puts on exhibitions, entertainments and markets from time to time. The village's 12th-century church contains interesting frescoes.

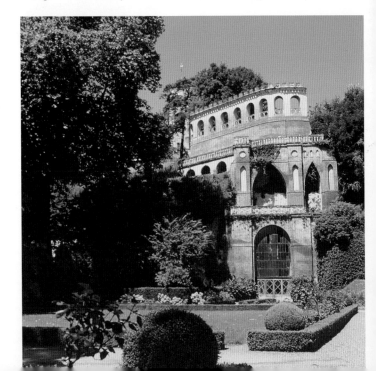

Right
Château, Poncé-sur-le-Loir

Opposite
Chapelle de St-Gilles, Montoire

TROO

ℹ️ **Troo Tourist Office** *At the Mairie;* *tel: 06 88 53 52 69;* *fax: 02 54 72 61 38;* *email: troo-st-jacques-de-guerets@fnotsi.net. Open daily Mar–Oct.*

🕐 **Tours** *Ask the tourist office about the train touristique and guided walks.*

This strange little village has several unusual features, especially the large number of cave houses rising up in tiers cut into the tufa cliffs. Their chimney stacks emerging from the ground strike a surreal note. Troo even has troglodyte streets and alleys – underground passageways and stairways – linking the subterranean homes. These underground galleries are known as *caforts*, originally from *caves forts*. Part of the village is beside the Loir, part on top of the escarpment and part buried in the hillside. Troo is an ancient community, once fortified, with remnants of the old ramparts and a massive feudal mound called La Butte. The 11th- to 12th-century St-Martin Collegiate Church has an unusual square tower in Angevin style, and 15th-century woodcarvings. Across the water, St-Jacques-des-Guérets Church dates from the same period, and has exceptional murals that are almost 1,000 years old; the best, in the apse, depict the *Crucifixion* and the *Resurrection of the Dead*. Maladrière Ste-Catherine, opposite the *Mairie* on the D917, is a 12th-century almshouse. At the bottom of the village, the Grotte Pétrifiant is a stalactite cave where objects are 'petrified' by limescale, while, at the top, is the *Grand Puits*, a large and deep covered well that is known for its echo.

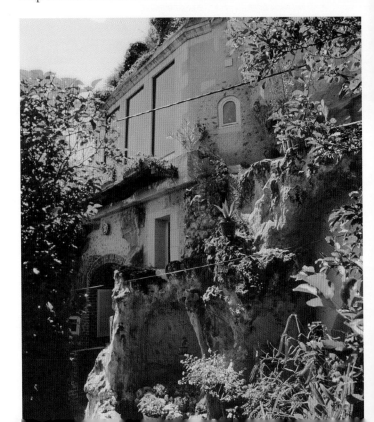

Right
Troglodyte houses, Troo

Opposite
Flying buttresses, Abbaye de la Trinité in Vendôme

VENDÔME

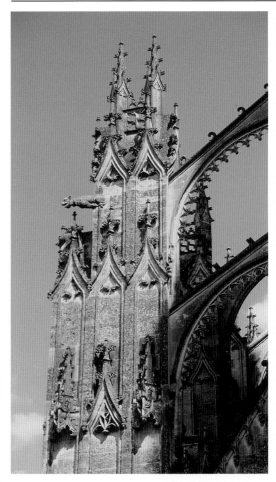

Don't be deterred by the extensive surrounding industrial and residential areas. At its heart a delightfully attractive and interesting town, old Vendôme's location is striking, standing across different arms of the Loir that form a group of river islands below a castle-topped escarpment grandly called La Montagne. The Loir channels are crossed by many bridges, and the flowing water gives charm to the streets and parks. Although very ancient – there was a Gallic settlement here – the town grew around the **Abbaye de la Trinité**, founded in 1040 as a Benedictine community. For centuries the town was a place full of pilgrims, who would come to see the *Sainte Larme de Vendôme* (the 'Holy Tear of Vendôme'), a drop of liquid brought here from the Holy Land in the 11th century by Geoffrey Martel, Count of Anjou, who claimed that it was the tear shed by Christ on Lazarus' tomb. Most of the surviving abbey church, and especially its 16th-century west façade, is a masterpiece of delicate Flamboyant Gothic stonework. Set apart is the remarkably tall (80m) 12th-century Romanesque bell tower. Inside the church only the transept survives from the 11th century. Notice the beautifully crafted 15th-century woodcarving on the stalls in the chancel.

In the 14th century old Vendôme was ringed by fortifications, of which the handsome Porte St-Georges is a remnant. In the town's main square, pl. St-Martin, you can see a 15th-century house called Grand St-Martin. Of the church that once stood on the square, only the Renaissance Tour St-Martin survives. The town hall, beside pleasant and shady Parc Ronsard in the town centre, was the college attended by Balzac – he hated it! There's also a 16th-century *lavoir* (wash house) on the edge of the park. It's a steep climb (some may prefer to drive) up to the sturdy 11th- and 14th- century **château**, with its 16th-century dungeons. The Promenade de la Montagne, beside the castle, gives superb views over the town and the River Loir.

ⓘ Vendôme Tourist Office *Hôtel du Saillant, Parc Ronsard;* tel: 02 54 77 05 07; fax: 02 54 73 20 81; www.vendôme.eu. *Open May–mid-Jun Mon–Sat 1000–1230 and 1400–1800, Sun & hols 1000–1300; mid-Jun–mid-Sept Mon–Sat 1000–1800, Sun & hols 1000–1300; mid-Sept–Apr Mon–Sat*

1000–1230 and 1400–1800, closed Sun, except Easter weekend 1000–1300.

🔁 The town is on the N10 between Tours and Chartres. From Paris (about 2 hrs' drive), take *autoroute* A10, then A11. Exit at Thivars (after Chartres), and take the N10 to Châteaudun, then Vendôme. Coming from the south, leave the A10 at Blois, and take the D957 to Vendôme. There are good rail links to towns in the region, and a TGV direct from Paris taking just 42min.

🅿 There is parking in central pl. St-Martin, and in several signposted car parks around the town centre.

🎧 **Guided tours** The tourist office organises 1–2hr themed guided walks throughout the summer. It also runs guided tours on water. In addition, it organises afternoon tours, walks and events for 6–12-year-olds, such as 'Animals and people in the Middle Ages'.

🏛 **Abbaye de la Trinité** € *r. de l'Abbaye; tel: 02 54 77 26 13. Open Wed–Mon 1000–1200 and 1400–1800.*

Château € *tel: 02 54 77 26 13. Open daily 0900–1900 (Jun–Aug closes 2000). Walk up from pl. du Château, or drive via r. Ferme and Faubourg St-Lubin.*

🎵 **Festivals** International Guitar Festival – *Apr, www.vendomeguitarfest.com;* Rockomotives – *last weekend in Oct.*

Accommodation and food in Vendôme

Auberge de la Madeleine €–€€ *6 pl. Madeleine; tel: 02 54 77 20 79; fax: 02 54 80 00 02.* Simple, unpretentious comforts, and a straightforward and inexpensive restaurant make this a good base or stopover.

Le Capricorne €€ *8 blvd de Tremault; tel: 02 54 80 27 00; fax: 02 54 77 30 63.* A relaxed and welcoming hotel with pleasant rooms arranged around a garden, the hotel also has a choice of two reliable, good-value eating places – one a simple bistro, the other a more ambitious restaurant.

Suggested tour

Total distance: 152km.

Time: 2 days.

Links: From La Flèche, you can travel 19km south via the D938 to link up with Baugé on the Western Châteaux tour (*see page 126*); or it is just 17km north on the N23 to La Fontaine-St-Martin on the Sarthe tour (*see page 170*).

Route: Start from **VENDOME ❶** on the Loir's picturesque north bank road, the D5. At **Villiers-sur-Loir** the church has 16th-century murals. There is also a good *cave co-operative* here selling white, red, rosé and sparkling wines of the Côteaux Vendômois, or you can buy direct from local producers in the village. From here, **Rochambeau castle** can be seen on the far side of the river – if you want a closer look, take the D67 and cross to the south bank, passing through **Thoré-la-Rochette**. The route and the view are perhaps more interesting than the castle itself, and there are several cave dwellings here. Continuing on the north bank, the little River Boulon flows into the Loir in green water meadows and reeds at **Le Guë-du-Loir**, where the Renaissance manor house La Bonaventure used to belong to the father of Henri IV, and later to the poet Alfred de Musset.

Instead of clinging to the riverside (via Asnières), take the direct road to **Les Roches-l'Evêque**, where – just before entering the village – there are remarkable dwellings cut into the cliff face, some with terraces and flowers around the entrances. It's a short distance into **MONTOIRE-SUR-LE-LOIR ❷**. Take the road to **TROO ❸**, its landmark bell tower visible much of the way. Then continue as far as the left turn to **Vieux-Bourg** and follow the little riverside road to this small village. Cross the water into Artins and follow the roadsigns to the **MANOIR DE LA POSSONNIERE ❹**. Pass through **La-Couture-sur-Loir** and cross the river back on to the north bank. Follow the river road through charming villages of pale tufa houses, many quite grand. Just before **PONCE-SUR-LE-LOIR ❺**, notice its château high on the wooded slope to the right of the road. The route is very picturesque along this stretch; passing by the vineyards of the Jasnières *appellation*, the road soon reaches **LA CHARTRE-SUR-LE-LOIR ❻**.

Leave town on the D305 but, at resorty little **Marçon**, turn right past the attractive old church on to the D61. Cross the river on a narrow bridge at **Le Port Gautier**, a former river port, and turn on to the D64. It's a surprise, at the next village, to discover that the Loir, like its grander namesake, has a **Vouvray**, and that this, too, is a winemaking village, simple and old-fashioned. From here comes very good Jasnières *appellation contrôlée* sweet wine. There's a tasting at the *Mairie* every weekend in summer – look out for it. Follow the signs into **CHATEAU-DU-LOIR ❼**.

Below
Montoire-sur-le-Loir

On the menu

This is a good region in which to sample *marmite sarthoise*, *rillettes* and *andouillettes* confectionery called *Roseau du Loir*. Among its wines, the reds, rosés and whites of the Côteaux du Loir, and the sweet wines of Jasnières, are well worth trying and buying.

Travel on the south bank road (via Nogent-sur-Loir) to **Vaas**. This is horsebreeding country, with many stables and stud farms. The waterside at Vaas, with its working corn mill and local museum (*tel: 02 43 46 70 22*) and its old *lavoir* (wash house), is picturesque. There's a good hotel-restaurant here (*see Château-du-Loir*) and a river beach and watersports, as well as riding, while just north in the **Forêt de Bercé** there are marked walking trails. Just beyond, the **Cherré** archaeological site stands at the junction of the D305 and D188. It's the site of a Gallo-Roman settlement occupied until the 4th century. You can see the remains of its theatre and some other structures. Continue into **LE LUDE** ❽. Travel on either side of the river for **LA FLECHE** ❾. If taking the main D306, south of the river, you first reach **Le Tertre Rouge** zoo beside the road on the left.

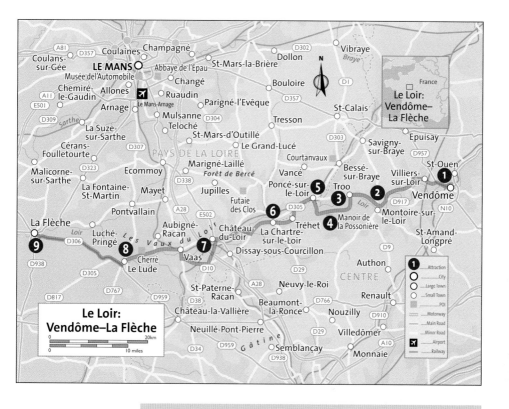

On the troglodyte trail

The Loir meanders through a valley cut into the tufa over 2 million years ago and, in many places, its white cliffs rise up to 60m from the valley floor. Quarrying of the soft white stone has left behind networks of caves and galleries, used as refuges in times of war, as places of pagan and Christian worship, as homes, barns, wine cellars, mushroom farms and even museums.

The stretch of river valley between Montoire-sur-le-Loir and Vendôme is very appropriately named Le Caveau (*tel: 02 54 85 31 11*). At Les Roches-l'Evêque there is a chapel with 14th-century frescoes, while Thoré la Rochette boasts some 15 wine cellars that can be visited by arrangement with the *Mairie (tel: 02 54 72 80 82)*. Just outside Villiers-sur-Loir, on the hillside at St-André, a 700m path leads to a troglodyte hamlet. Exhibitions and guided tours take place at *weekends Jul–Sept (tel: 02 54 72 90 83)*. Also at St-André is a mushroom farm offering tours of its galleries and selling its produce, as well as a troglodyte picnic area with a wood fire (*tel: 02 54 72 78 10*).

Finally, if all this has given you a taste for troglodyte life, ask at local tourist offices about *gîtes troglodytes*.

Le Mans

Ratings

Architecture	●●●●●
Sport	●●●●●
Gastronomy	●●●
History	●●●
Museums	●●●
Roman remains	●●●
Shopping	●●●
Entertainment	●●

For many, the name Le Mans is inextricably linked with the epic 24-hour motor race and dismissed from a cultural point of view. That's a mistake, as this riverside town has a fine renovated medieval heart that, in turn, is enclosed within a large Roman city wall, legacy of the Gallo-Roman town, *Vindinium*. The town centre is divided in two: the mainly modern sector, with shops, banks and administrative buildings, and *Le Vieux Mans* spread out on the hilltop. Thanks to its scores of half-timbered houses, cobblestone streets and quiet courtyards, it has become a very fashionable place to live. Subtle illumination and a plethora of restaurants enhance its appeal at night. A major tunnel, from the 1870s, cuts under the old town and is named after aviator Wilbur Wright (1867–1912) who undertook aviation trials here. Other former Le Mans residents include Kings Henri II (1139–89) and Jean le Bon (1319–64), and the poet Paul Scarron (1610–60).

Getting there and getting around

ⓘ Le Mans Tourist Office *r. de l'Etoile;*
tel: 02 43 28 17 22;
fax: 02 43 28 12 14;
www.lemanstourisme.com.
Open Mon–Fri 0900–1800,
Sat 0900–1200 and 1400–
1800, Sun 1000–1200.

By road
Le Mans is located at a central point in France: two major *autoroutes* (the A11 from Nantes to Paris and the A81 from Rennes) meet here. Access to Paris, 205km away, takes just 2hr.

By rail
The TGV links Le Mans with Paris, Montparnasse in 54min.

By air
The nearest international airport is Paris-Orly.

Parking
Le Mans' street parking is generally metered. The best option is to leave your car in the underground parking in pl. des Jacobins, or head

Le Mans

RUE DU PRÉ
RUE DE LA CALANDRE
QUAI LEDRU-ROLLIN
RUE VOLTAIRE
RUE SIEYES
RUE DENFERT-ROCHEREAU
QUAI LOUIS BLANC
RUE HENRY DELAGENIÈRE
RUE LIONEL ROYER
RUE MONTBARBET
RUE DU DONJON
PONT YSSOIR
Église Notre-Dame-du-Pré
RUE MONTESQUIEU
RUE ROBERT TRIGER
PLACE DU CARDINAL GRENTE
Musée de Tessé
AVENUE DE PADERBORN
Parc de Tessé
QUAI LEDRU-ROLLIN
La Sarthe
RUE DES CHAPLAINS
RUE DES CHANOINES
PLACE ST-MICHEL
Cathédrale St-Julien
N
QUAI LOUIS BLANC
RUE ST-HILAIRE
RUE DE VAUX
SQUARE JACQUES DUBOIS
Musée de la Reine Bérengère
PLACE DU JET D'EAU
GRANDE RUE
RUE WILBUR WRIGHT
PLACE DES JACOBINS
RUE DU 33E MOBILES
RUE DU CIRQUE
Gallo-Roman Walls
RUE DE LA FÉFÈRE
PLACE DU HALLAI
PLACE ST-PIERRE
GRANDE RUE
RUE ST-FLACEAU
Collégiale St-Pierre la Cour
AVENUE DE ROSTOV-SUR-LE-DON
PLACE ST-BENOÎT
AVENUE P MENDES-FRANCE
RUE DES ARÈNES
RUE DE LA GALÈRE
RUE GAMBETTA
PLACE DE L'ÉPERON
RUE DE LA BARILLERIE
RUE DE LA JUVERIE
i
RUE DE L'ÉTOILE
RUE DE L'ÉTOILE
PLACE LIONEL LECOUTEUX
RUE GOUGEARD
RUE VICTOR BONHOMMET
RUE ST-MARTIN
RUE DE BOLTON
CARREFOUR ST-NICOLAS
RUE DE LA PAILLE
RUE DE PARIS
RUE BARBIER
AVENUE DU GENERAL DE GAULLE
Place de la République
RUE COURTHARDY
RUE DU PORT
RUE DES MINIMES
RUE DU LEROY
BOULEVARD RENE LEVASSEUR
AVENUE FRANÇOIS MITTERAND
RUE BERTHELOT
PLACE ARISTIDE BRIAND

0   100 metres
0   100 yards

○ ....Attraction
  ....Important Building
  ....Park
  ....Main Road
  ....Other Road
i ....Information

ⓘ Comité Départemental du Tourisme *19bis r. de l'Etoile, Le Mans; tel: 02 43 40 22 50; fax: 02 43 40 22 51; www.tourisme-en-sarthe.com. Open Mon–Thur 0900–1230 and 1400–1745, Fri 0900–1330 and 1400–1730.*

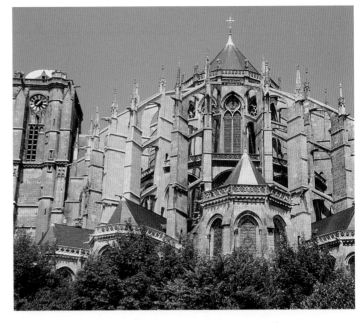

Right
Cathédrale St-Julien

for the area slightly north of the centre around Eglise Notre-Dame-du-Pré (where street parking is still free). Then cross the Pont Yssoir and you are in the *vieille ville* or 'old town'.

Sights

ⓗ Cathédrale St-Julien *Open 0900–1200 and 1400–1800.*

Cathédrale St-Julien

Consecrated in the name of the first bishop of Le Mans, this is one of France's finest Romanesque cathedrals. Its imposing western portal, nave and finely carved stone capitals date from the end of the 11th century, while the choir and apse chapels are all 13th century. It's worth walking round the cathedral's exterior to admire the 82 flying buttresses that sustain the roof – works of art in themselves. The 12th-century stained-glass windows depicting biblical scenes (including the celebrated 1140 interpretation of the *Descent from the Cross*) are matched by other magnificent works executed in the 13th and 15th centuries. The tomb of Charles IV (d. 1472) is the work of celebrated Sicilian sculptor Francesco Laurana. Leaning against a corner of the western portal, like a shrouded figure, stands an ancient menhir attesting to the significance of this site in pagan times.

Gallo-Roman walls

Some 1,700 years ago the Gallo-Romans constructed these sturdy walls, towers and tunnels around their 9ha town *Vindinium*.

ⓘ Musée de la Reine Bérengère € *7–11 r. de la Reine Bérengère; tel: 02 43 47 38 80. Open summer Tue–Sun 1000–1230 and 1400–1830, winter Tue–Sun 1400–1800.*

Musée de Tessé € *2 av. de Paderborn; tel: 02 43 47 38 51. Open Sept–Jun daily except Mon, 0900–1200 and 1400–1800; Jul–Aug Mon–Sat 1000–1230 and 1400–1830, Sun & national hols 1000–1200 and 1400–1800.*

Right
Gallo-Roman walls, Le Mans

Subsequent generations have built on these ancient fortifications, embellishing them with carved designs, coloured stonework or geometric brick decorations. The Tours Madeleine and du Vivier are particularly fine.

Grande Rue

This is a focal point in the old town, for it still retains a number of interesting 15th- and 16th-century façades with some quirky details and plenty of grandiose portals. The listed Maison d'Adam et Eve (the superb two-figure relief that gave the house its nickname is now believed to represent Bacchus and Ariane) was built for the astrologer Jean de l'Epine. The house represents French Renaissance architecture at its finest. The Maison des Deux Amis, once property of the 15th-century poet Nicolas Denizot, has an intriguing sculpted image of two figures outside, giving it its common name. The Maison du Pilier Rouge, on the corner of r. du Pilier Rouge and Grande Rue, is named after the 16th-century twisted barleysugar stone column with red paintwork that supports part of the house's façade. Nearly opposite is the 16th-century pillar giving the Maison du Pilier Vert its sobriquet.

Musée de la Reine Bérengère

This historical and ethnographic museum, built in the mid-15th century, holds some beautiful paintings of old Le Mans, including work of local painter Jules-Alfred Hervé-Mathé (1868–1953), a collection of locally produced pewterware and a fine range of pottery and faience from the Sarthe and Maine regions.

Musée de Tessé

Once the home of the influential Tessé family, this museum now houses a fascinating and eclectic collection of old paintings, including works by Philippe de Champaigne, Georges de la Tour, Nicolas Tournier and the Sienese painter Pietro Lorenzetti.

Place du Cardinal Grente

Located in front of the cathedral, this square is characterised by the elegant 16th-century Hôtel du Grabatoire, now the city's bishopric. In much the same style, but with a delightful round corner tower, is the Maison de la Tourelle, decorated with stone lucarne windows.

Above
Le Vieux Mans

Time out from sightseeing

The **Parc de Tessé** is a pleasant place to relax, as is the 5ha **Jardin d'horticulture**, a classified garden, nearby on r. de Flora. It was conceived in part as a formal French garden, and in part as an English one. The French rose garden is not to be missed, while the English-style park-garden, with its lake, islands and waterbirds, is always popular with the young.

Festivals and events

- Spring Festival – *beginning Apr*; Onion Festival – *first Fri in Sept*;
- Les Quatre Jours du Mans – festival *during first fortnight of Sept*;
- Les 24 Heures du Mans – *for cars, staged from Sat to Sun during the middle to end of Jun each year; for motorbikes it is staged in Apr, and for lorries/utility vehicles in Oct. www.lemanstourisme.com*

Les 24 Heures du Mans

In June 1906 the first Automobile Club de la Sarthe endurance race was staged on regional roads. The drivers raced 130km between Le Mans, St-Calais and La Ferthé-Bernard. Through the years it gained in prestige to become a 24-hour endurance test, for all classes of motorcars, and is now held each June on a 13.6km-long circuit just south of Le Mans. The record distance clocked up has now exceeded 5,000km during the 24 hours.

Accommodation and food in and around Le Mans

Le Grenier à Sel €–€€ *26 pl. de l'Eperon; tel: 02 43 23 26 30; fax: 02 43 77 00 80. Open daily except Sun pm.* A bright restaurant in an attractive period building, serving a good traditional menu with local specialities.

Auberge de la Foresterie €€ *route de Laval; tel: 02 43 51 25 12; fax: 02 43 28 54 58. Open all year.* Five minutes out of town, a tranquil, modernised hotel with full services and an excellent restaurant.

Hôtel Chantecler €€ *50 r. de la Pelouse; tel: 02 43 14 40 00; fax: 02 43 77 16 28; www.hotelchantecler.fr. Open all year.* A very well-kept hotel in a quiet part of town close to the railway station and river. No restaurant.

La Ciboulette €€ *14 r. de la Vieille-Porte; tel: 02 43 24 65 67; fax: 02 43 87 51 18. Closed Sat and Sun.* A gourmet address that offers consistently good food.

Auberge des Matfeux €€€ *D147 at Arnage (9km); tel: 02 43 21 10 71; fax: 02 43 21 25 23; www.aubergedesmatfeux.fr.* In a traditional *auberge*, a classical French menu is served with elegance.

Suggested walk

Total distance: About 1.5km.

Time: Allow about 4 hours to enjoy this walk.

Route: The **PLACE DU CARDINAL GRENTE ❶**, in front of the cathedral's western portal, is a good spot to admire the **CATHEDRALE ST-JULIEN ❷** itself before walking past the menhir and turning left along the cathedral's flank, to pl. St-Michel. Behind you, note the southern portal: it's a beautiful 12th-century entrance in carved stone. At No 1, the rather rundown Renaissance house was once owned by Paul Scarron.

Backtrack a few metres and turn left into **r. Bérengère**. In the elegant building on the left is the **MUSEE DE LA REINE BERENGERE ❸**. Continue along this narrow street into the Square Jacques Dubois where, on the corner ahead, stands the **Maison du Pilier Rouge**. Turn left, past the café, in r. du Pilier Rouge which leads through the **pl. du Hallai**, past the **Hôtel de Ville**, built on the former Plantagenet royal palace, and into the **pl. St-Pierre**. On the south side are the 14th-century remains of the **Collégiale St-Pierre la Cour**, which overlook the vestiges of Le Mans' **Roman baths**. Leave the square by **r. de l'Ecrevisse** and head for the **GRANDE RUE ❹**. Turn left and walk downhill until you reach the

Above
Maison d'Adam et Eve, detail of carvings

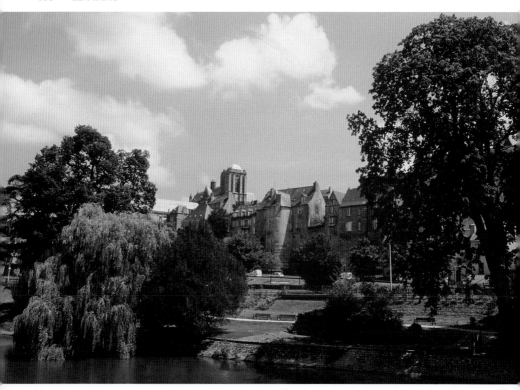

Above
River view at Le Mans

L'Obéissante

The French automobile industry has Le Mans resident Amédée Bollée (1844–1917) to thank for the debut of the car. His first vehicle, making its appearance in 1873, was oddly named *L'Obéissante* (The Obedient One). He was the first person to place the engine in front of the driver, rather than behind. His likewise-named son (1867–1926) carried on the research, but concentrated on speed rather than utility.

turning on the right into **r. St-Pavin-de-la-Cité**, a quiet street that curves back and runs into **r. du Bosquet**. Straight ahead at the bottom of this street are the imposing portals of the **Hôtel de Vaux**, former residence of painter J-A Hervé-Mathé. The tranquillity and gardens of **r. de Vaux** make it a prime residential address. Turn left and walk along to the flight of steps that leads through the **GALLO-ROMAN WALLS ❺** and out to the grassy lawns along **r. St-Hilaire** and the river. Walk northwards along the walls to opposite the **Pont Yssoir**, catching a glimpse of the Romanesque **Eglise Notre-Dame-du-Pré**, once part of the female Benedictine Abbaye St-Julien-du-Pré, before turning towards the long flight of steps that leads up to the **r. des Chanoines**. Turn left here and walk along to the end of the road that rejoins the pl. du Cardinal Grente. Although it is not in Vieux Mans, the **MUSEE DE TESSE ❻**, just 500m along the **av. de Paderborn** from the cathedral, should also be visited.

Le Mans

0   100 metres
0   100 yards

RUE DU PRÉ
RUE DE LA CALANDRE
QUAI LEDRU-ROLLIN
QUAI LOUIS BLANC
RUE DENFERT ROCHEREAU
RUE HENRY DELAGENIÈRE
RUE LIONEL ROYER
RUE MONTBARBET
RUE DU DONJON

RUE VOLTAIRE
RUE SIEYES
RUE MONTESQUIEU

PONT YSSOIR
Eglise Notre-Dame-du-Pré
QUAI LEDRU-ROLLIN
QUAI LOUIS BLANC

RUE DES CHAPLAINS
RUE DES CHANOINES
PLACE DU CARDINAL GRENTE
PLACE ST-MICHEL
Cathédrale St-Julien
RUE ROBERT TRIGER
AVENUE DE PADERBORN
Musée de Tessé
Parc de Tessé
N

La Sarthe
RUE DE VAUX
SQUARE JACQUES DUBOIS
Musée de la Reine Bérengère
PLACE DU JET D'EAU

RUE ST-HILAIRE
GRAND'RUE
RUE WILBUR WRIGHT
PLACE DES JACOBINS

Gallo-Roman Walls
RUE DE LA VERRERIE
PLACE DU HALLAI
PLACE ST-PIERRE
RUE DU CIRQUE

GRAND'RUE
RUE ST-FLACEAU
Collégiale St-Pierre la Cour
RUE DE ROSTOV-SUR-LE-DON
AVENUE DU 33E MOBILES
RUE DES ARÈNES

PLACE ST-BENOIT
AVENUE P MENDES-FRANCE
RUE DE L'ÉTOILE
PLACE LIONEL LECOUTEUX
RUE GOUGEARD

RUE DE LA GALERE
RUE DE LA BARILLERIE
RUE DE LA JUIVERIE
CARREFOUR ST-NICOLAS
RUE DE L'ÉTOILE

RUE GAMBETTA
PLACE DE L'EPERON
RUE VICTOR BONHOMMET
RUE ST-MARTIN
RUE DE BOLTON
RUE DE LA PAILLE

RUE DE PARIS
AVENUE DU GENERAL DE GAULLE

Place de la République
RUE COURTHARDY
RUE BARBIER
RUE DU PORT
RUE DES MINIMES
BOULEVARD RENÉ LEVASSEUR
RUE DU LEROY
AVENUE FRANCOIS MITTERAND
RUE BERTHELOT

PLACE ARISTIDE BRIAND

1 .... Attraction
.... Important Building
.... Park
.... Main Road
.... Other Road
i .... Information

The Sarthe

Ratings

Châteaux	●●●●
Churches	●●●●
Forests	●●●●
Children	●●●
Gardens	●●●
Scenery	●●●
Gastronomy	●●
History	●●

Surrounding the city of Le Mans is the *département* of the Sarthe, taking its name from the navigable river that diagonally cuts it in two. Like the Loire, the Sarthe provided a lifeline and transport system for the villages and towns that grew along its banks and, like the Loire, it has retired from continuous transport and now accommodates the more leisurely traffic of boating holidaymakers. Within this area are some large forested tracts, such as the Perche, once the sparring ground of the English and French during the Hundred Years War. From those distant times, we still find historic dolmens, ancient feudal manors and little churches. Small towns and villages still boast traditional, Renaissance half-timbered houses and old wash houses. Sometimes barely touched by the advancing centuries, the role of these communities was to support and nurture the noble residence in their midst. Give this area the time and attention it deserves and its rewards will be many.

ABBAYE DE L'EPAU

Abbaye de l'Epau
€€ Le Mans (near exit for motorway);
tel: 02 43 84 22 29.
Open Mar–Sept 0930–1200 and 1400–1800;
Oct–Feb 0930–1200 and 1400–1730.

Le Mans' soulless modern suburbs are in direct contrast to the serenity of this Cistercian abbey – one of France's most attractive – founded in 1229 by Queen Bérengère (Richard the Lionheart's widow), who also ended her days here. The Abbaye de l'Epau was torched during the Hundred Years War but was partially rebuilt between 1400 and 1444. The coloured glass windows in the choir date from this rebuilding, while the grey and black glass window antedates this, having been designed in the 13th century during a ban on the use of coloured glass. The abbey is laid out around grassy cloisters, with the collegial church to its north side. The beautifully vaulted Salle Capitulaire, probably the most impressive part of this abbey, shelters the stone effigy of Queen Bérengère, while the bare interior of the deconsecrated church highlights the simplicity of Cistercian architecture. Three chapels are of moderate interest, though one has an odd altarpiece showing the *Martyrdom of Saint Sebastian*. The Sacristy has been

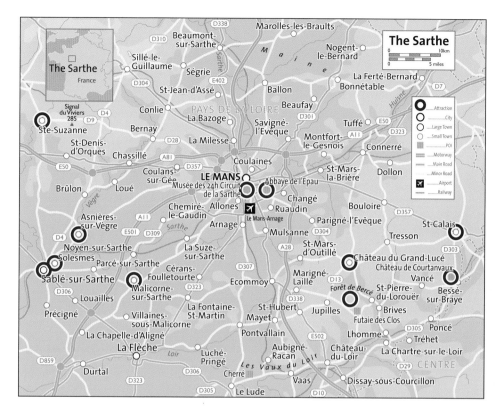

restored to its original state and boasts a couple of beautifully carved capitals and 14th-century wall paintings; so, too, the renovated dormitory (now also used for seminars), which is believed to have been constructed before the rest of the abbey buildings.

Accommodation and food near the Abbaye de l'Epau

Novotel Le Mans Est €€€ *blvd R Schuman; tel: 02 43 85 26 80; fax: 02 43 75 31 76. Open year-round.* A large and very comfortable hotel just minutes from the abbey and the centre of Le Mans. Its restaurant has a good reputation with locals.

ASNIÈRES-SUR-VÈGRE

There are parts of rural France where you dream of going back in time. In Asnières-sur-Vègre you are plunged into another era, one in which the painter John Constable would feel at home. A pretty little river weaves lazily between its banks, ducks paddle nonchalantly on its

Association Patrimoine d'Asnières-sur-Vègre
tel: 02 43 92 40 47.
Open Jul & Aug Tue–Sun 0900–1700, guided visits at 1630; Apr–Jun & Sept Sun only, 1630 for guided visits.

waters, thick foliage droops into the stream, ancient houses are found along crooked little roads, and a stone bridge has witnessed the passage of wheels and pedestrians for over 800 years. This is a gem of a village and one that, for its own preservation and for visitors' pleasure, should ban cars from its centre. Each way you turn there is an old building to admire: the solid small church dedicated to St Hilaire boasts a fine cycle of wall paintings depicting scenes from the *Life of*

Christ, executed nearly 1,000 years ago (look at those terrified chaps in chain mail cringing at the demons from hell, and the wonderful rendition of *Christ's Baptism*); the Cours d'Asnières, a 13th-century manor house with a pepperpot tower, is a massive limestone building, with attractive ochre-coloured mortar and a very severe grey slate roof; have a look at the old *pigeonnier* (dovecote) in the field behind it. The Vieux Pont, one of the focal points of the village, is next to the mill and leads over the Vègre to the medieval building known as the Basse Cour. There is also a notable wash house around the Fontaine de St-Aldic.

Accommodation and food in Asnières-sur-Vègre

Right
Asnières-sur-Vègre café

Opposite
Cruising on the River Sarthe

Manoir des Claies €€ *La Malvoyère; tel: 02 43 92 40 50; fax: 02 43 92 65 72; www.manoirdesclaies.fr. Open Apr–mid-Nov.* This is a large, privately owned *chambres d'hôtes* in a restored building dating from the 15th century. Comfortable and secluded. Meals on request.

CHÂTEAU DE COURTANVAUX

Château de Courtanvaux €
Bessé-sur-Braye; tel: 02 43 35 34 43. Open Easter– 1 Nov daily except Mon. Guided visits 1000, 1100, 1400, 1500, 1600 & 1700.

The attractive entrance gate, designed with twin rounded towers and decorative windows, and the beautifully maintained parkland, suggest the château's former grandeur, but the large, high-ceilinged rooms of this château are disappointingly bare. There are guided tours when the building is not hosting more lucrative private functions. However, the gardens are open irrespective of these. A château was originally erected here in Gothic times but most of what we see today is 15th and 16th century and was last owned by the Montesquiou family (the Comtesse was employed by Napoleon as a governess) who sold it to the state in

Right
Château de
Courtanvaux

1976. The cobblestone courtyard affords a good point from which to look at the stone castle's different styles. Beyond it you can enjoy its pretty, formal French garden and lush parkland. With over 70ha of woodland, a lake and a small river – all accessible by good footpaths – this is probably the most attractive part of the château.

Food near the Château de Courtanvaux

La Petite Auberge €–€€ *Bessé-sur-Braye, 8km south of town, on D303; tel: 02 43 44 45 08; fax: 02 43 44 18 57. Closed Wed and, out of season, Tue pm.* A popular, rustic restaurant with pretty decoration. Creative cuisine using fresh, local produce.

FORÊT DE BERCÉ

The 5,379ha Forêt de Bercé is a vast area, the remains of an extensive Gallic forest, thickly wooded with beech, chestnut and oak trees – it is a rare treat for the nature lover and amateur ornithologist. Over the centuries Bercé has been protected by royal warrant, but today selective logging is permitted in parts of the forest and, amid the brackens hidden by the dappled light, there are often huge piles of stacked logs. There are numerous places to picnic, walk and drive through this area: if you don't follow the suggested route (*see page 180*), try going on the D13, through **Jupilles** and then via the die-straight avenue from Rond-Wautot to the Rond-du-Clocher and out via **St-Pierre-du-Lorouër**. Don't miss the Chêne Boppe, a huge and ancient oak tree, the Futaie des Clos, where trees still date from the 1650s, and the Fontaine de la Coudre, source of the River Dinan.

CHÂTEAU DU GRAND-LUCÉ

Château du Grand-Lucé €€ *9 pl. de la République, Le Grand-Luce; tel: 02 43 40 85 56; fax: 02 43 40 94 97. Phone for details of visits.*

Le Grand-Lucé is a fine 18th-century château in neoclassical style with 30ha of equally magnificent gardens. It was built for Jacques III Pineau de Viennay as a summer residence between 1760 and 1764 (unfortunately, he died just as it was completed), and is light and airy in ambience, designed to incorporate the new ideas of the French Enlightenment. The gardens include greenhouses, wooded park, vegetable gardens and, of course, a formal French garden.

MALICORNE-SUR-SARTHE

Malicorne Tourist Office *3 pl. du Guesclin; tel: 02 43 94 74 45; fax: 02 43 94 59 61; www. ville-malicorne.fr. Open Apr–Sept daily 0900–1230 and 1430–1700; rest of year Wed–Sat 0900–1200 and 1400–1700.*

Musée de la Faïencerie d'Art de Malicorne *18 r. Bernard Palissy; tel: 02 43 94 81 18; www.faiencerie-malicorne.com. Open Mon–Sat 0900–1200 and 1400–1830, Easter–Sept Sun 1400–1830.*

Faïenceries du Bourg-Joly *16 r. Carnot; tel: 02 43 94 80 10. Open Mon–Sat 1000–1200 and 1400–1830, Easter–Sept Sun 1400–1830.*

Château de Malicorne €€ *tel: 02 43 94 84 65. Open daily Jul–Aug except Mon & Tue 1500–1800.*

A quintessentially French town with its languid river, pleasure boats and elegant 18th-century brick and stone architecture, Malicorne is, however, better known for its unusual faience. Potters have been working here since 1747, and much of the work that they produce is still decorated by hand. Its trademark style is created by cutting away shapes in each piece, and by enlivening its white base with details in colour. Bowing to the changes in taste, the major producers in Malicorne now also create faience that follows contemporary trends. The **Musée de la Faïencerie d'Art de Malicorne** traces the development of the craft, while the two major **factory outlets** welcome visitors. The old mills used for grinding material for the ceramic industry, the town's renovated 17th-century **château** and its delightful 11th-century **Eglise St-Sylvestre** are all in the western part, as you come in from Sablé or Parcé.

Right
Malicorne faience

L'Espace Faïence €
tel: 02 43 48 07 17.
Open daily 1000–1900.

Market Fri am.

Food in Malicorne-sur-Sarthe

Restaurant La Petite Auberge € *pl. du Guesclin; tel: 02 43 94 80 52. Open daily except Mon.* A pretty, traditional inn, next to the river, offering local dishes with a creative flair.

Musée des 24h Circuit de la Sarthe

Musée des 24h Circuit de la Sarthe €€ 9 pl. Luigi Chinetti Circuit des 24 Heures, Le Mans; tel: 02 43 72 72 24; www.lemusee24h. com. Open Apr–Sept daily 1000–1800; Oct–Mar Wed–Sun 1100–1700.

This museum will seduce even those not interested in racing or cars. It is laid out beautifully in a modern hangar-like building near the famous circuit and is divided into two sections. The first starts with the origins of the vehicle, and includes steam-run examples dating from 1769, vehicles pioneered by Nicolas Joseph Cugnot and James Watt. Then there are the first 'bikes' dating from 1861, each with a big front wheel and small back one. From the turn of the 20th century and its early years there are some beautiful cars: a Peugeot dating from

Right
A Lagonda M45 in the Musée des 24h Circuit de la Sarthe

1906–10, a 1930s Mercedes, a Rosengart cabriolet, even a Bugatti, and in the midst of these antiquities there is an 'exploded' 1990s Renault that shows how all the component parts of a modern car fit together. The second part of the museum is dedicated to cars – and motorbikes – that have taken part in the 24-hour endurance race. Between these two sections a walled area has dozens of video screens that play back footage of historic moments in racing.

SABLÉ-SUR-SARTHE

ℹ️ Sablé-sur-Sarthe Tourist Office pl. Raphaël Elizé; tel: 02 43 95 00 60; fax: 02 43 92 60 77; www.sable-sur-sarthe.com. Open Mon–Sat 0930–1230 and 1400–1800.

🅿️ The best places to leave a car are either in front of the château or in the pl. de la République.

🍞 Markets Mon am and Fri am.

🚤 Cruising the Sarthe For short trips contact **Croisière Sabolienne**, tel: 02 43 95 93 13; fax: 02 43 95 99 14; www.sablesien.com; for residential houseboats contact **Anjou Navigation**, Sablé-sur-Sarthe; tel: 02 43 95 14 42; fax: 02 43 92 26 06.

⛪ Eglise de Notre-Dame € Open only during religious services.

Situated at the confluence of three rivers, Sablé evolved as a port for transporting sand (*sable* in French) on the Sarthe and as a bridging point across this large river. Today, transport is in the form of pleasure boats that ply the river and its basins, while its economy has shifted from sand and anthracite to agriculture and tourism. Its charm lies in its little island, formed by the rivers and the unexpected backwaters that encircle its oldest part. The town is dominated by the 18th-century **Château des Colberts**, named after Colbert de Torcy, Marquis de Sablé and nephew of the better-known Jean-Baptiste Colbert (minister to Louis XIV), who commissioned its construction in 1711. Colbert erected this handsome building on the site of a much earlier fortified castle. Unfortunately, it is closed to the public as it now houses the Bibliothèque de France's centre for book restoration. The town's rather unattractive neo-Gothic church, the **Eglise de Notre-Dame**, was built at the end of the 19th century on the site of its previous church. The building doesn't entice visitors, which is a pity since it houses some magnificent stained-glass windows (including the huge *Crucifixion* commissioned by the Dukes of Nemours in 1494), which, declared a Historic Monument in 1894, were reinstalled in the modern church and have been subsequently painstakingly restored. Sablé still boasts homes constructed between the 15th and 18th centuries, some to be found along the Grande Rue, while the pl. Raphaël Elizé (where the tourist office is, and where the weekly market is held) is an elegant example of 19th-century architecture.

Accommodation and food in Sablé-sur-Sarthe

Villa Roma € *1 r. de l'Île; tel: 02 43 92 43 93. Open daily except Mon.* This is a popular pizzeria but its biggest draw is its position right by the Sarthe, where it has a pleasant terrace overlooking the river.

Le Saint-Martin €–€€ *3 r. Haute St-Martin; tel: 02 43 95 00 03; http://lesaintmartin-restaurant-traiteur.fr. Closed Mon.* A first-class traditional-style *traiteur*, on the south side of the centre, with a better-known gastronomic restaurant.

ST-CALAIS

ⓘ St-Calais Tourist Office pl. de l'Hôtel de Ville; tel: 02 43 35 82 95; fax: 02 43 35 15 13; www.payscalaisien.com. Open Tue–Fri 1030–1230 and 1430–1730 (1800 Mar–Sept), Sat 1030–1230 (and 1400–1700 Mar–Sept).

ⓝ Eglise Notre-Dame € pl. de l'Eglise; tel: 02 43 35 82 95. Open daily 0900–1800.

ⓞ Market Sun am.

Karileph, the saint who indirectly gave his name to this town, was a monk from the Auvergne who founded a simple abbey here in the 6th century. The large 15th-century **Eglise Notre-Dame** is dedicated to this pious fellow. With its ornate Italianate façade one would expect a decorative interior: this is not the case. Massive Gothic columns support a high ceiling, leaving the huge nave bare. Karileph's 7th-century shroud, a very rare piece of religious reliquary, is kept in the *Mairie*. Ask to see it or look out for a postcard of this unusual cloth. Among the town's most attractive aspects are its shady *quais* running along the banks of the River Anille. Built to protect the town from flooding, they are beautifully maintained and a favourite rendezvous with locals. The old *lavoir*, or wash house, is a particularly fine example of its type and worth a visit. The renovated *Halle*, with its fancy decorative brickwork, is once more the site of the Sunday market and is also used as a public meeting hall.

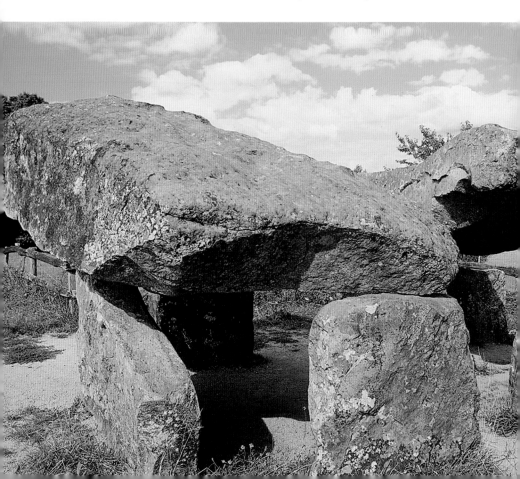

STE-SUZANNE

ⓘ Office du Tourisme des Coevrons 1 r. Jean de Bueil; tel: 02 43 01 43 60; fax: 02 43 01 21 12; www.sainte-suzanne.com. Open Sept–Jun Mon–Sat 0900–1230 and 1400–1800; Jul–Aug daily 1000–1230 and 1400–1900. Closed Sun am.

ⓜ Musée de l'Auditoire € 7 Grande Rue; tel/fax: 02 43 01 42 65. Open summer daily 1400–1800.

Château de Ste-Suzanne € Open daily Jul–Aug 1000–1900, May, Jun & Sept 0900–1800, Oct–Apr daily except Mon 0930–1230 and 1330–1800.

Dolmen des Erves € Open at all times.

Topped by towers and turrets, Ste-Suzanne is still encircled by its fortified walls, forming a perfect, shield-shaped little medieval town of crooked stone buildings and narrow streets perching above the River Erve. This is definitely a place to park and stroll, to soak up its historic atmosphere. William the Conqueror camped outside the town, and it was a strategic point in the Hundred Years War. Medieval life is on show in the small **Musée de l'Auditoire**, where, through documents, exhibits and life-sized maquettes, the daily life of Ste-Suzanne's predecessors takes form. Tangible evidence of the town's past includes the remains of the 11th-century rectangular dungeon and the handsome but smallish 17th-century **château**. However, Ste-Suzanne's history dates back even further, as the Neolithic **Dolmen des Erves** attests. This monument was erected some 6,500 years ago and the site, just 2km north of town, may be visited. There is no information concerning the dolmen actually on-site so it's best to pick up a leaflet from the tourist office before heading out there.

Accommodation and food in Ste-Suzanne

Hôtel Restaurant Beauséjour €–€€ 4 r. de la Libération; tel: 02 43 01 40 31; fax: 02 43 01 46 21; www.hotelstesuzanne.com. Open daily in summer, closed Sun in winter. A small hotel with a popular restaurant. The menu features traditional cuisine with some interesting additions.

SOLESMES

ⓔ Eglise de l'Abbaye de Solesmes € For information, tel: 02 43 95 03 08. Open 0915–1815; services in Gregorian chant at 1000, 1300, 1350, 1700 & 2030.

With its honey-coloured stone buildings and profusion of flowers, Solesmes could just as easily be in England's Cotswolds. The village is beautifully maintained and breathes a gaiety that the austere 19th-century Abbaye St-Pierre de Solesmes – reminiscent of Le Mont-St-Michel – lacks. The abbey (still occupied by the Benedictines) dates from the 11th century and is closed to the public, but its 11th- to 16th-century **church** is open, and attending a service sung in Gregorian chant is a memorable occasion. A shop near the entrance to the abbey sells recordings made by the brothers, as well as books about this ancient and beautiful form of worship. Of particular note in the church are its Renaissance sculptured 'Saints of Solesmes' and the extraordinary rendition of *Christ's Entombment*, a three-dimensional work composed of many different figures and sculpted architectural elements, dating from 1496.

Opposite
Dolmen des Erves, Ste-Suzanne

Accommodation and food in Solesmes

Grand Hôtel de Solesmes €€–€€€ *16 pl. Dom Guéranger; tel: 02 43 95 45 10; fax: 02 43 95 22 26; www.grandhotelsolesmes.com. Open year-round.* This attractive period mansion has been renovated to form a mid-sized hotel with a notable gastronomic restaurant.

Suggested tour

ⓘ Comité Départemental du Tourisme *40 r. Joinville, Le Mans; tel: 02 43 40 22 50; fax: 02 43 40 22 51; www.tourisme-en-sarthe.com. Open Mon–Fri 0900–1230 and 1400–1730.*

Total distance: 240km.

Time: 2 days.

Links: The N138 south of Ecommoy links with Château-du-Loir on the Loir: Vendôme–La Flèche tour (*see page 146*).

Route: Leave **Le Mans** (*see page 162*) on the N157 (and continue for 3km past the university), then branch off right for some 33km on the D28 via Bernay and Torcé-Viviers-en-Charnie. Here you turn left and drive through the village, leaving on the D9 to **STE-SUZANNE ❶**. The best view of this small town is from behind the château or, as you leave, just off the D7. The road goes due south through the forest of Grande Charnie, crosses the motorway and leads into Epineux-le-Séguin. Here we cut across to the Vègre Valley by turning left on to the D560 and arrive at Polle-sur-Vègre. This stretch of the D190 is very pretty, and meanders down to medieval **ASNIERES-SUR-VEGRE ❷**. The D22 leads towards the larger town of **SOLESMES ❸**.

Following the banks of the River Sarthe, and passing by Juigné-sur-Sarthe (there's a great view back up to the village as you cross the iron bridge), the D138 leaves the countryside behind for the busy town of **SABLE-SUR-SARTHE ❹**.

Getting out of the car: The gardens of the château at Juigné are delightful, with panoramic views.

Cross the main D306 highway and head for the car park at the edge of the old town. The Sarthe's course is sinuous, but the straight D309 heads to the stone town of **Parcé-sur-Sarthe**. Pick up the D8, which hugs the river for a while and heads southeast to the attractive town of **MALICORNE-SUR-SARTHE ❺**. The same D8 continues towards the deciduous Forest of Courcelles.

It is another cross-country run from here via the quaint village of **La Fontaine-St-Martin**. Stop and look at the few old buildings that cluster around the privately owned château. Of interest is the house belonging to Louis Simon, a self-taught peasant, who learnt to read and write, played six instruments and found employment as sacristan, aubergist and tax collector. Here, you change to the D32 to **Ecommoy**, and turn south on the D338. Just 8km later, at **St-Hubert**,

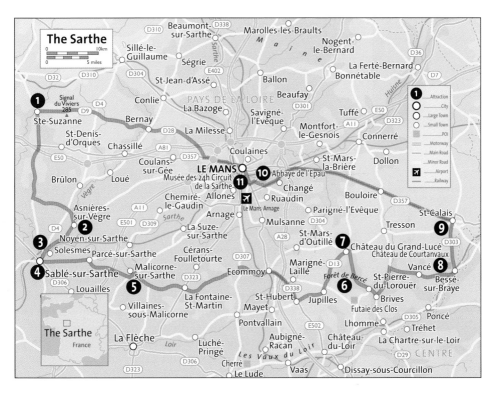

the D13 crosses this road and you turn left to enter the **FORET DE BERCE** ❻. This large area is criss-crossed with roads and tracks but you remain on the D13, a pretty road through the thick forest that passes through Pruillé-l'Eguillé and goes on to **Le Grand-Lucé**. Fork right as you enter the town and the **CHATEAU DU GRAND-LUCE** ❼ is on your right. Leave by the D304 towards La Chartre-sur-le-Loir and head along the increasingly attractive road to **Brives**. You take the left turn on to the D64, which joins the D63 in Courdenmache and heads north through pockets of wooded area to St-George-de-la-Couée. Turn in the direction of **Vancé** on the D176 and the D34, which leads towards the woodmilling town of **Bessé-sur-Braye**. It's just a further 1km north on the D303 to the **CHATEAU DE COURTANVAUX** ❽.

Picking up the D303 again, it's a 15-minute drive to **ST-CALAIS** ❾ on the River Anille. The main Le Mans road skirts St-Calais and heads northwest, arriving at the city just by the **ABBAYE DE L'EPAU** ❿. Although the abbey is in the midst of the suburbs, it is well signposted. Before returning to the centre of Le Mans, take the fast N23 ring road, following the signs to the **Circuit Automobile** and then signs to the **MUSEE DES 24H CIRCUIT DE LA SARTHE** ⓫. The road back into the heart of Le Mans is well indicated.

Chartres

Ratings

Architecture ● ● ● ● ●

History ● ● ● ● ●

Medieval art ● ● ● ● ●

Views ● ● ● ● ○

Museums ● ● ● ○ ○

Restaurants ● ● ● ○ ○

Children ● ● ○ ○ ○

Shopping ● ● ○ ○ ○

The name Chartres at once brings to mind not a town but a building: the beautiful early Gothic stonework and famous stained glass of one of Europe's best-known churches. For over 700 years crowds of pilgrims have been admiring it, marvelling at it and praying in it. For the modern visitor, there is the added rarity of seeing a medieval cathedral that has hardly been changed since the day it was completed. Yet Chartres is not just a cathedral. It is also a busy working town, one of the oldest in northern France, with a rich religious history going back to Druidic times, and a medieval quarter at its centre, picturesque with lanes and waterside cottages and stone bridges across the River Eure. As well as the cathedral, there are many other impressive historic churches. Once reached by the pious only after long journeys on foot, Chartres is now an easy and popular day trip from Paris, and an ideal stopover between the Channel and the Loire.

Getting there and getting around

ⓘ Chartres Tourist Office *pl. de la Cathédrale; tel: 02 37 18 26 26; fax: 02 37 21 51 91; www.chartres-tourisme.com. Open daily Apr–Sept Mon–Sat 0900–1900, Sun 0930–1730; Oct–Mar Mon–Sat 1000–1800, Sun 1000–1300 and 1430–1630.*

By road
Chartres is an easy 100km drive from Paris on *autoroute* A11. From the Channel ports, the best way to reach the town is via Rouen, on expressway N154. A busy ring road bypasses Chartres completely, while another inner ring road, made up of separate boulevards, avoids the old centre. Take any turn to the *Centre Ville*.

By air
Paris-Orly international airport is under an hour's drive away.

By rail
Trains leave from Paris approximately every 2hr during the day; the journey takes around 1hr. There are rail links to Le Mans, Nancy, Tours and other major towns in the region.

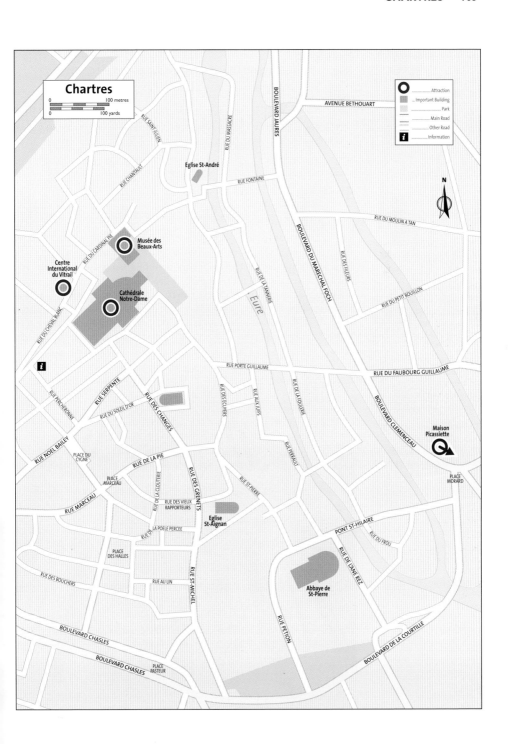

Chartres

0   100 metres
0   100 yards

○ .... Attraction
▨ ... Important Building
▨ .... Park
━━ .... Main Road
.... Other Road
𝒊 .... Information

N

AVENUE BETHOUART
BOULEVARD JAURES
RUE SAINT-JULIEN
RUE DU MASSACRE
Eglise St-André
RUE FONTAINE
RUE CHANTAULT
RUE DU MOULIN A TAN
BOULEVARD DU MARECHAL FOCH
RUE DES FILEURS
RUE DU PETIT BOUILLON
RUE DU CARDINAL PIE
Musée des Beaux-Arts
Centre International du Vitrail
RUE DE LA TANNERIE
Eure
Cathédrale Notre-Dame
RUE DU CHEVAL BLANC
RUE PORTE GUILLAUME
RUE DU FAUBOURG GUILLAUME
RUE FERCHERONNE
RUE SERPENTE
RUE DES ÉCUYERS
RUE AUX JUIFS
RUE DE LA FOULERIE
BOULEVARD CLEMENCEAU
RUE DU SOLEIL D'OR
RUE DES CHANGES
RUE PERRAULT
Maison Picassiette
RUE NOEL BAILEY
PLACE DU CYGNE
RUE DE LA PIE
RUE ST-PIERRE
PLACE MORARD
PLACE MARCEAU
RUE DE LA CLOUTERIE
RUE DES GRENETS
RUE MARCEAU
RUE DES VIEUX RAPPORTEURS
Eglise St-Aignan
PONT ST-HILAIRE
RUE DU FROU
LA POELE PERCEE
RUE DE L'ANE REZ
PLACE DES HALLES
Abbaye de St-Pierre
RUE DES BOUCHERS
RUE AU LIN
RUE ST-MICHEL
RUE PETION
BOULEVARD DE LA COURTILLE
BOULEVARD CHASLES
BOULEVARD CHASLES
PLACE PASTEUR

W *www.ville-chartres.fr*
(official site of the
town of Chartres, mainly
for residents);
www.chartres-tourisme.com
(site of the town's tourist
office); *www.chartres.com*
(independent site
promoting Chartres, in
English and French);
www.diocesechartres.com
(official site of the
Chartres diocese and
cathedral, French only).

Markets *Sat am in
r. des Changes.* Flower
market *Tue, Thur & Sat in r.
du Cygne.*

Festivals There are
important concerts
and other musical events
throughout the year,
including Musical Saturdays
and Lyric Days. *Festival de
Jazz* – *Mar; Harpsichord
Festival – May; Le Festival
International d'Orgue*
(International Organ
Festival) *– Jul–Aug.*

Théâtre Municipal *blvd
Chasles; tel: 02 37 23
42 79.* Puts on frequent
performances ranging from
children's shows to
modern dance.

Parking
There is car parking off the inner ring-road boulevards.

Guided tours
Tours of the Old Town are available through the tourist office, either
with a guide or with a 1hr audio-cassette. It is also enjoyable to get an
overview of the town from a horse-drawn carriage or on the little
train.

Sights

Cathédrale Notre-Dame
One of the great buildings of the world, this UNESCO World Heritage
Site does not disappoint when you arrive. Vast and beautiful, it is
heralded from afar by two curiously dissimilar spires, one simple and
elegant, the other higher, fussier, more elaborately Gothic, soaring
high above the rooftops of the town. Constructed at speed – it was
completed in 25 years – and incorporating the west front and the
crypt of its late Romanesque predecessor, which had been destroyed
by fire in 1194, the new building employed revolutionary new Gothic
ideas to create a masterpiece of grace and craftsmanship. By good

Cathédrale Notre-Dame € *tel: 02 37 21 75 02; fax: 02 37 36 51 43; tour office tel: 02 37 28 15 58; email: visitecathedrale@ diocesechartres.com. Open generally 0830–1845 (hours sometimes vary). http://whc.unesco.org/en/list/ 81 (UNESCO webpage on Chartres Cathedral).*

fortune, it escaped serious damage during the Wars of Religion, the Revolution and the two World Wars.

On the west front, the Romanesque triple doorway of the Royal Portal includes a multitude of small figures and statuary. The impressive tympanum above the central doorway shows *Christ in Majesty*. The south tower is the Romanesque survivor, while the taller north tower in Flamboyant Gothic style was added in the early 16th century. The sharp contrast between the two is intriguing and pleasing. Around to the right of the building, the beautiful South Porch is also richly carved.

The most striking features on entering the building are its massive dimensions (it has the widest nave of any church in France), and the phenomenal quantity and quality of richly coloured stained glass. The three rose windows, especially, are remarkable. The effect is, of course, at its most vivid on a sunny day. In all, there are more than 150 windows, their total surface area adding up to an astonishing 2,600sq m. The colour and workmanship of the glasswork, depicting biblical stories, are exceptional. The finest of the windows are the west rose window, the *Tree of Jesse* window, also on the west side, and the *Blue Virgin* window in the apse close to the south door.

During the Middle Ages the building was often filled with people sleeping inside it, many of them sick and hoping for a miracle cure. The labyrinth laid into the nave floor (these used to be a common feature of churches) was followed by pilgrims on their knees, and symbolises the Way of the Cross; it usually took about an hour to complete. In the absidal chapel is displayed the Veil of the Virgin, which pilgrims worshipped as a sacred relic.

Visiting the cathedral

Explanatory signs (in English) are displayed around the cathedral. Tours in English, starting from the gift shop, are offered *twice daily at 1200 and 1445* by the noted authority on the cathedral, Malcolm Miller. If there are fewer than 12 participants, a tour may be cancelled.

Tours of the crypts: *Apr–Oct 1100 (except Sun and hols), 1415, 1530, 1630 & 1715 (in high season), Nov–Mar 1100 (except Sun and hols) & 1615.*

Centre International du Vitrail € *5 r. du Cardinal Pie; tel: 02 37 21 65 72; fax: 02 37 36 15 34; www.centre-vitrail.org. Open daily 0930–1230 and 1330–1800.*

Centre International du Vitrail

Close to the cathedral is the remarkable International Stained Glass Centre. It is housed in the beautifully restored 13th-century vaulted crypt of the Greniers de Loëns, originally the grain warehouse of the cathedral chapter. Dedicated to research and education, the centre has a vital role in the preservation and development of stained glasswork. Demonstrations by skilled artists, hands-on workshops and classes, a museum and a documentation centre reveal the secrets of designing and making stained glass both in the Middle Ages and today.

Above
Clock, Cathédrale
Notre-Dame

Maison Picassiette
€ Off r. St-Barthélémy;
tel: 02 37 34 10 78. Open
from about Easter to end
Sept 1000–1200 and
1400–1800. Closed Tue
(and sometimes Mon).

Maison Picassiette

Raymond Isidore (1900–64) was one of those eccentrics whose obsession eventually comes to be admired. Every day, after work, this local tram conductor would set to work using fragments of broken glass, glazed pottery, pieces of smashed plates and other scraps to make sculptures, mosaics and murals all over his house and garden, even covering furniture. Guided tours of his home show the mosaic of Jerusalem, a replica of the cathedral and numerous other unique works.

Musée des Beaux-Arts € 29 cloître
Notre-Dame; tel: 02 37 90
45 80; fax: 02 37 90 45 90;
email: musee.beaux-
arts@ville-chartres.fr. Open
Wed–Mon 1000–1200 and
1400–1700 (or 1800).
Closed Tue, Sun am &
national hols.

Musée des Beaux-Arts

The Fine Arts Museum, located inside the former Bishops' Palace adjacent to the cathedral, displays small but important collections of paintings and other artwork from the 15th to the 20th century. Highlights include a fine group of tapestries, some interesting portraits, and 12 large enamels depicting the Apostles, made in 1547 by Léonard Limousin. More modern work includes a collection of paintings by Vlaminck, and frequent interesting temporary exhibitions.

Accommodation and food in Chartres

Mid-priced chain hotels can be found near the railway station and on the boulevards around the town centre.

Hôtel Ibis Chartres Centre € *14 pl. Drouaise; tel: 02 37 36 06 36.* Chartres has few hotels of character but several chain hotels. Many are close to highways about 4km from the city centre, but the functional, inexpensive Ibis Centre is well placed by the river, close to the city centre and cathedral.

St-Hilaire €€ *11 r. Pont St-Hilaire; tel: 02 37 30 97 57.* A small, charming and friendly place beside Pont St-Hilaire over the Eure, the restaurant strongly features the best of all that is local to Chartres and its region.

Grand Hôtel Monarque €€€ *22 pl. des Epars; tel: 02 37 18 15 15; fax: 02 37 36 34 18; www.bw-grand-monarque.com.* This landmark establishment stands on the edge of the old town centre. A fine 18th-century façade covers an older, well-preserved mansion that offers spacious, attractively decorated rooms. The restaurant is one of the best in town, with a noted wine cellar.

Suggested walk

Total distance: About 2km, or 4km with the detour.

Time: 2 hours.

Route: Start from the west side of the **CATHEDRALE NOTRE-DAME** ❶ and walk over to parallel r. du Cardinal Pie for the **CENTRE INTERNATIONAL DU VITRAIL** ❷. Continue along this street for the **MUSEE DES BEAUX-ARTS** ❸, behind the cathedral. Follow Tertre St-Nicolas down towards the river. The Romanesque church of **St-André**, on the left, was once the place of worship for a densely populated working-class district alongside the riverbank. Now deconsecrated, it is used for concerts and exhibitions. Reaching the River Eure, cross on the footbridge to **r. de la Tannerie**, following this upstream past restored old houses and picturesque wash houses, and views of the cathedral. Walk as far as **Pont St-Hilaire**.

Detour: At Pont St-Hilaire, turn away from the river on **r. de la Porte Morard**, and cross the next arm of the Eure to reach pl. Morard. Leave the square on the street on the left to **r. St-Barthélémy. MAISON PICASSIETTE** ❹ is signposted (*end of detour*).

On Pont St-Hilaire, with its attractive view downstream, cross back over to the left bank to reach the church of the former 6th-century Benedictine **Abbaye de St-Pierre** (originally St-Père-en-Vallée), which

Right
Gate and façade,
Musée des Beaux-Arts

has beautiful 13th-century early Gothic stained-glass windows. The building itself was constructed mainly in the 12th and 13th centuries, but includes remnants of much older structures. The porch-belfry is pre-Romanesque, and may date as far back as the 10th century.

Wander on **r. St-Pierre** and **r. des Ecuyers** through the old quarter, perhaps turning off right along **r. Perrault** and **r. aux Juifs** for part of the way. Several beautiful old houses line the steep narrow streets and lanes; some date back to the 14th, or even the 13th, century. Go along r. de la Porte Cendreuse to the point where it meets **r. des Changes**, where there are many lovely old houses. Turn left along r. des Grenets to see **St-Aignan** church, which has good stained glass and is attached to the town's original 9th-century ramparts. Returning to the crossroads, **r. de la Pie** leads into central pl. Marceau and pl. du Cygne. **R. du Soleil d'Or** leads back down into r. des Changes, where you turn left to return to the cathedral.

Right
Vieux Chartres

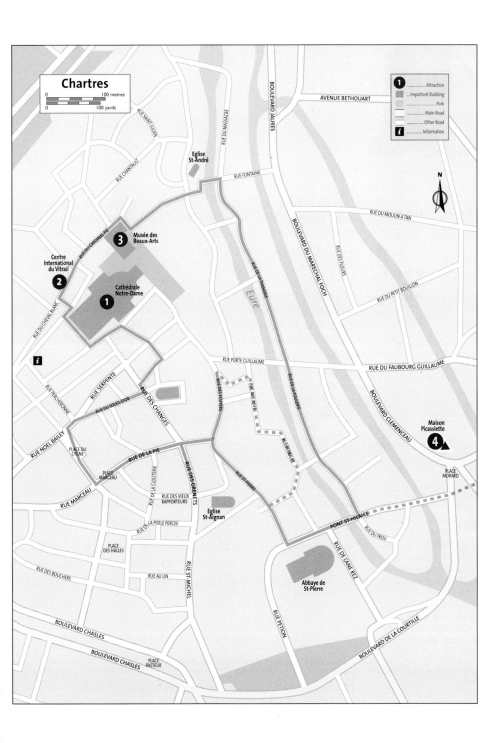

Chartres

0 ___ 100 metres
0 ___ 100 yards

❶ .... Attraction
░ .... Important Building
░ .... Park
___ .... Main Road
___ .... Other Road
𝑖 .... Information

BOULEVARD JAURES

AVENUE BETHOUART

RUE SAINT-JULIEN

RUE DU MASSACRE

RUE CHANTAULT

Eglise
St-André

RUE FONTAINE

RUE DU MOULIN A TAN

N

RUE DU CARDINAL PIE

❸ Musée des
Beaux-Arts

BOULEVARD DU MARECHAL FOCH

RUE DES FLEURS

Centre
International
du Vitrail

❷

Cathédrale
Notre-Dame

❶

RUE DE LA TANNERIE

Eure

RUE DU PETIT BOUILLON

RUE DU CHEVAL BLANC

𝑖

RUE PORTE GUILLAUME

RUE DU FAUBOURG GUILLAUME

RUE PERCHERONNE

RUE SERPENTE

RUE DU SOLEIL D'OR

RUE DES CHANGES

RUE DES ECUYERS

RUE AUX RUFFE

RUE DE LA FOULERIE

RUE DE L'EAU

BOULEVARD CLEMENCEAU

Maison
Picassiette
❹ ▲

RUE NOEL BAILLY

PLACE DU
CYGNE

RUE DE LA PIE

RUE DE LA CLOUTERIE

RUE DES GRENETS

RUE ST-PIERRE

PLACE
MIDRARD

PLACE
MARCEAU

RUE DES VIEUX
RAPPORTEURS

RUE MARCEAU

RUE DE LA POELE PERCEE

Eglise
St-Aignan

PONT ST-HILAIRE

RUE DU FROU

PLACE
DES HALLES

RUE DE L'ANE REZ

RUE DES BOUCHERS

RUE AU LIN

RUE ST-MICHEL

Abbaye de
St-Pierre

BOULEVARD CHASLES

RUE PETION

BOULEVARD DE LA COURTILLE

BOULEVARD CHASLES

PLACE
PASTEUR

Eure-et-Loir

Ratings

Windmills	●●●●●
History	●●●●○
Medieval architecture	●●●●○
Activities	●●●○○
Dungeons	●●●○○
Museums	●●●○○
Châteaux	●●●○○
Scenery	●●○○○

The relatively flat land surrounding the major city of Chartres falls into the *département* of Eure-et-Loir, which, in turn, takes its name from the two major rivers that flow through it. In the eastern part, it is a land of wide-open spaces ideal for the cultivation of cereals, and the western part is a landscape of undulating hills and a patchwork of forests that forms the region of the Perche. By the Middle Ages the local gentry were growing in power and authority, with the result that they expanded and fortified their substantial residences, and constructed impregnable dungeons to protect themselves in times of siege. The region's proximity to Paris meant also that royalty were often present in its châteaux. But if castles and towers are one feature of the landscape, the other rather more quaint feature is the scores of windmills that break the often-flat horizon of the Beauce's cereal lands.

BONNEVAL

ⓘ Bonneval Tourist Office *2 square Westerham; tel: 02 37 47 55 89; email: contact@ bonnevaltourisme.com; www.bonnevaltourisme.com. Open Apr–Sept 0900–1200 and 1400–1830; Oct–Mar 0930–1200 and 1400–1800. Closed Sun–Mon, except Jul–Aug, open Sun 1000–1200.*

◓ Market *Mon all day.*

Just 14km north of its better-known neighbour, Châteaudun, Bonneval is a small, fortified town beside the Loir. It grew up in the 14th century around the Benedictine Abbaye de St-Florentin, the remains of which are now occupied by a psychiatric hospital behind a grandiose entrance gate. It's an engaging little town of old stone buildings, towers and gates, and many man-made channels that run into the Loir. The Gothic Eglise Notre-Dame in the centre of Bonneval dates from the 13th century and has an attractive rose window.

Accommodation and food in Bonneval

Hostellerie du Bois Guibert €€ *Hameau de Guibert; tel: 02 37 47 22 33; fax: 02 37 47 50 69; www.bois-guibert.com.* A relatively inexpensive

hotel (for its comfort and style), located in a 17th- to 18th-century manor house. Its highly rated gastronomic restaurant has an innovative and excellent menu.

CHÂTEAUDUN

ℹ Châteaudun Tourist Office *1 r. de Luynes; tel: 02 37 45 22 46; fax: 02 37 66 00 16; www.ville-chateaudun.com. Open mid-Jun–mid-Sept Mon–Sat 0900–1230 and 1400–1830, Sun 1000–1200; rest of year Mon–Sat 0900–1230 and 1400–1830; closed national hols.*

⛪ Château de Châteaudun €€ *tel: 02 37 94 02 90. Open May–Aug 1000–1300 and 1400–1800; Sept–Apr 1000–1230 and 1400–1730. Closed major national hols.*

Musée des Beaux-Arts et d'Histoire Naturelle *€ 3 r. Toufaire; tel: 02 37 45 55 36. Open Oct–Mar 0930–1200 and 1330–1700; Apr–Jun & Sept 0930–1200 and 1330–1800; Jul–Aug 0930–1830. Closed Tue out of high season and 1 Jan, 1 May & 25 Dec.*

Grottes du Foulon €€ *r. des Fouleries; tel: 02 37 45 19 60; fax: 02 37 45 80 02. Open Jun–Sept 1000–1200 and 1400–1800, Apr–May 1400–1800, winter Sat, Sun & national hols 1400–1800. Closed Mon.*

🛒 Market *Thur all day.*

The small town of Châteaudun, situated on a rocky outcrop overlooking the valley of the Loir, grew from the foundations of a 6th-century fortification that was largely rebuilt into a **château** during the 12th century. Despite its proximity to Chartres, it remains a provincial town with relatively few tourists. The heart of the *Vieille Ville* is the castle (once the property of Joan of Arc's companion, Jean de Dunois), a building erected in medieval and Gothic style with Renaissance additions. Its most important features include the 30m-high circular dungeon, used as a bolt hole during times of war or siege, which was originally accessible only from the second floor. Its pepperpot tower is a much later addition. Next to it, the Sainte Chapelle shelters some fine 16th-century sculpture, while the exquisite French and Flemish tapestries in the château are breathtaking. The gardens, too, are interesting for they are the re-creation of a medieval garden, complete with medicinal herbs.

Beyond the castle walls lies the largely pedestrian-only *Vieux Quartier*, the oldest part of Châteaudun that was spared the catastrophic fire of 1723. An area of cobblestone streets, ancient buildings and quiet courtyards, it merits leisurely exploration. Within this area the huge Hôtel-Dieu, founded in 1062 but remodelled in the 18th and 19th centuries, and the Church of the Madeleine, once part of the abbey of the same name, are impressive sights. Near the pl. du 18 Octobre, the geographic centre of Châteaudun, lies the **Musée des Beaux-Arts et d'Histoire Naturelle** with an eclectic display of over 2,500 stuffed birds, plus archaeological items from Egypt and local sources.

Also beyond the ancient city walls, and accessible from the Loir Valley below, is a series of grottoes, the limestone **Grottes du Foulon**, which, after a guided tour, are enlivened with a *son-et-lumière* performance.

Accommodation and food in Châteaudun

Aux Trois Pastoureaux €–€€ *31 r. André Gillet (corner r. du Coq); tel: 02 37 45 74 40; fax: 02 37 66 00 32; www.aux-trois-pastoureaux.com.* You'll receive a warm welcome in this restaurant located just a few minutes' walk from the centre. Gastronomic and creative cuisine, all prepared in-house, using local ingredients.

Hôtel Saint-Michel €€ *28 pl. du 18 Octobre; tel: 02 37 45 15 70; fax: 02 37 45 83 39; www.hotelstmichel.net.* An unusual and inexpensive small

18th-century hotel in the centre of town, within easy walking distance of all the principal sights.

Le Saint-Louis €€ *41 r. de la République; tel: 02 37 45 00 01; fax: 02 37 45 16 09.* A combination of comfortable hotel, brasserie, restaurant, pizzeria and piano bar, with the bonus of a delightful terrace for summer dining. The brasserie in particular is a favourite with locals.

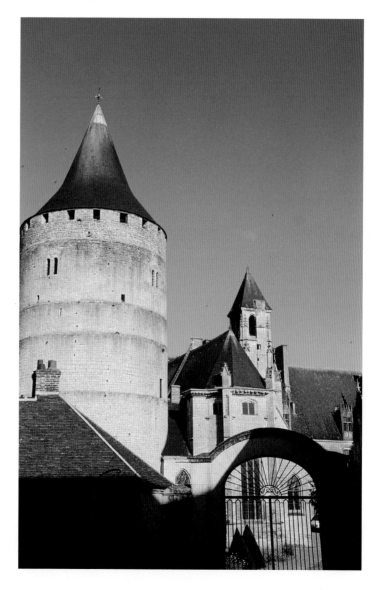

Right
Château de Châteaudun

GALLARDON

ℹ **Gallardon Tourist Office** *Impasse de la Tour; tel: 02 37 31 11 11; fax: 02 37 90 90 06. Open Apr–Oct Sat & Sun 1500–1800.*

 Market *Tue am.*

The slim remains of what was once a circular 12th-century dungeon bring history buffs to Gallardon. This was part of Gallardon's former castle, which was razed in 1421 by the Dauphin, Charles VII. In the main square there is also a well-preserved, carved, timber-frame house, known simply as the Maison de Bois. It dates from the 16th century and boasts 88 carved wooden columns and old, diamond-shaped, glass windowpanes. The church, dedicated to Saints Peter and Paul, was first consecrated in the 11th century and enlarged to its present form in the 16th century. It has a carved wooden vault and old stained-glass windows.

Food in Gallardon

Restaurant Le Commerce € *12 pl. de l'Eglise; tel: 02 37 31 00 07. Closed Sun, Tue pm and Wed.* Next to the church, with inexpensive traditional menus. Inside and outside seating.

ILLIERS-COMBRAY

ℹ **Illiers-Combray Tourist Office** *5 r. Henri Germond; tel: 02 37 24 24 00; fax: 02 37 24 21 79. Open daily except Mon Apr–Oct 1030–1200 and 1430–1730, rest of year except Fri & Sat 1000–1230 and 1430–1700. Guided visits on request.*

🏛 **Musée Marcel Proust** €–€€ *4 r. du Docteur Proust; tel: 02 37 24 30 97. Open mid-Jan–mid-Dec, guided tours 1430 & 1600, except mid-Jun–mid-Sept, guided tours 1430, 1530 & 1630. Closed Mon except national hols and 1 & 11 Nov.*

Jardin du Pré Catelan € *route de Tansonville; tel: 02 37 24 24 00; fax: 02 37 24 21 79. Open 0900–1730 (2000 in summer).*

For Marcel Proust *cognoscenti*, a trip to Illiers-Combray is *de rigueur*. For the rest of us, it is perhaps less of a highlight. It was here in the medieval town of Illiers (on the pilgrimage route to Santiago de Compostela) that the celebrated author spent childhood holidays and drew inspiration for his great work, *A la Recherche du Temps Perdu*, 'In Search of Lost Time'. The **Musée Marcel Proust**, located in the home where the author stayed with his aunt (Maison de Tante Léonie), displays documents, photos and family memorabilia. The **Jardin du Pré Catelan**, created by Proust's Uncle Jules in 1850, offers a pleasant detour on the banks of the River Loir. With Proust having immortalised the town of Illiers under the imaginary name of Combray, a decision was taken on the centenary of Proust's birth in 1971 to rename the town Illiers-Combray.

Food in Illiers-Combray

Le Saint-Hilaire € *10 rue Saint-Hilaire; tel: 02 37 24 16 80.* Among the handful of modest eating places in the little town is this pleasant and satisfyingly inexpensive establishment serving simple, familiar and well-prepared dishes, ranging from salads, crêpes and pizzas to fish terrine and *magret de canard*.

Marcel Proust

Considered by many to be France's greatest author, Marcel Proust (1871–1922) was born in Paris but spent some of his school holidays with his paternal aunt, Elizabeth (Léonie), and her husband, Jules Amiot. However, suffering from hayfever and severe asthma, the young writer had to forsake his visits as he grew up. After Léonie's death in the autumn of 1886, he saw their house for the last time. His visit brought back his impressions of Illiers, its homes and inhabitants, and of childhood walks along the Thironne in neighbouring Méréglise. These images marked Proust and were to provide the inspiration for *Du Côté de chez Swann*.

MAINTENON

ⓘ Maintenon Tourist Office *pl. Aristide Briand; tel/fax: 02 37 23 05 04. Open Apr–Sept Mon, Wed, Thur & Fri 1430–1800, Sat 1000–1200 and 1430–1800.*

ⓗ Château de Maintenon €€
tel: 02 37 23 00 09. Open Apr–Oct Mon & Tue–Sat 1400–1830, Sun & hols 1000–1200 and 1400–1830; Nov–Mar Sat, Sun & hols 1400–1730; closed Tue & Christmas week.

A pretty town straddling the Eure and bursting with flowers, Maintenon might not have made its mark on the tourist circuit were it not for its most famous resident, Françoise d'Aubigné, the Marquise de Maintenon. Widow of poet Scarron but later to become the secret wife of Louis XIV, she bought the castle in 1674, revamping the feudal building into an elegant **château**, and employed noted landscape architect Le Nôtre to lay out the park and gardens. Vauban's unfinished aqueduct (commissioned by Louis XIV to bring water to Versailles) provides an unexpected backdrop. Beside the entrance to the château is the Eglise St-Nicolas, built in 1521 by Jean Cottereau (1458–1530), François I's treasurer. Nearby, in Maintenon-Pierres, there is a beautiful medieval garden, the **Jardin Médiéval de Bois-Richeaux**, pleasantly laid out and full of interest to gardeners and laypeople alike.

Accommodation and food in Maintenon

🏛 **Jardin Médiéval de Bois-Richeaux €**
Tel: 06 11 88 20 20. Open daily except Mon 1000–1200 and 1400–1800.

🍴 **Market** *Thur am.*

⚫ For a bird's-eye view of Maintenon in the early morning, a local company offers hot-air ballooning trips. **Montgolfières Air-Magic €€€** *5 r. de l'Aqueduc, Houx; tel: 02 37 32 38 06; fax: 02 37 27 10 20; www.air-magic.com*

Le Bistro d'Adeline € *3 r. Collin d'Harville; tel: 02 37 23 06 67. Closed Sat–Mon.* This charming little restaurant just along from the château serves good, old-fashioned home cooking at low prices. Its size and value means it's always busy, so book in advance.

Brasserie du Soleil € *5 pl. Aristide Briand; tel: 02 37 23 05 22.* A pleasant brasserie in the centre of town.

Royal Maintenon € *5 pl. Aristide Briand; tel: 02 37 27 14 09; fax: 02 37 23 03 91.* In the heart of town, a small yet pleasant hotel with an excellent Asian restaurant.

NOGENT-LE-ROTROU

ℹ️ **Nogent-le-Rotrou Tourist Office** *44 r. Villette Gâté; tel: 02 37 29 68 86; email: contact@ nogentlerotrou-tourisme.fr; www.nogentlerotrou-tourisme.fr. Open Mon–Fri 0800–1200 and 1330–1730, Sat 0900–1200 and 1400–1700, Sun at château 1000–1200 and 1400–1800.*

🏛 **Château St-Jean** € *tel: 02 37 52 18 02. Open Wed–Mon 1000–1200 and 1400–1800. Closed 1 Jan, 1 May, 1 Nov & 25 Dec.*

Mausoleum of the Duke of Sully *r. de Sully. Open daily 0900–1630.*

🍴 **Market** *Sat all day.*

Capital of the forested region of the Perche, and rising above the River Huisne, Nogent-le-Rotrou is a delightful market town, with some historic old homes and ancient churches. It is best known for its **Château St-Jean**, containing the **Musée du Perche**, and for its attached 1,000-year-old dungeon. The visible origins of the town date back to the Middle Ages (though it may well date from Roman times) when the knoll above the river was walled and a fortification erected. In the 10th century the first of the powerful Rotrou family took up residence, giving his name to the burgeoning town. The two Demoiselles d'Armagnac, daughters of the beheaded Duc of Nemours, inherited the castle in 1503 and are responsible for much of its current aspect. In 1624 the Duc de Sully assumed ownership of the castle and built a small pavilion on the northern side. The museum documents the history of Nogent-le-Rotrou and displays items relating to country life in the Perche. Within the town, the white marble **Mausoleum** of Sully and his wife, Rachel, can be visited in the Rotunda next to the recently renovated Eglise Notre-Dame. The latter was once the chapel of an almshouse for pilgrims en route to Santiago de Compostela.

Accommodation and food around Nogent-le-Rotrou

Restaurant l'Alambic € *20 av. Paris, at Margon (1.5km from Nogent); tel: 02 37 52 19 03.* Not so long ago a modest roadside eatery, this is now a good restaurant serving classic French dishes at very modest prices.

Le Lion d'Or €€ *28 pl. St-Pol; tel: 02 37 52 01 60; fax: 02 37 52 23 82; www.hotel-chartres-le-mans.com.* A traditional, small and surprisingly quiet hotel in the main square in the centre of Nogent-le-Rotrou. Attractively modernised rooms.

Le Moulin de Villeray €€€ *route de Rémalard, near Condeau (8km from Nogent); tel: 02 33 73 30 22; fax: 02 33 73 38 28* and **Le Château de Villeray €€€** *tel: 02 33 83 36 83.* A choice between staying in the hotel complex built around an old windmill or in the 17th-century château. Either way, the service and rooms are impeccable. The cuisine at the Moulin is arguably the best in the region.

Suggested tour

ⓘ Comité Départemental du Tourisme *10 r. du Docteur Maunoury, Chartres; tel: 02 37 84 01 00; fax: 02 37 36 36 39; email: infos@tourisme28.com; www.tourisme28.com. Open Mon–Fri 0900–1300 and 1400–1800 but not open to public visits.*

🏭 Guided tour of Moutiers' historic mill *tel: 02 37 99 93 25; by appointment only.*

Le Grand Moulin, Ouarville € *tel: 02 37 22 13 87; guided visits in summer on Sun & national hols pm.*

Total distance: 240km, and 15km for the detour.

Time: Allow 2 days.

Links: A fast national road connects Châteaudun with Orléans (*see page 240*), while another good national road links Nogent-le-Retrou with the city of Le Mans (*see page 162*).

Route: Leave **Chartres** (*see page 182*) on its northern side (following directions initially to Drieux) and branch off in the suburbs on to the D906, which goes to **MAINTENON ❶** and Rambouillet. Crossing the River Eure, you leave Maintenon on the D18 and pass under the high arches of Vauban's aqueduct. Following the River Voise, the road leads to **GALLARDON ❷**. Leave by the D116 in the direction of **Auneau** and its 14th-century château. Leave Auneau on the D7 and drive 9.5km southwards before turning left on to the D939 to **Ouarville**. Rising to a height of 10.85m, with sails extending over 14m, the Grand Moulin is a local landmark and is visible from the road as you near the village of Ouarville. Take the D107 via Louville-la-Chenard to enter **Moutiers**. The 18th-century wooden mill is just beside the road leaving the village on the south side. Continue on this road to **Ymonville** where there is another interesting mill. Keep following the D107 southwards through large tracts of open fields to Orgères-en-Beauce. Here, you'll pick up the faster D927 in the direction of **CHATEAUDUN ❸**, or you may follow the detour first.

Detour: For aficionados of windmills, there is a superb, restored example of a stone windmill at **Niverville**. Take the D144 via Harville and cross the D955 heading for Morgues and Niverville. In its present form, the Moulin à Vent de Frouville-Pensier (*open 1430–1830 in summer*) is largely 19th century, though its origins date back to the 13th. From Niverville, pick up the D31 back towards Châteaudun (*end of detour*).

Exit on the N10 in the direction of Chartres, passing Flacey, and drive for another 5km when you take the slip road into the centre of

Auberge de l'Abbaye € 15 r. du Commerce, Thiron-Gardais; tel: 02 37 49 54 18; fax: 02 37 49 49 17. Closed Sun pm. A modest, traditional auberge restaurant on the main road, offering local specialities and grills in the garden area during summer.

BONNEVAL ❹. Back on the N10, turn left on to the D281 just after the end of town. It leads to **Alluyes**, a pretty village straddling the River Loir. Note its round dungeon, similar to that of Châteaudun, now integrated into a building that forms part of the local psychiatric hospital. The D281 continues from Alluyes for another 10km, when it joins the D941 and enters **ILLIERS-COMBRAY ❺**. Continuing through the sometimes-wooded Perche by the picturesque D922, via Chassant and **Thiron-Gardais**. This town grew up around its Eglise Abbatiale de la Sainte-Trinité built during the 12th and 13th centuries. Only its church remains, just by the main road. From here, it is just 14km to **NOGENT-LE-ROTROU ❻**. The N23 is the quickest way to return to Chartres.

Windmills

Windmills have been part of the landscape in the Beauce plains since the Middle Ages. They were used to grind the local oats or wheat. Those that remain date from the 17th–19th century and are built of wood or stone, with either wood or canvas panels. Constructed on a central pivot, they have the unique distinction of a long, wooden 'tail', which is used to rotate the whole building in order to catch the wind at the best angle. The Beauce style of mill was copied throughout Europe and adapted for not only milling flour, but cutting and pulping wood for paper.

Right
Moutiers' windmill

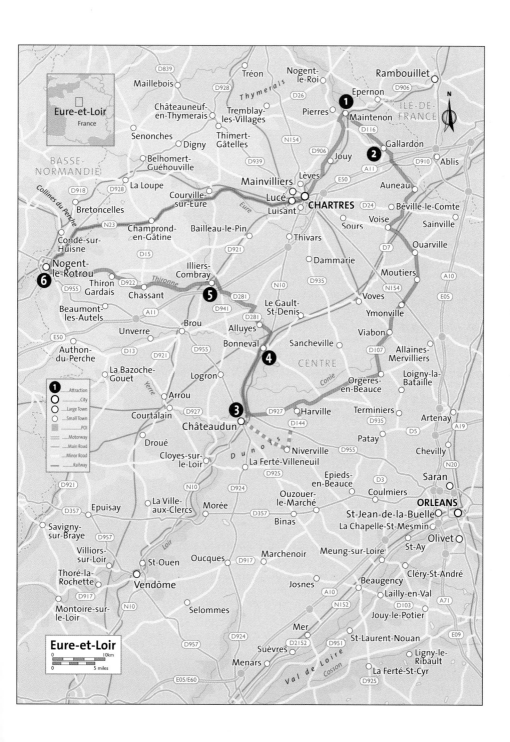

Eure-et-Loir
France

BASSE-
NORMANDIE

ÎLE-DE-
FRANCE

CENTRE

Eure-et-Loir

0   10km
0   5 miles

Legend:
- ❶ Attraction
- ○ City
- ○ Large Town
- ○ Small Town
- ■ POI
- Motorway
- Main Road
- Minor Road
- Railway

Blois

Ratings

Architecture	●●●●●
Châteaux	●●●●●
History	●●●●●
Entertainment	●●●●○
Children	●●●○○
Museums	●●●○○
Restaurants	●●●○○
Shopping	●●●○○

From across the river, the elegant buildings of Blois, in pale and dark grey, stepping up in long terraces to the town's lofty château, look supremely dignified. The vast Château Royal, first constructed over a thousand years ago on an easily defended ledge of rock rising from the Loire, has been substantially rebuilt and enlarged in different reigns and under different regimes. Yet it remains the heart of Blois. From their rocky platform, the château façades look down upon the steep streets, lanes and stairways of the old town. In these narrow streets stand many Renaissance mansions, often built by the officials, courtiers, financiers, friends and hangers-on of the French kings. Yet, though proud of its historic, aristocratic and royal connections, Blois is thoroughly vivacious, busy and productive, a modern commercial centre for the surrounding rural area. It is noted for excellent local produce, high-quality pâtisserie and confectionery, and some good restaurants.

Getting there and getting around

ℹ️ **Blois Tourist Office**
23 pl. du Château; tel: 02 54 90 41 41; fax: 02 54 90 41 49; email: info@ bloispaysdechambord.com. Open mid-Oct–mid-Apr Mon 1000–1230 and 1400–1800, Tue–Sat 0900–1230 and 1400–1800, Sun & hols (except 25 Dec and 1 Jan) 0930–1230; rest of year Mon–Sat 0900–1900, Sun & hols 1000–1900. The tourist office offers a wide

By road
The town is 2 hours' drive from Paris. Many roads converge on Blois, coming from every direction. *Autoroute* A10 and the N152 on the north bank of the Loire, and the quieter D751/D951 on the south bank, connect Blois to Tours and Orléans. On reaching the town from any direction, head for the *Centre Ville*, and then for the château.

By rail
There are frequent rail links from Tours and Orléans.

Parking
There is a large multi-storey car park, partly underground, less than 5 minutes' walk from the château.

Blois

Key	
O	Attraction
	Important Building
	Park
	Main Road
	Other Road
i	Information

0 — 100 metres
0 — 100 yards

variety of services, including hotel reservations, currency exchange, booking for local events and tours.

W *www.bloispaysde chambord.com* (Blois tourism site); *www.ville-blois.fr* (the town's official site).

Markets *Tue, Thur & Sat weekly, and second Sun of each month. Local produce market every Thur pm Jul–Aug.*

Guided tours

Free tours of the Old Town are available on request, depending on numbers; ask at the château. Tours by horse-drawn carriage start in front of the château.

Combined ticket

A low-priced all-in-one ticket (*Billet Jumelé*) gives access to the château, a *son-et-lumière* show and the Maison de la Magie, or any two. Available at the château.

Right
Château Royal de Blois gardens

Sights

Château Royal de Blois

On the outside wall of the château, the Flamboyant Gothic brick and stone main entrance faces on to pl. du Château. Once a walled farmyard, this is now a large, attractive and sunny plaza with a tree-shaded esplanade. Peaceful gardens to one side give a good view across the town and river. Set in the wall above the château's main gate is a 19th-century equestrian statue of Louis XII. To the right is the gable end of the 13th-century Salle d'Etats, and to either side the window corbels are decorated with robust stone carvings.

The fortified entrance gives access to the château's bright, spacious inner courtyard, recently restored. Four entirely dissimilar styles of architecture, representing four eras of French history, almost completely enclose the paved courtyard: from the feudal period, two 13th-century Gothic structures stand diagonally opposite one another; the late Gothic (Louis XII) wing and chapel on the left; the exquisite Renaissance (François I) wing on the right, with its stupendous open staircase; and the 17th-century classical wing directly ahead.

The repeated crowned porcupine motif was the emblem of Louis XII, while the crowned salamander was the chosen symbol of François I. It is striking that just 14 years passed between the construction of the Louis XII and François I wings. In that time a revolutionary change in taste had been brought about by exposure to Italian design during the Italian war campaigns. Notice Italianate decoration on the Gothic structures. The builder of the classical section was Gaston d'Orléans, brother of the king, Louis XIII. The architect was Mansart. He had already demolished about half of the existing château to construct the new wing, and was already knocking down the lovely Renaissance wing when his work stopped abruptly in 1638 when Louis XIII had a son (meaning Gaston was no longer next in line to the throne). Note the strange break between the two wings, and the off-centre position of the spiral staircase. Go inside the classical wing to see Mansart's intriguing and beautiful cupola. Gaston's demolitions also created the gap between the church and the new wing, giving access to the terrace, with magnificent town and river views. The church contains modern stained glass by Max Ingrand.

Inside François' Renaissance section, the Royal Apartments on the first floor are decorated with bright floor tiles, colourful patterned walls, painted beams and gilded fireplaces. In the Galerie de la Reine the floor has recently been laid with surprising new glazed floor tiles in blue, yellow, black and white. Apparently, these are based on historical evidence. In the smaller Study the narrow gilded wood panelling is original, and supposedly conceals secret hiding places. On the second floor are Henri III's apartments and the Guise Hall, devoted to a museum of paintings on the theme of the 1588 assassination of the Duc de Guise. He was killed on 23 December 1588, in the king's

Chronology of the château

10th century: built by Thibault I.

12th century: Count of Blois marries William the Conqueror's daughter; their son, Stephen, becomes Count of Blois and King of England.

1440: Charles d'Orléans demolishes part of the feudal fortress and rebuilds in brick and stone.

1462: future Louis XII born in the château; after 1498 it is the principal royal residence.

Early 16th century: François I frequently in residence, adds Renaissance wing.

1588: Henri III has Duc de Guise assassinated at the château; three days later Catherine de Medici (the king's mother) dies in the château.

1635: Gaston d'Orléans commissions Mansart to demolish the château and rebuild in classical style. Completes just one wing before stopping in 1638.

Above right
Château interior

Overleaf
Château courtyard and spiral staircase

bedchamber. His brother, the Cardinal of Lorraine, was also murdered. The influential Guise and his followers were fanatically anti-Protestant, wished to form an alliance with Spain and seemed intent on deposing the king.

Returning to the first floor, the **Musée des Beaux-Arts** (Fine Arts Museum) contains a large number of 16th- and 17th-century portraits, several good later works and many Flemish tapestries. Pass through the guardroom to reach the large restored *Salle des Etats-Généraux* (the meeting place of the medieval French Parliament). This is the oldest part of the château, as well as one of the oldest and largest surviving feudal assembly halls in France. Despite a spell in the 19th century as an army gymnasium, it is in excellent condition, with an impressive ceiling of twin barrel vaults supported by central pillars. Here, free classical concerts are held on summer evenings. On the ground floor a **Musée Archéologique** (Archaeological Museum) is located in former château kitchens.

Eglise St-Nicolas €
r. St-Lauren. Open daily.

Maison de la Magie €€€
1 pl. du Château; tel: 02 54
90 33 33; fax: 02 54 90 33
30; www.maisondelamagie.fr.
Open 25 Mar–30 Jun &
1–24 Sept 1000–1230 and
1400–1800 (closed Mon
except national hols); Jul–Aug
daily 1000–1230 and
1400–1830; 26 Oct–
5 Nov daily 1000–1230 and
1400–1800. Exact dates
liable to change – depends
on French school holidays.

Eglise St-Nicolas

Formerly a Benedictine abbey church, St-Nicolas was built in an interesting experimental transitional style in the early 12th century when the Gothic style was a novelty. Inside, there is some good stone carving, interesting stained glass and a 15th-century altarpiece. An unusual dome covers the crossing. The large abbey and its ecclesiastical quarter once played an important part in the life of medieval Blois. The abbey's 18th-century dependencies, in classical style, stretch down to the Loire.

Maison de la Magie

A huge and implausible dragon pokes its six heads through the windows of this large, 19th-century brick-and-stone mansion opposite the château, dedicated to Robert Houdin. The 'father of modern magic', Houdin – no relation to the famed Houdini – was a brilliant illusionist and entertainer. This engaging museum gives some background to 'magic', and many amusing examples. The underground *Théâtre des Magiciens* stages excellent conjuring shows (at 1145, 1530 & 1700 daily).

Below
Statue of Robert Houdin

Accommodation and food in Blois

Streets in the town centre have dozens of inexpensive brasserie-style eating places, with tables set outside in summer. Chain hotels in all price ranges can be found close to the town centre.

Le Bistrot du Cuisinier €–€€ *20 quai Villebois-Mareuil; tel: 02 54 78 06 70; fax: 02 54 78 00 98.* Right beside the water on the south bank, close to the bridge, this convivial and informal bistro with its big dining room has a wonderful view of the town. It makes a point of specialising in wine rather than any particular style of cuisine. For all that, the food is very good, with local dishes emphasised despite periodic specials from around the world. Excellent value for money. Keeps relatively late hours, too – you can order until 2330.

Au Rendez-vous des Pêcheurs €€ *27 r. du Foix; tel: 02 54 74 67 48; fax: 02 54 74 47 67; www. rendezvousdespecheurs.com.* Relaxed and enjoyable, one of the best restaurants in town, this Michelin-rosetted address is near the river, a few paces downstream from the Eglise St-Nicolas. The speciality is imaginative fish and seafood dishes perfectly prepared, but the game, sauces, vegetables and desserts are all excellent, too. There is a good-value set menu and local wine list.

L'Orangerie du Château €€€ *1 av. Dr J Laigret; tel: 02 54 78 05 36; fax: 02 54 78 22 78; www.orangerie-du-chateau.com.* This is the place for a special treat in Blois, a top of the range, classic, elegant, traditional restaurant. Being located inside the château's Orangerie, just off pl. Victor Hugo at the foot of the Façade des Loges, adds to the pleasure. Cooking with flair, using the best ingredients, accompanied by an excellent wine list and crisp, friendly, efficient service.

Suggested walk

Total distance: About 3km.

Time: Half a day.

Links: Blois is the point at which three tours meet and can be linked: the Grands Châteaux: Tours–Blois (*see page 52*); Blois–Orléans (*see page 228*); and Cher and the Sologne (*see page 212*).

Route: Start from **pl. Victor Hugo** (or square Augustin Thierry), at the foot of the château. On the square's north side is the 17th-century Jesuit church of **St-Vincent**. On the west side of the square, the **Jardin du Roi** is a last small remnant of the once extensive park and gardens of the château (which reached about as far as today's SNCF railway station). Nearly opposite is the charming Renaissance **Pavillon Anne de Bretagne** (now the tourist office) and the **Orangerie**, which were once in the king's gardens and directly accessed by a footbridge from the château's Royal Apartments. Along one side, pl. Victor Hugo is overlooked by the impressive **Façade des Loges**, the exterior of the château's Renaissance wing, a long, Italianate, elegant terrace, four storeys high, of which two storeys are open galleries, or *loges* (from Italian *loggia*).

Walk up the steps that lead from pl. Victor Hugo to r. de la Voûte-du-Château and up past the Loges façade to reach pl. du Château, the fine traffic-free space in front of the **CHATEAU ROYAL DE BLOIS ❶**. Before entering the château, admire the quiet rose gardens on the far side of the square; they have a good view down to the river, crossed by the town's beautiful old bridge. After visiting the château, **MAISON DE LA MAGIE ❷** is at the far end of the square.

At the southwestern corner of pl. du Château (that is, at the far left-hand end of the château as seen from the square), a flight of steps leads steeply down to r. St-Lubin. Turn right into this street, and right again, to see the **Façade Gaston d'Orléans**, the imposing exterior of the château's classical wing. Steps down from r. St-Lubin lead to the **EGLISE ST-NICOLAS ❸**. Near the back of the church, in r. des

Above
Place du Château, Blois

Jacobins, the town's **Natural History** and **Religious Art museums** are housed in former abbey buildings. Walk back along **r. St-Lubin**, which has houses dating from the 15th and 16th centuries, to busy **pl. Louis XII**, the main square, destroyed in 1940 and rebuilt. Take **r. St Martin** and cross r. du Commerce – convivial, crowded, pedestrianised old shopping streets – into r. des Trois Clefs. Cross over **r. Denis Papin**, the main street of the town; ironically, it is named in honour of the great 17th-century physicist, a native of Blois who, being Protestant, was driven out of the town and hated the place for the way it had treated him and his family.

There are interesting old façades, several half-timbered, along all these streets. Turn right down **r. des Juifs**, so called for the Jewish community of about 200 living here in the Middle Ages. Thirty-five members of the Jewish community were burnt alive on 26 May 1171 after 'the Jews' were blamed for the death of a child. The whole community was again arrested in 1181 and freed after payment of a crippling ransom. There is no Jewish community here today. There are fine Renaissance houses in the street; especially at No 3, **Hôtel Condé,** which was built in 1540 and has a gallery and spiral staircase in the courtyard. Turn left for **r. du Puits Châtel**, where again there are several fine mansions, some with courtyards based on that of the château (note Nos 3, 5 and 7). Off to the left, via the atmospheric little Petits Degrés St-Louis, is the **Cathédrale St-Louis**, an ancient church rebuilt (in Gothic style) in the 17th century. It stands on a steep ledge overlooking the river. Behind the church and lower down the slope is the **Hotel de Ville** (town hall), with beautiful rose gardens, and a little beyond are the **Jardins de l'Evêché** (the Bishop's Gardens), which afford wonderful river views.

Walk along r. du Palais and r. St-Honoré, backstreets with occasional wide views across the town and river. Nos 56–48 r. St-Honoré have 16th-century arched shopfronts; the façade of No 50 displays the salamander of François I. At the end of the street, turn left and right to follow the wider r. Porte du Côté back to pl. Victor Hugo.

Cher and the Sologne

Ratings

Activities	●●●●
Châteaux	●●●●
Children	●●●●
Nature	●●●●
Gastronomy	●●●
History	●●●
Picturesque villages	●●●
Wildlife	●●●

The Sologne was one of the country's great gaming grounds in pre-Revolution days. Royal hunting lodges, elaborate châteaux amid huge parklands, and smaller royal towns pepper a landscape of forests, marshes, small lakes and undulating hills that thin out as they extend towards the Cher and the Loire valleys to the west and north. Amid this bucolic background, the battles between Catholic and Protestant were waged during the Wars of Religion, while the intrigues of kings and courtiers were played out in their favourite châteaux and noble mansions. Nature lovers find the peace and beauty of the Sologne a tonic after city life, while many of the châteaux have nurtured alternative attractions – small zoos, the rearing of exotic birds and animals, and small museums presenting local lifestyles – in their spacious parks. A region of poor, sandy soil, the Sologne is known today for its excellent strawberries and asparagus, and its variety of game and wines, all of which constitute a regional cuisine to delight the gourmet.

CHÂTEAU DE BEAUREGARD

Château de Beauregard €€
Cellettes; tel/fax: 02 54 70 36 74; www.beauregard-loire.com. Open Apr, May, Jun & Sept 0930–1200 and 1400–1830, Jul–Aug 0930–1830, Oct–Mar 0930–1200 and 1400–1700 except Wed. Closed Jan and the first 3 weeks in Dec.

Originally a hunting lodge for François I, this château passed into the hands of Jean du Thier, Henri II's Secretary of State, and it was he who, in the middle of the 16th century, commissioned the Cabinet des Grelots, a small room decorated in oak, carved and gilded, as his own study. The intricate work, depicting man's varied occupations, was executed by master craftsman and cabinet-maker to Henri II, Italian Scibec de Carpi, who had also undertaken work at Fontainebleau. In 1617 Beauregard belonged to Paul Ardier, a former treasurer to Henri IV. During his time he hosted Cardinal Richelieu (*see page 99*) who had been travelling with King Louis XIII and his court when the king stopped at Blois to meet his mother, Marie de Medici. Fearing a conspiracy, Richelieu slipped away with his faithful musketeers and took shelter in Beauregard. It was Ardier who commissioned the celebrated Galerie des Illustres. It's the equivalent of a 'who's who' of France's royals and notables, as well as famous foreign personalities,

Cher and the Sologne

France

Cher and the Sologne

Talcy
Lailly-en-Val
Jouy-le-Potier
D103
N20
D921
La Ferté-St-Aubin
Mer
Ligny-le-Ribault
D924
A10
N152
St-Laurent-Nouan
D2152
D951
Suèvres
Val de Loire
Menars
Cosson
La Ferté-St-Cyr
D957
Herbault
E05/E60
La Chaussée-St-Victor
Chambord
D925
A71
E09
D922
BLOIS
D766
Vineuil
Château de Villesavin
Neung-sur-Beuvron
Beuvron
D923
St-Gervais-la-Forêt
Château de Beauregard
Bracieux
Chouzy-sur-Cisse
Cour-Cheverny
Fontaines-en-Sologue
D923
Onzain
D751
Cellettes
Château de Troussay
Château de Cheverny
Marcilly-en-Gault
Loire
N152
Chaumont-sur-Loire
D956
D765
D120
D13
D922
D751
Sambin
Fougères-sur-Bièvre
Soings-en-Sologne
D63
Pontlevoy
D764
Contres
Mur-de-Sologne
Selles-St-Denis
La Ferté-Imbault
Sauldre
Montrichard
D85
Château du Gué-Péan
Chémery
Château du Moulin
D20
D59
D724
Romorantin-Lanthenay
D675
D956
CENTRE
Pruniers-en-Sologne
St-Georges-sur-Cher
E604
N76
Thésée-la-Romaine
St-Romain-sur-Cher
A85
Villefranche-sur-Cher
Mennetou-sur-Cher
N76
A85
D17
Selles-sur-Cher
Gièvres
Cher
E60
St-Aignan
Noyers-sur-Cher
D764
Meusnes
Chabris
D675
D33
Plateau de Ste-Maure
Villentrois
D37
D4
St-Christophe-en-Bazelle
Genouilly
Montrésor
Château de Valençay
Poulaines
Massay
Chartreuse du Liget
D11
Nouans-les-Fontaines
D960
Graçay
Loché
Luçay-le-Mâle
D960
D922
Ecueillé
D43
Vatan
D975
Champagne Berrichonne
A20
Indre
Bouges
D956
E09
Levroux
221
Issoudun
D926
Villegongis
N151

○ .....Attraction
◎ .....City
○ .....Large Town
○ .....Small Town
■ .....POI
■ .....Motorway
— .....Main Road
— .....Minor Road
— .....Railway

N

0   16km
0   8 miles

Above
Château de Beauregard

for it includes 327 portraits. Hundreds of eyes focus on you as you wander around the room. Look down, too: the blue Delft tile floor is a fine piece of 17th-century faiencework. The south gallery holds some impressive Belgian tapestries as well as various items of remarkable period furniture. The château is currently in private hands and the owners live in the left wing.

In complete contrast to the historical aspect of this château, the owners commissioned a modern garden in the 70ha park that was created by a notable contemporary French landscape gardener, Gilles Clément.

Accommodation and food near Beauregard

Hôtel du Château and **Le Restaurant de l'Agriculture** €€ *37 r. de la Mairie, Tour-en-Solonge; tel: 02 54 46 50 20. Closed Christmas and Feb school hols, Sun pm and Mon.* An attractive hotel with a highly reputed restaurant specialising in local produce and game, in season. It is 10km eastwards on the D77 from Cellettes, and is located near Villesavin.

CHÂTEAU DE CHEVERNY

ⓘ Cour-Cheverny Tourist Office *12 r. du Chêne des Dames, Cour-Cheverny; tel: 02 54 79 95 63; fax: 02 54 79 23 90; email: otcheverny@aol.com. Open Feb–Dec daily 1030–1800 (1900 Jun–Aug).*

This is one of the most classic of the Loire châteaux and is well organised for tourists, children included. Huge parking areas usher in visitors and encourage them to get out and walk. The immaculately maintained château dates from the 17th century – it was built between 1604 and 1634 by Count Hurault de Cheverny – and its slate roof and cool stone façade have not been altered since. The château will seem familiar to lovers of Hergé's *Tintin* – his fictional Château Moulinsart was inspired by this castle. The château is beautifully furnished in period style with dozens of rare items, and the decoration

Château de Cheverny €€€
Cheverny; tel: 02 54 79 96 29; fax: 02 54 79 25 38; email: chateau.cheverny@ wanadoo.fr; www.château-cheverny.fr. Open Nov–Mar 0945–1700; Apr–Jun & Sept 0915–1815; Jul–Aug 0915–1845; Oct 0945–1730.

Market *Cour-Cheverny, Tue pm.*

of some of its principal rooms is exquisite. Among the most interesting is the Salle d'Armes with a fine collection of ancient arms and Gobelin tapestries, and the king's bedroom with its magnificent painted ceiling and stone fireplace held aloft by atlantes figures, its tapestries and its rich silk baldaquin bed. The 17th-century tapestries in the Tapestry Chamber are woven copies of works by the famous Flemish painter Teniers. Visitors to the 100ha park have a choice of discovering the woodlands and fauna either by a small electric car, by boat on the château's canal or on foot. Cheverny is also noted for its hunting, and it boasts a 90-strong pack of hounds. Their afternoon feeding time is a popular occasion with younger visitors.

Accommodation and food near Cheverny

Le Béguinage € *D765, Cour-Cheverny; tel: 02 54 79 29 92; fax: 02 54 79 94 59; www.lebeguinage.fr.st.* A lovely and tranquil *chambres d'hôtes* with an established garden, just outside the centre. An excellent base for regional visits.

Restaurant Le Pinocchio €–€€ *pl. de l'Eglise, Cheverny; tel: 02 54 79 97 23; fax: 02 54 79 24 03. Open daily in season, closed Sun and Mon out of season.* Cleverly located at the château's exit gates opposite the little church (worth a quick look, too), a small restaurant with outdoor and indoor seating and Italian-style dishes.

Hôtel des Trois Marchands €€ *pl. Victor Hugo, Cour-Cheverny; tel: 02 54 79 96 44; fax: 02 54 79 25 60; www.hoteldes3marchands.com.* A mid-sized hotel in the centre of town, with garden and highly rated restaurant. The ambience is that of Louis XIII elegance, and all dishes are made entirely in the kitchens.

Below
Chateau de Cheverny

CHÂTEAU DU GUÉ-PÉAN

Château du Gué-Péan *Monthou-sur-Cher; to contact the riding centre only, tel: 02 54 71 10 71.*

Under its new owners, this very handsome privately owned château, dating from the 16th and 17th centuries, can only be visited by clients of its riding centre, but its beautiful situation in the Forêt Choussy makes it well worth pausing to see. It is said that it was here that Louis XII's widow, Anne of Brittany, secretly married her lover, the Duke of Suffolk. The fine château with asymmetrical towers (three are round with pepperpot roofs, the fourth has a bell-shaped roof) has an important *cour d'honneur*, entirely enclosed by the château and its ancillary buildings.

CHÂTEAU DU MOULIN

Château du Moulin €€ *Lassay-sur-Croisne; tel: 02 54 83 83 51. Open Apr–Sept Thur–Tue 1000–1230 and 1400–1830.*

This beautiful fortified château is hidden in the forests just near the village of Lassay-sur-Croisne. It was built in 1492 by royal architect Jacques de Persigny for Philippe du Moulin, captain to Charles VIII. Complete with its original dungeon, round towers, an impressive keep and water-filled moat, this privately owned (and still inhabited) castle presents a picture-postcard image of a Renaissance château.

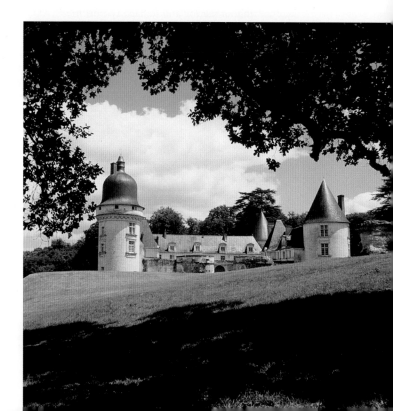

Right
Château du Gué-Péan

CHÂTEAU DE TROUSSAY

Château de Troussay and Musée de Sologne €–€€
Cheverny; tel: 02 54 44 29 07. Open Apr–Jun & Sept daily 1030–1230 and 1400–1800; Jul–Aug daily 1000–1830 (Tue in Jul–Aug till 2200); Oct weekends 1030–1230 and 1400–1730.

Hidden in a lovely tract of woodland is the privately owned Château de Troussay. It probably dates back to 1450 – though the first deeds are from 1545 – and, extraordinarily, this building has only been sold twice (in 1732 and 1900) during the last 600 years. It was constructed for Robert Bugy who was controller of the all-important salt reserves in Blois under François I. It was subsequently owned by the 19th-century historian Louis de la Saussaye, who was responsible for much of its embellishment. His portrait hangs in the Salon Louis de la Saussaye. What we see today is a gentleman's residence, a mansion with human proportions and symmetrically designed service buildings either side of the *Cour d'honneur*. The best views of this ensemble are from the park, behind the château where the decorative stonework is far more appreciable; it wasn't designed to be seen from today's entrance. The château's ceilings and furniture keep up its 18th-century ambience. A small **Musée de Sologne** is lodged in the old stables and distillery and displays a collection of traditional farming and agricultural implements.

Accommodation and food near Troussay

Château du Breuil €€€ route de Fougères, Cheverny; tel: 02 54 44 20 20; fax: 02 54 44 30 40; email: info@chateau-du-breuil.fr; www.chateau-du-breuil.fr. Closed Jan–mid-Mar. In its own wooded parkland, this 18th-century château has been remodelled into a smallish luxury hotel. Good restaurant.

CHÂTEAU DE VALENÇAY

Valençay Tourist Office 2 av. de la Résistance; tel/fax: 02 54 00 04 42. Open May–Oct daily 0930–1230 and 1400–1900; winter 0930–1230 and 1400–1800.

www.pays-de-valencay.fr

Château de Valençay €€–€€€ tel: 02 54 00 15 69; email: message@chateau-valencay.com; www.chateau-valencay.com. Open Mar–Jun & Sept–Nov 0930–1800; Jul–Aug 0930–1930; winter

This Renaissance château, just inside the Berry, took its inspiration from Chambord. It was built around 1540 but bought in 1803 by the Prince of Talleyrand (Napoleon's Foreign Minister) who revamped it to entertain foreign dignitaries. Its excellent proportions lend themselves to fine decoration, and all the rooms are well furnished with period pieces and reflect the personalities of those who once inhabited them. These numbered the Duchess of Dino, Talleyrand himself (look out for his elaborate clothing) and Ferdinand, later King of Spain. The large underground kitchen was the domain of the illustrious Chef Carême. Beside it, the cellars still boast a magnificent, albeit dusty, collection of wines. The park is also a big draw and very child-friendly. Apart from deer, there are llamas and other exotic creatures. The peacocks, ducks and geese have the free run of the formal French garden. During the summer months costumed actors bring the castle back to life: fencing matches take place, the kitchen bustles with activity as Chef Carême 'prepares a meal' and the courtiers move through the state rooms.

open only for groups by appointment. Closed 1 Nov.

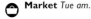 **Market** *Tue am.*

Accommodation and food in Valençay

Hôtel Le Relais du Moulin €–€€ *94 r. National; tel: 02 54 00 38 00; fax: 02 54 00 38 79; www.hotel-lerelaisdumoulin.com. Closed mid-Nov–1 Apr.* A modern, mid-sized hotel, with pool, just 800m outside town. Two restaurants with local and gourmet menus.

Valençay cheese

Gourmets should look out for Valençay's goat's cheese. This creamy, crumbly delight is formed in the shape of a pyramid with a flat top – it is best enjoyed with a local red Sauvignon wine such as the AOC Valençay or Reuilly.

CHÂTEAU DE VILLESAVIN

Château de Villesavin €€ *Tour-en-Sologne; tel: 02 54 46 42 88; fax: 02 54 46 09 49; www.chateau-de-villesavin. com. Open mid-Feb–May 1000–1200 and 1400–1900; Jun–Sept 1000–1900; Oct–Nov 1000–1200 and 1400–1800; Dec Sat–Sun & school hols 1000–1200 and 1400–1800.*

This Renaissance-style château only rises two storeys yet creates an imposing impression with its elegant wings. Although it is used for receptions, it is also open to the public on guided tours. Some 350 diadems form part of its unusual collection of objects and costumes grouped around the theme of marriage. On display, too, is a series of horse-drawn carriages and, a highlight for children, their herds of breeding donkeys.

Accommodation and food near Villesavin

Au Bistrot d'Arian € *231 route d'Arian, Tour-en-Sologne; tel/fax: 02 54 46 42 85. Closed Thur.* A small restaurant with a shady garden, conveniently situated for Villesavin. Traditional and regional dishes, and friendly service.

Right
Entrance to Château de Villesavin

FOUGÈRES-SUR-BIÈVRE

ⓘ Château de Fougères-sur-Bièvre € *tel: 02 54 20 27 18. Open early May–early Sept Wed–Mon 0930–1200 and 1400–1800; rest of year Wed–Mon 1000–1200 and 1400–1630; closed 1 Jan, 1 May, 1 & 11 Nov, & 25 Dec.*

Right
Château de Fougères-sur-Bièvre

Amid pine forests and fields of asparagus sits the small town of Fougères. It unfurls around its **château** built by Pierre de Refuge, Louis XI's treasurer at the turn of the 15th century. No pure architectural lines here. His sturdy concept of architecture was tempered by the more attractive additions commissioned subsequently by his son-in-law, Jean de Villebresme, with the result that it's a bit of a hotchpotch. Towers capped with pointed roofs, flat arches and a Renaissance gallery inspired by the château at Blois, the building was entirely constructed, unusually for its importance, by local artisans.

Accommodation and food near Fougères-sur-Bièvre

Relais des Landes €€–€€€ *Ouchamps; tel: 02 54 44 40 40; fax: 02 54 44 03 89; www.relaisdeslandes.com. Open Mar–Nov.* Just 5km from Fougères, this is a luxurious hotel, housed in a converted mansion and its cottages. Excellent gourmet restaurant.

ROMORANTIN-LANTHENAY

ⓘ Romorantin-Lanthenay Tourist Office *pl. de la Paix; tel: 02 54 76 43 89; fax: 02 54 76 96 24; www.tourisme-romorantin.com (tourist office's own website), www.romorantin.fr (town's official site for residents and visitors). Open Mon 1000–1215 and 1400–1830, Tue–Fri 0845–1215 and 1330–1830, Sat 0845–1215 and 1330–1800.*

When the 1498 plague threatened Amboise, young François I fled with his mother to take up residence in his château in Romorantin. Not much of the château now exists in this beautiful town – the sub-prefecture occupies the remains – but there are plenty of ancient homes, built of brick and wood, and a number of watermills. Romorantin grew up as an important drapery centre, and the materials for its trade were prepared in the numerous mills along the River Sauldre, one of which was still active until 1970. The **Musée de Sologne** is situated in a couple of these renovated (and built onto) buildings, the **Moulin du Chapitre** and the **Moulin de la Ville**. Once used to mill flour and oil, and for pressing raw materials for fabric, these mills now house an interesting collection dedicated to the life, history and economy of the Sologne, including that of its capital, Romorantin-Lanthenay.

℗ Parking pl. Jean Moulin, in the south, or pl. de la Paix, in the centre.

ℹ️ Musée de Sologne € tel: 02 54 95 33 66; fax: 02 54 95 33 60; www.museedesologne.com. Open Wed–Mon 1000–1200 and 1400–1800, Sun & national hols 1400–1800. Closed Tue.

Musée d'Archéologie € 21 r. de la Pierre; tel: 02 54 76 22 06. Open Jul–Aug except Thur, Sun & national hols 1430–1830; rest of year by appointment.

Espace Automobiles Matra €€ 17 r. des Capucins; tel: 02 54 94 55 55; fax: 02 54 94 55 56. Open Mon & Wed–Fri 0900–1200 and 1400–1800, hols, Sat & Sun 1000–1200 and 1400–1800. Closed 1 Jan, 1 May & 25 Dec.

⌷ Markets Wed all day, Fri am.

Tarte Tatin

The two 19th-century Tatin sisters made culinary history at the Solognot village of Lamotte-Beuvron. They invented (though one wonders if it was by accident) the much-loved French dessert, *tarte Tatin*, in which the standard apple pie is reversed and the caramelised apples appear sitting on their pastry base.

Romorantin's other trump card is its collection of old buildings that line the various arms of the River Sauldre, some still half-timbered and almost all in good condition. The **Musée d'Archéologie** is a must just for its 600-year-old building, the Carroir Doré. Its brick and timber walls are embellished by finely carved wooden columns. St Michael about to stab the dragon is particularly well preserved. The collection (small, as is the building) incorporates finds from the region, including prehistoric tools, Gallo-Roman pottery and medieval locks. Nearby, on an islet encircled by more arms of the river, is the well-kept **Parc Ferdinand Buisson**, a quiet and favourite place for the locals to relax. It backs onto the very elegant 19th-century mansion that now houses the *Mairie*. Lastly, Romorantin-Lanthenay used to be known as the centre of the now defunct Matra car production, a company with close links to Renault (Matra pioneered the *Espace*, for instance, which Renault markets). The **Espace Automobiles Matra**, an exhibition of 50 of Matra's vehicles, including racing, experimental and saloon cars, is open to the public in the old Beaulieu factory once responsible for producing Super 8 movie cameras.

Accommodation and food in Romorantin-Lanthenay

La Pyramide € r. Pyramide; tel: 02 54 76 26 34. Modern and functional but attractively decorated hotel with its own modestly priced restaurant, a short distance from the town centre.

Auberge de Lanthenay €€ pl. de l'Eglise, r. Notre-Dame-du-Lieu (2km from centre); tel: 02 54 76 09 19; fax: 02 54 76 72 91. Closed Christmas and New Year period, first half Jul, Sun pm and Mon. Perennially popular restaurant with gastronomic and local cuisine, and a family-run inn with ten rooms. Good, friendly service. Book early for weekend meals.

Grand Hôtel du Lion d'Or €€€ 69 r. Georges Clemenceau; tel: 02 54 94 15 15; fax: 02 54 88 24 87; www.hotel-liondor.fr. A member of the prestigious *Relais & Châteaux* group, this largely Renaissance mansion has been beautifully converted to a small luxury hotel. Its award-winning gourmet restaurant also has a remarkable selection of fine wines.

The Sologne

The Sologne is a vast area of often-misty ponds, dense heath and extensive forests. Conifers, birches and oaks hide prolific wildlife: indeed, under the Second Empire some 340 châteaux were built for hunting. In those days game was everywhere; today, the area counts just 20 different species of mammal but 200 species of bird. And, in its 3,000-odd ponds, there are carp, tench, pike and perch. It is a haven for nature lovers.

ST-AIGNAN

St-Aignan Tourist Office 60 r. Constant Ragot; tel: 02 54 75 22 85; fax: 02 54 75 50 26; www.tourisme-valdercher-staignan.com. Open Mon–Sat 0930–1230 and 1400–1800, summer Sun 1000–1200 and 1500–1800.

Park in front of the Hôtel de Ville.

In summer there are 90-min cruises on the *Val-du-Cher* from the embarkation point on the Cher. Tel: 02 54 71 40 38.

Below
St-Aignan, view from château

This town is best known for its white lions in the **Zoo Parc de Beauval**, 4km to the south. It is a fine place to visit, especially with children, but the medieval town also has plenty of charm. It is a place to park and walk through its tiny alleys, exploring streets with ancient homes such as the 15th-century, half-timbered house or the Gothic Maison de la Prévôté that was formerly the Palais de Justice. The château is not open to the public but the **Eglise Collégiale de St-Aignan** merits a serious visit. This Romanesque church – one of the Loire region's finest – has superb capitals and a fabulous series of original 11th- to 15th-century frescoes in the choir, in a chapel dedicated to St John, and above all in the crypt, which was the site of its previous church, the Eglise St-Jean. No need for a guide here as, for a small fee, a pre-recorded *son-et-lumière* show lights up and explains each space in turn. The energetic can climb up the bell tower and view medieval St-Aignan from a novel angle. Crowning the skyline is the château – remains of which date back to the 9th and 11th centuries: Foulques Nerra (*see page 98*) took the town in 1030 and remodelled part of the fortified castle. It then became the home of the Ducs de Beauvillier. The views over the River Cher from the far end of the *Cour d'Honneur* are impressive.

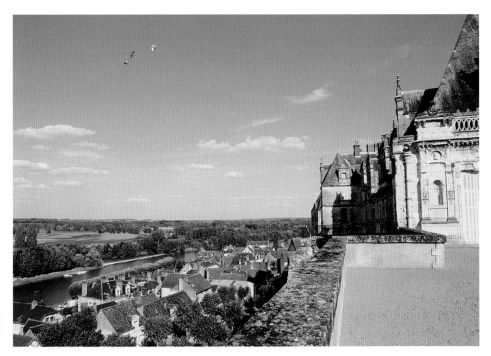

Zoo Parc de Beauval €€ *tel: 02 54 75 50 00; fax: 02 54 75 50 01; www.zoobeauval.com. Open daily 0900–dusk.*

Eglise Collégiale de St-Aignan € *r. Constant. Open 0930–1200 and 1400–1830.*

Market *All day Sat.*

The much-publicised zoo is certainly worth a visit, especially for the young. It was conceived to help conserve endangered species and has evolved into a centre dedicated to research and conservation, offering help and financial assistance in countries requiring conservation measures. Various different climatic environments have been re-created on the 15ha estate, including tropical greenhouses and savanna grasslands. The large collections of cats and primates are a big attraction, but it is interesting to find that they also have over 2,000 birds, many of which are tropical and spectacularly plumed. One of the most delightful and newer aspects of the zoo is the introduction (to the public) of its nursery where abandoned young are bottle-fed and reintegrated as they mature with their respective species.

Accommodation and food in and around St-Aignan

Restaurant Chez Constant € *pl. de la Paix; tel: 02 54 75 10 75. Closed Mon and Tue out of season.* This pleasant restaurant is named after Constant Ragot, the Mayor of St-Aignan. It offers diners a good traditional menu, and friendly service.

Grande Hôtel St-Aignan €–€€ *quai Jean-Jacques Delorme; tel: 02 54 75 18 04; fax: 02 54 75 12 59. Closed part-Feb, part-Nov; out of season Sun, Mon and Tue am.* A pretty, small hotel right on the banks of the Cher offering comfortable rooms and a good restaurant.

Hôtel Le Clos du Cher €€ *2 r. Paul Boncour, Noyers-sur-Cher; tel: 02 54 75 00 03; fax: 02 54 75 03 79; www.closducher.com. Closed Wed pm and Thur out of season.* Located in parkland, this restored 18th-century home has been converted into a comfortable small hotel. There is also a restaurant offering regional menus.

SELLES-SUR-CHER

Selles-sur-Cher Tourist Office *28 r. de Sion; tel/fax: 02 54 95 25 44; www.mairie-selles-sur-cher.fr. Open Oct–Apr Mon 1430–1800, Tue, Wed & Fri 1000–1230 and 1430–1800, Thur & Sat 0900–1230 (Sat pm 1400–1800); May–Sept Mon 1500–1900, Tue–Fri 1000–1230 and 1500–1900, Sat 1000–1800.*

Market *Thur all day.*

It is a pity that you can't visit the Renaissance château at Selles-sur-Cher, for its impressive profile reflecting in the waters of the Cher hints at a once-grandiose past. Content yourselves with the Eglise St-Eusice. This Merovingian church dates back some 1,500 years (have a look at the ancient 6th-century sarcophagus containing the remains of St Eusice in the crypt, and the paintings in the apse depicting his life), though much of its form shows its 13th- to 16th-century remodelling.

Accommodation and food in Selles-sur-Cher

Le Lion d'Or €–€€ *14 pl. de la Paix; tel: 02 54 97 40 83; fax: 02 54 97 78 36.* This staging point has been feeding travellers since 1664 and, although its interior is modern, it is still a favourite rendezvous. Apart from the restaurant, it also has five bedrooms.

Right
Selles-sur-Cher church façade

Selles-sur-Cher cheeses

Selles-sur-Cher is known for its soft, round goat's cheese, which has its own *appellation contrôlée*. Round or cylindrical, rolled in herbs or left to mature on its own, it is one of the fine cheeses from the Sologne area. For more cheesy know-how and the chance to sample local produce, visit the *Fromagerie P Jacquin & Fils €, off the D956 (between Selles-sur-Cher and Valençay), tel: 02 54 95 30 60; fax: 02 54 97 47 46. Open by appointment only Feb–Oct daily except Sun & national hols 0900–1100, min 5 people.*

Suggested tour

Comité Départemental du Tourisme de Loir-et-Cher *5 r. de la Voûte du Château, Blois; tel: 02 54 57 00 41; fax: 02 54 57 00 47; www.tourismeloir-et-cher. com. Open 0900–1300 and 1400–1700.*

W *www.chambordcountry. com*

Overleaf
Selles-sur-Cher

Total distance: About 165km.

Time: Allow 2–3 days. The distances are not particularly great but there are so many interesting sights that it's impossible to do them justice in less than 2 days.

Links: From Montrichard, the D176 heads westwards to Chenonceaux on the Grands Châteaux: Tours–Blois route (*see page 52*). Were you to travel 20km south from Valençay to Levroux, you'd link up with the Berry route (*see page 268*), while at Bracieux the D120 leads straight to Chambord, on the Blois–Orléans route (*see page 228*).

Route: Leaving **Blois** (*see page 202*) by the southbound D956, it is just 8km to the small village of Cellettes. Turn first left, following the signs for **BEAUREGARD ❶**. It's just a short road through the corn fields to the château. Leave by the same route into Cellettes and drive through

La Magnanerie €€
4 chemin de la Croix-
Bardin, Bourré; tel: 02 54 32
63 91. Open Apr–Aug daily
except Tue, guided visits at
1100, 1500, 1600 & 1700;
Sept–Nov Thur–Mon 1500,
1600 & 1700. Raising silk
worms.

La Ville Souterraine €€
40 route des Roches, Bourré;
tel: 02 54 32 95 33; fax: 02
54 32 56 09. Open Palm
Sunday–mid-Nov daily
1000–1800. Champagne-
style wine cellars,
mushroom cellars and
troglodyte village.

Musée Archéologique
€€ Mairie de Thésée-la-
Romaine; tel: 02 54 71 00
88. Open Jul–Sept daily
except Tue 1400–1830
(1800 Sat).

**Restaurant-Hôtel
de l'Ecole €–€€**
12 route de Montrichard,
Pontlevoy; tel: 02 54 32 50
30; fax: 02 54 32 33 58. A
handsome-looking small
hotel with an elegant
restaurant, La Closerie, and
garden dining in fine
weather. Personalised
service and warm welcome.

**Hostellerie du Moulin
de la Renne €€** 11 route de
Vierzon, Thésée-la-Romaine;
tel: 02 54 71 41 56; fax: 02
54 71 75 09. Closed mid-
Jan–mid-Mar, Sun pm & Mon
out of season. A small hotel
just behind the old
watermill, on the D176
road towards Noyers-sur-
Cher. Traditional restaurant
decorated in rustic style.
Pleasant gardens.

the village, branching off to the left on the D77 signposted to Bracieux and **CHEVERNY ❷**. The nearby town (1km) of **Cour-Cheverny**, on the D765, is a better bet for a hotel and for dining. Leaving the château at Cheverny, make for the D52 and turn left at the junction. It is just 1km to the turning marked **TROUSSAY ❸**.

You pick up the D52 again leaving Troussay and head southwest towards Sambin, arriving in the pretty town of **FOUGERES-SUR-BIEVRE ❹**. Its large, fortified château is on the left, just across the River Bièvre. Continue along the D52 to Sambin and turn left on to the D764 in the direction of **Pontlevoy**. The vast and impressive Abbaye de Pontlevoy has been renovated to become the EACIEA (European American Center for International Education Association), a cross-cultural educational institute. It is a pleasant place to stop and stroll. There is an interesting open-air exhibition of sepia photographs placed strategically around town, showing how Pontlevoy looked a century ago. Take the D85, marked to Monthou-sur-Cher, and turn in the direction of the signposted **LE GUE-PEAN ❺**.

The small road back to the River Cher, via Monthou, comes to **Thésée-la-Romaine**. This pleasant town was once an important Gallo-Roman site. Renowned for its pottery, it has a remarkable small museum with archaeological finds from this era and the remains of its 2nd-century town walls; it is also known for its troglodyte homes. From Thésée, take the bridge across the river, marked to Pouillé. The D17 follows the Cher and takes you towards **ST-AIGNAN ❻**, crowned by its château. It is a pleasant run eastwards along the D17. There is a historic dovecote on the right side of the road, at Le Colombier, just short of Couffy. The D33A and the D33, to the south of **Meusnes**, follow the small River Modon. At Villentrois you take a left on to the D37, which passes through the thick **Forêt de Gâtiné** before joining the D956 at **VALENCAY ❼**. The straight D956 heads for the Cher, and the town of **SELLES-SUR-CHER ❽**. Take the exit road from the north of Selles to the highway, N76, and turn eastwards. This will bring you to the capital of the Sologne, **ROMORANTIN-LANTHENAY ❾**. Leave Romorantin by the D59, which is marked to Gy-en-Sologne, and then turn on to the D20 in the direction of Lassay-sur-Croisne where the moated **CHATEAU DU MOULIN ❿** is located just 1km away.

The D20 goes to **Mur-de-Sologne**, a little town in the heart of this flat area. Continue onwards on the D63 via **Courmemin**, where you turn on to the D120 to **Fontaines-en-Sologne** and stay on the road to **Bracieux**. This town is known for little else than its highly rated restaurant, one of the region's best. At the junction just before the town, take the D102A to Arian, for just over the River Beuvron is the château of **VILLESAVIN ⓫**. The simplest way back to Blois is to pick up the D102 and head for Cour-Cheverny, turning right at the main junction on to the D765.

Cher and the Sologne

Blois–Orléans

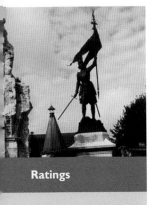

Ratings

Châteaux	●●●●●
History	●●●●●
Entertainment	●●●●○
Activities	●●●○○
Museums	●●●○○
Wine tasting	●●●○○
Children	●●○○○
Scenery	●●○○○

At Orléans, the Loire has turned west to face the sea, and opens out to create a region of cultivation and plenty in the broad river plain. It is also a region of heath and forest, once preserved as hunting lands for the nobility. As it continues downstream, the river valley carves into the soft rock of the Beauce plateau on the north bank, and forms fertile meadows from sandy alluvial deposits on the south bank. The Loire itself is often seen only from afar. Much of the history of France has been made on this stretch of the valley. At Blois Joan of Arc had her standard blessed, and from there rode with her men to force the English to retreat from Orléans. So began their withdrawal from the whole of France. Later, as the kings of France moved restlessly from château to château, they often travelled with more than 10,000 people to Chambord and Blois.

BEAUGENCY

ℹ Beaugency Tourist Office 3 pl. Dr Hyvernaud (or pl. de l'Hôtel de Ville); tel: 02 38 44 54 42; fax: 02 38 46 45 31; email: tourisme.beaugency@wanadoo.fr. Open daily.

Ⓟ It is difficult to drive or park in the town. It's easier to park by the riverside and walk.

It is best to approach Beaugency from the south, on the old bridge. The long, narrow, medieval stone structure that crosses the Loire, with its irregular arches and humped not in the middle but closer to the north bank, has determined much of the little town's history. When Loire bridges were few, they had great strategic importance. During the Hundred Years War Beaugency was frequently besieged, changing hands between English and French forces four times. In 1429, when Joan of Arc was marching from Blois to Orléans, she wanted to cross the river at Beaugency but was unable to do so because English soldiers held the bridge. Having driven the English from Orléans, she returned to Beaugency and defeated them here, too. Little more than a century later, the town and its bridge were again the focus of fighting, between Catholics and Protestants. In 19th- and 20th-century wars Beaugency's bridge was also fiercely contested. The present structure is believed to date mainly from the 12th and 14th centuries.

France

Blois–
Orléans

Sancheville
Bonneval
Allaines-
Mervilliers
Janville   Toury
D2020
D107
D927
Bazoches-les-
Gallerandes
Orgères-
en-Beauce
Loigny-la-
Bataille
A10
E05
Aschères-
le-Marché
D927   D955   D927   Harville
Terminiers
Artenay
A19
D935
Neuville-
aux-Bois
D144
Châteaudun
Patay
D5
Chevilly
Cloyes-sur-
le-Loir
Niverville
D955
Orléanais
N20
D97
La Ferté-Villeneuil
Saran
Fleury-les-
Aubrais
D925
N10
Epieds-
en-Beauce
D3
St-Jean-
de-Braye
D924
Ouzouer-
le-Marché
Ingré
Morée
Coulmiers
St-Jean-de-la-Buelle
ORLEANS
D357
Binas
La Chapelle-St-Mesmin
St-Ay
Olivet
Marchenoir
D917
Meung-
sur-Loire
Sandillon
Oucques
Josnes
Cléry-St-André
N20
CENTRE
Beaugency
Marcilly-
en-Villette
A10
Château de Talcy
Lailly-en-Val
N152
D103
D921
Jouy-le-Potier
La Forêt-
St-Aubin
D924
Mer
St-Laurent-Nouan
Suèvres
D951
Ligny-
le-Ribault
D957
D2152
Cosson
A71
Muides-
sur-Loire
La Ferté-St-Cyr
E09
Menars
E05/E60
D922
Herbault
La Chaussée-
St-Victor
Chambord
Lamotte-Beauvron
D766
BLOIS
D925
D923
St-Gervais-la-Forêt
Vineuil
Château de
Villesavin
Bracieux
Nouan-le-Fuzelier
Chouzy-
sur-Cisse
Château de
Beauregard
Onzain
Cour-
Cheverny
Fontaines
Neung-sur-
Beuvron
D923
D751
Cellettes
Château de Troussay
Château de
Cheverny
Marcilly-
en-Gault
N152
Chaumont-
sur-Loire
D765
D120
D13
D922
Sambin
Fougères-
sur-Bièvre
D956
Soings-en-
Sologne
Contres
D63
Mur-de-Sologne
D764
Pontlevoy
Romorantin-
Lanthenay
D956
A89
Château du
Gué-Péan
D675
Montrichard
Chémery
Château du
Moulin
D20
D59

Blois–Orléans
0   10km
0   5 miles

Attraction
City
Large Town
Small Town
POI
Motorway
Main Road
Minor Road
Railway

N

Château Dunois and Musée des Arts et Traditions de l'Orléanais €€ *pl. Dunois; no phone. Open Wed–Mon 1000–1100 and 1400–1700 (1600 in winter).*

Markets *All day Sat. Big annual markets fill the streets on 1 May, third Sun in Jun, and (wine and gastronomy fair) third Sun in Sept.*

Summer events There is a programme of concerts, cultural events and *son-et-lumière* every summer – contact the tourist office for details.

Attractive cobbled streets and lanes, lined with old stone and timber houses, rise away from the river to the main square with its Renaissance town hall at the top of the town. A few paces higher up, Tour de l'Horloge is a remnant of medieval ramparts. Among pretty, smaller squares, pl. St-Firmin (together with pl. Dunois) has two huge towers – one is all that survives of a 15th-century church, the other, called Caesar's Tower, was a keep that formed part of the 11th-century fortifications. Old street lamps give the squares a special charm after dark.

Lower down, the **Château Dunois** was converted in the 15th century from a small fortress into a luxurious mansion. Heavily restored, and with an interesting medieval garden at the back, it now contains the **Musée des Arts et Traditions de l'Orléanais**. This small museum of local culture and history has an eclectic assortment of furnishings, dolls and toys, and material on local celebrities. Alongside it, the **Eglise Notre-Dame** is a restored 11th-century Romanesque abbey church.

The devil's bridge

The legend has long been told in Beaugency, in song and in rhyme, of how it was the devil who first built the town's ancient bridge across the Loire. He built it in a single night, without the use of any tools, on condition that he could have and keep the first soul that crossed it. The wily folk of Beaugency agreed – and pushed a cat on to the bridge before anyone else. The cat ran across, too fast and too agile to be caught even by the devil.

Below
Vieux Beaugency

Accommodation and food in Beaugency

Hostellerie de l'Ecu de Bretagne €–€€ *5 r. de la Maille d'Or; tel: 02 38 44 67 60; fax: 02 38 44 68 07; www.ecudebretagne.fr.* A long, low coaching inn just off the (quiet) main square, this atmospheric, creaky old 2-star hotel (dating from the 17th century) and excellent restaurant provide a very enjoyable stay at a modest price. The imaginative three-course set lunch menu is a bargain.

The Joan of Arc story

A focus for French nationalism, reverence for Joan of Arc reaches its height at Blois and Orléans. The main street of Orléans bears her name and a large equestrian statue of her stands in the centre of the main square. The cathedral has modern stained-glass windows devoted to her. Every year, on 7–8 May, the city celebrates its liberation by Joan of Arc.

Jeanne d'Arc was born to a peasant family in Domrémy, in northern France, in 1412. At the age of 17, while tending sheep, she began hearing voices, which she believed to be those of Saints Catherine and Michael. They told her that she would drive the English out of France (the Hundred Years War had been waging since 1337) and that the uncrowned king of France, Charles VII, would be crowned king in Reims. The English were at that moment besieging Orléans and looked likely to take the whole of France.

With six male companions, Joan set off to the Loire Valley, arriving on 6 March 1429 at Chinon, where Charles was residing. She asked to be given an audience with him, and was admitted to the château. Although Charles was mixing with courtiers in the Great Hall, and not wearing royal robes, Joan identified him immediately and told him of the prophesy. She was taken to a religious court in Poitiers to determine whether she was inspired by the devil. The court came to the conclusion that she was inspired by God, and she was taken to Tours to be provided with armour and troops. On 29 April, marching east from Blois, where her standard had been ritually blessed, she arrived at Orléans, its citizens starving and demoralised after the long siege. Opposed by the town's officials, who tried to prevent her, Joan so roused the local people that they were able to expel the English forces the following week, on 7 and 8 May. Joan went on to defeat the English at Jargeau, Beaugency and Patay. On 1 July she accompanied Charles to Reims for his coronation.

Joan was then captured by Burgundians, allies of the English, to whom she was handed over. English authorities sentenced her to death by burning, carried out in Rouen in 1431. But the English were now retreating and, by 1453, they had been driven from France. Joan of Arc was finally made a saint in 1920.

CHAMBORD

ℹ Chambord Tourist Office *pl. St Louis; tel: 02 54 33 39 16.*

Ⓦ *www.chambord.org (the official site of the château and forest of Chambord); http:// whc.unesco.org/en/list/933 (UNESCO's Loire Valley pages).*

Ⓟ Château de Chambord €€–€€€ *tel: 02 54 50 40 00; fax: 02 54 20 34 69. Open daily Apr–Sept 0900–1815 (1915 for part of Jul–Aug), Oct– Mar 0900–1715. Last entry 30min before château closes. Closed 1 Jan, 1 May & 25 Dec.*

☉ Entertainment at the château *Le Cheval Roi (equestrian display) – May–Sept daily 1145; Son-et-Lumière (the colourful show Chambord, Rêve de Lumières) – Jun–Sept evenings. To book for these events, or for more information, tel: 02 54 50 40 00, or see the website: www.chambord.org*

More than any other château, Chambord is fit for a king. Enclosed by a vast private oak forest, the pale castle is itself gigantic, and covered with a huge black roof of wild, fantastic complexity. The sheer monumental madness of its grandeur and size seems to convey what it was to be monarch in 16th-century France. Construction of the **Château de Chambord** began in 1519, and took 15 years, thousands of men being employed on the site. It is entirely Renaissance in style. Erected for François I, it became his favourite château – even though he stayed there only 40 nights during 15 years. The building is three storeys high, and consists of a simple rectangular outer structure with round towers at each corner, and a massive square keep on the north-west side, also with towers.

Inside the château, everything is huge. Rising up through the centre of the keep is the vast *Escalier à Double Revolution*, an astounding idea, believed to be the work of Leonardo da Vinci, who was working for François I at the time. Two staircases in one (one above the other), it is so arranged that two people may use it at the same time without meeting. However, side openings would allow them to converse.

In the keep and the rest of the château, only about 80 rooms – a small proportion of the total – are open to the public. Though sparsely furnished, they are lavish enough in decoration and size to give an intriguing glimpse into château life.

On the first floor the *Chambre du Comte de Chambord* contains a large, draped four-poster bed, under a ceiling of massive timbers, and a floor patterned with wood tiles. The *Chambre aux Lauriers Roses* shows the 18th-century move towards greater decoration, refinement and comfort. The Royal Apartments of the 17th century are decorated with

Right
Château de Chambord reflected in its moat

Overleaf
Château de Chambord

huge tapestries. The *Chambre du Roi*, installed in 1681 for Louis XIV, is rich in sculpted, gilded wood and plasterwork. In contrast, the delicate *Chambre de la Reine* is decorated entirely in blue fabric, covering walls, ceiling and furniture. The *Chambre du Roi* in the François I apartments is heavy with red and gold fabrics, and a massive fireplace is still in use.

On the second floor vaulted stone ceilings covered with carved coffers depicting royal emblems – notably the salamander and the letter F, both symbols of François I – are impressive. On that floor a group of rooms is devoted to a **Museum of Hunting and Nature**. The central staircase climbs to the roof, where the profusion of windows and turrets resembles a lofty village with fine views over the parkland, the River Cosson and the dark forest concealing game and wildlife. There is also a village of about 50 houses within the forest.

With 440 rooms, Château de Chambord is the largest of the Loire castles. Its estate of 5,440ha is the most expensive in Europe, and it is enclosed by the longest wall in France – 31km – which took from 1542 until 1645 to construct.

Accommodation and food in Chambord

There are several popular eating places just outside the château.

Hôtel du Grand Saint-Michel €€ *pl. St Louis; tel: 02 54 20 31 31; fax: 02 54 20 36 40; www.saintmichel-chambord.com.* Ideally situated just opposite the château entrance, yet moderately priced, this family-run 2-star hotel has comfortable rooms (three with views of the château) and a good restaurant with affordable menus. After the château is closed and the visitors gone, everything is entirely peaceful. Book months ahead.

Visiting the château

It is best to arrive early at the château. A visit takes about 2hr. Long queues build up during the day, and the building becomes more and more crowded. Tours in English are at 1100 daily (taking 1½–2hr); audioguides are available for a 1½hr self-guided tour. Also available is a *tour ludique* – a 1hr tour 'led by a personality from the past'.

Château de Talcy

In a rural setting, behind a sober and dignified exterior, Talcy turns out to be one of the most comfortable and appealing of all the region's châteaux. It is richly decorated and furnished, mainly in Renaissance style but with a pleasing degree of restraint. Most notable are several medieval tapestries. A 16th-century kitchen also survives. Outside are attractive gardens, outbuildings and two courtyards. The first courtyard is galleried and has an old well, while the second has an extraordinarily large dovecote with 1,500 pigeon-holes. There is a huge 300-year-old winepress, too, still in working order and able to fill 10 barrels in a single pressing. The château has the air of a grand farmhouse.

It was purchased in 1520 by a well-to-do Florentine financier, Bernardo Salviati, who had the castle rebuilt in its present style. His daughter, Cassandre, when only 15, was the inspiration for Pierre de Ronsard's series of sonnets *Les Amours de Cassandre*, written over a 10-year period.

Château de Talcy €€ *tel: 02 54 81 03 01; email: talcy@ chateauxcountry.com. Open Apr–Sept daily 0930–1200 and 1400–1800 (no midday closing Jul–Aug), rest of year Wed–Mon 1000–1200 and 1400–1630. Closed national hols.*

Festivals and events The château is the setting for summer concerts and a literary festival in May. Contact the château for details.

Market At Mer, Thur pm.

CLÉRY-ST-ANDRÉ

ℹ Cléry-St-André Tourist Office *111 r. du Maréchal Foch; tel: 02 38 45 94 33; fax: 02 38 45 94 33; email: o-tourismedeclery@wanadoo.fr; www.clery-saint-andre.com. Open 0930–1230 and 1430–1800.*

🏛 Basilica € *tel: 02 38 45 70 05. Open daily (Apr–Nov guided tours pm).*

🛒 Market *Sat am.*

⚑ Events *Son-et-Lumière – end Jul; pilgrimage of Notre-Dame de Cléry, with other events on the same day – 8 Sept.*

The simple village is dominated by its large Flamboyant Gothic **basilica** dedicated to the much-venerated Notre-Dame de Cléry. In 1280 a local peasant ploughed up ancient pottery shards, bones and other relics, including a figurine in female form that was promptly hailed as a miraculous appearance of the Virgin. Placed in a church, the statue attracted many pilgrims, and Notre-Dame de Cléry became a stop on the route to the shrine of Santiago de Compostela. The original Cléry church was destroyed by English soldiers as they passed through on their way to Orléans in 1428; a single tower that survived is incorporated into the present building. Dunois, the companion at arms of Joan of Arc, began the reconstruction of the church. Louis XI – who had vowed to give his weight in silver to Cléry if he were victorious in the siege of Dieppe, and kept his vow – continued the work of building the Gothic basilica (it was completed under his son Charles VIII). Louis formed a close attachment to Cléry: he used to visit the church, going up the spiral staircase to a private oratory from which he could follow the service and, at his own wish, was buried there. His tomb, together with the statue of Our Lady of Cléry, was destroyed by Protestants in 1563. The wooden statue of the Virgin now over the altar is a later replacement, and the marble of Louis XI kneeling before her was made by Michel Bourdin in 1622. The rest of the king's tomb was a 19th-century addition. In vaults below it are the remains of Louis and his wife, except for their two skulls, which are in a glass case; on the other side of the nave is buried the heart of Charles VIII. A separate highly ornate Gothic chapel is dedicated to St James, while another houses the Dunois family vaults. Across the road from the basilica is the house where Louis XI used to stay while in Cléry.

MEUNG-SUR-LOIRE

ℹ Meung-sur-Loire Tourist Office *Moulin Massot, 7 r. des Mauves; tel: 02 38 44 32 28; fax: 02 38 44 72 22; email: infos@visitez-meung.com; www.visitez-meung.com. Open summer daily (closed Sun pm), winter Mon pm–Sat. Free 1hr guided tours of the town are bookable at the tourist office.*

Penetrate the outskirts of this little town to reach the picturesque old riverside village at its heart. A stream, the Mauves, runs through the middle, with several old mills alongside (mostly now converted into apartments or houses). In the village centre there's a market square and a fine covered market with a timber-framed roof. The village has a large Romanesque and early Gothic church, and a large **château**, standing in a park at the foot of the village.

The château, from the 12th to the 18th century the residence of the bishops of Orléans, is still occupied. Much updated over the years, it preserves almost every style, ranging from remnants of its medieval entrance to 19th-century interiors. It contains priceless furniture, some of it 14th century, and several Aubusson and Flemish tapestries. Beneath the building's oldest section there is a surprising underground chapel. Also hidden below the castle are dungeons and torture

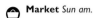

Château €€ *tel: 02 38 44 36 47; fax: 02 38 44 29 37; email: contact@chateaudemeung. com; www.chateaudemeung. com. Open daily 1000–1200 and 1400–1900. Guided visits available.*

Market *Sun am.*

chambers, and in the grounds is the *oubliette* where the bishops of Orléans confined prisoners on a starvation diet until they did indeed die of starvation (as bishops, they felt it would be unchristian actually to sentence people to death). The *oubliette* was in the form of a deep well; prisoners were lowered down by rope on to a dark ledge, where they had to remain in the blackness, hoping that they would not fall off. A small amount of bread and water was lowered once a day – the same amount no matter how many prisoners were inside – and prisoners remained there until they died. Among the few ever to be brought out alive was the poet François Villon, known for his crimes of burglary and violence as well as for tender lyric verse. As Louis XI was passing through the town, he was told that the popular poet was in the *oubliette*, and ordered him to be released.

Accommodation and food in Meung-sur-Loire

Auberge St Jacques €–€€ *60 r. Gén. de Gaulle; tel: 02 38 44 30 39; fax: 02 38 45 17 02.* It is claimed that the musketeer d'Artagnan lodged at this simple, inexpensive 2-star hotel on the main N152. Rooms are adequately equipped (although can be noisy on the main road side) and there is a good restaurant.

Suggested tour

Total distance: 65km, and a detour of 45km.

Time: The driving will take under 2 hours, but allow most of a day for the sightseeing.

Links: At Blois (*see page 202*) this route connects with the Grands Châteaux: Tours–Blois tour (*see page 52*), and at Orléans (*see page 240*) with that of the Upper Reaches (*see page 248*).

Route: Start out from **Blois** by crossing to the south side of the river on the main ring road and following signs, via Vineuil, to **CHAMBORD ❶**. The road follows the little River Cosson. Access to the château is on the private roads through the extensive, pretty woodland of the Parc de Chambord and Forêt de Boulogne. On leaving the château, follow signs to Orléans but, on reaching a junction where it is straight on for Orléans and left for Muides-sur-Loire, take the left. This road – from Chambord to Muides – is called the *Route François I*. Today, the cooling towers of a nearby riverside nuclear power station, steam clouds streaming into the sky, dominate the view.

Detour: At Muides continue over the Loire into **Mer**. From Mer, turn back towards Blois on the N152 to visit the **Château de Ménars**, a grand 17th- and 18th-century riverside palace that became one of the

W *www.chambordcountry.* *com* (website of the Loir-et-Cher *département*, with packages and special offers. English and French); *www.loiret.com* (for the Loiret *département,*. magazine-style, full of information and news. French only).

The *autoroute* A10 (from Paris) and the N152 on the north bank, and the quieter D951 on the south bank, give access to Blois and Orléans and all points in between. There is a frequent rail service from Paris direct to Orléans and Blois. Local trains also run along the valley between the two towns.

homes of Madame de Pompadour, the mistress of Louis XV. It has beautiful gardens. Returning to Mer, turn north, away from the river, on the rose-lined road to the **CHATEAU DE TALCY ❷**. Return to Mer, and back over the river to Muides (*end of detour*).

From Muides, turn towards Orléans on the D951, the main south bank road. It would be equally possible to continue on the north bank – the drive is not very interesting on either side of the river – but the south bank gives a much better approach into **BEAUGENCY ❸**, which is entered by crossing the town's old bridge. Continue on the north bank to **MEUNG-SUR-LOIRE ❹**. From here, cross the Loire again, on the little suspension bridge, to **CLERY-ST-ANDRE ❺**. Stay on the D951 to Orléans.

Right
Boulangerie in
Meung-sur-Loire

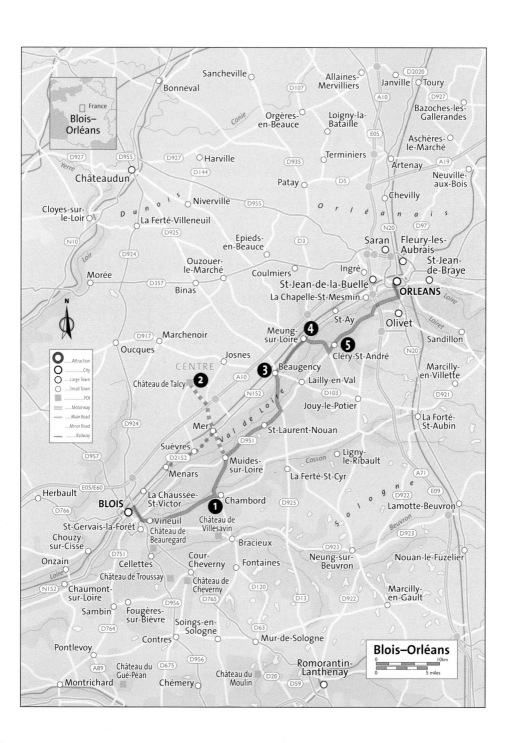

Blois–
Orléans

France

Sancheville

Bonneval

Allaines-
Mervilliers

Janville Toury

D2020

A10

D927

Bazoches-les-
Gallerandes

Conie

Orgères-
en-Beauce

Loigny-la-
Bataille

D107

E05

Aschères-
le-Marché

D927

D955

D927

Harville

Terminiers

Artenay

A19

Neuville-
aux-Bois

Yerre

D144

D935

Châteaudun

Patay

D5

Chevilly

Orléanais

Cloyes-sur-
le-Loir

Niverville

D955

N20

D97

La Ferté-Villeneuil

Dunois

D925

Epieds-
en-Beauce

D3

Saran

Fleury-les-
Aubrais

St-Jean-
de-Braye

N10

Ouzouer-
le-Marché

Coulmiers

Ingré

Loir

D924

Morée

D357

Binas

St-Jean-de-la-Buelle

La Chapelle-St-Mesmin

ORLEANS

Loire

N

St-Ay

Olivet

Loiret

Marchenoir

Meung-
sur-Loire

4

Sandillon

D917

 Oucques

Josnes

5

Cléry-St-André

N20

Marcilly-
en-Villette

Attraction

CENTRE

A10

3

Beaugency

D921

City

Château de Talcy

2

Lailly-en-Val

Large Town

N152

D103

Small Town

Jouy-le-Potier

POI

Val de Loire

Mer

St-Laurent-Nouan

La Forté-
St-Aubin

Motorway

D924

Main Road

Suèvres

D951

Minor Road

D957

D2152

Muides-
sur-Loire

Cosson

Ligny-
le-Ribault

Railway

Menars

La Ferté-St-Cyr

A71

Herbault

E05/E60

La Chaussée-
St-Victor

Chambord

D925

D922

E09

Lamotte-Beauvron

BLOIS

1

D766

St-Gervais-la-Forêt

Vineuil

Château de
Villesavin

Beuvron

D923

Chouzy-
sur-Cisse

Château de
Beauregard

Bracieux

Sologne

Nouan-le-Fuzelier

Onzain

D751

Cellettes

Cour-
Cheverny

Fontaines

Neung-sur-
Beuvron

D923

Loire

N152

Chaumont-
sur-Loire

Château de Troussay

Château de
Cheverny

D120

D13

D922

Marcilly-
en-Gault

Sambin

Fougères-
sur-Bièvre

D956

D765

Soings-en-
Sologne

Pontlevoy

D764

Contres

D63

Mur-de-Sologne

Blois–Orléans

D956

A89

Château du
Gué-Péan

D675

10km

Montrichard

Chémery

Château du
Moulin

D20

D59

Romorantin-
Lanthenay

5 miles

Orléans

Ratings

Architecture ●●●●●

History ●●●●●

Entertainment ●●●●○

Gardens ●●●●○

Restaurants ●●●●○

Museums ●●●○○

Children ●●○○○

Wine tasting ●○○○○

Orléans stands on the north bank of the Loire, at the most northerly point of the river's course, and is the nearest Loire Valley town to Paris. This positioning once gave it great commercial and strategic importance. An ancient, royal city, it has now become large and industrial. Its name is synonymous with Joan of Arc, the 'Maid of Orléans', object of fervent adoration since she was beatified in 1905. Although her only visit here lasted just a matter of days, the pivotal events of her patriotic mission occurred here. The superb cathedral at the heart of Orléans has become inescapably associated with her. The cathedral quarter and the area around the main square, pl. du Martroi, are majestic with fine avenues. There's a huge municipal renewal project under way. Restoration of some of the town's many Renaissance houses is continuing, as is work on the older neighbourhood between the cathedral and the riverside. The railway station is being spectacularly rebuilt, while already up and running is a modern tram system through the centre of Orléans. The city of Orléans, with its suburbs, has a population of about 270,000, of whom 27 per cent are under 20.

Getting there and getting around

ℹ **Orléans Tourist Office** 2 pl. de l'Etape; tel: 02 38 24 05 05; fax: 02 38 54 49 84; email: infos@tourisme-orleans.com; www.tourisme-orleans.com. Open all year Tue 1000–1300 and 1400–1800, Wed–Sat 0930–1300 and 1400–1800, except 1 Jan, 1 May, 1 Nov, 11 Nov & 25 Dec.

The tourist office organises free guided tours of the town.

By road
The main roads into Orléans are *autoroutes* A10 (Paris, Orléans, Tours, Bordeaux), A71 (Orléans–Clermont-Ferrand), N152 and N20. On reaching the town on the Loire's north bank, traffic is fed on to a ring road of boulevards. Take any turn for *Centre Ville*.

By rail
At least 40 trains run daily from Paris to Orléans, taking about one hour. Other rail services run to the city from towns throughout the region. For rail information, *tel: 08 36 35 35 35*.

Driving and parking
Driving and parking are difficult in the town centre. There are many one-way streets. Parking areas are small, and usually full. There is parking on some of the boulevards surrounding the centre, especially

Orléans

Below
Joan of Arc window showing
Joan leading the troops,
Cathédrale Ste-Croix

blvd Alexandre Martin, north of the cathedral. The underground car park at Campo Santo is convenient for the city centre. Other town-centre car parks include St-Pierre Lentin, just behind the south side of the cathedral, and Châtelet, at the covered market near Pont George V.

Getting around town

The old central area is small and easily accessible on foot. For longer journeys, consider using the bus or tram. For local transport information contact:

Semtao *tel: 0800 012000 (free); www.semtao.fr*
Gare Routière *2 r. Marcel Proust; tel: 02 38 53 94 75.*

Sights

Campo Santo

Just north of the cathedral, this 12th-century cemetery – known as the Martroi-aux-Corps until 1912 – is now a tranquil garden edged with elegant 16th-century arcades, entered by a Renaissance portal. It ceased being used for burials over 200 years ago, and today, the stonework beautifully renovated, it is the setting for many cultural events.

Cathédrale Ste-Croix

Quite apart from its pale and ornate façade, and its two curious circular towers (popularly likened to a wedding cake decoration), most striking of all about the cathedral in Orléans is its grandiose 19th-century setting. A broad and handsome avenue in pale stone leads straight to the imposing west front, with an immense parvis in front of the building. Everything seems filled with light, space and majesty.

The town appears to revolve around the cathedral. Main streets converge on the building, and the administrative offices of the town and the *département*, as well as its Conservatoire de Musique and Musée des Beaux-Arts, are all around the cathedral square.

The architecture of the cathedral is a testament to the enduring appeal of the Gothic style. Although begun in the 13th century, at the height of the Gothic period, the construction continued over several centuries, and even into the 19th century – but all the work was done according to the original Gothic design. Almost all of the interior decorative work, seemingly medieval, was added in the 19th century. A series of ten stained-glass windows deals with the life of Joan of Arc. A new window devoted to her was added in the year 2000. Fine woodcarvings in the choir were a gift to Orléans from Louis XIV, the 'Sun

Festivals and events

Festivals and events *Grande Brocante* – big annual street market, 5–6 May; *Fêtes Johanniques* – celebrating the liberation of Orléans by Joan of Arc, 7–8 May; *Orléans Jazz* – international jazz festival, usually held in Jun.

Campo Santo € *r. Fernand Rabier; for phone enquiries call tourist office. Open Oct–Mar daily 0800–1730, rest of year 0730–2000.*

Cathédrale Ste-Croix € *pl. Ste-Croix; for phone enquiries call tourist office. Open daily 0915–1200 and 1415–1700 (later closing in summer).*

Eglise St-Aignan € *r. Neuve St-Aignan; for phone enquiries call tourist office. Open Jul–Aug 1400–1800. May also be open in Sept.*

Hôtel Groslot € *pl. de l'Etape. Open daily 0900–1800.*

Groslot Gardens € *Entrance in r. d'Escures. Open Oct–Mar 0800–1730, rest of year 0730–2000.*

Maison Jeanne d'Arc € *3 pl. du Gén. de Gaulle; tel: 02 38 52 99 89; fax: 02 38 79 20 82; www.jeannedarc.com.fr. Open May–Oct Tue–Sun 1000–1215 and 1330–1800, rest of year pm only.*

Musée Historique et Archéologique € *pl. de l'Abbé Desnoyers; tel: 02 38 79 25 60. Open Oct–Apr Wed, Sat & Sun 1400–1800, May, Jun, Sept Tue & Sun only 1400–1800, Jul–Aug Tue–Sun 1000–1215 and 1330–1800 (Sun pm only).*

King'. In his honour, the rose windows in the transept have a radiant sun design.

Outside the cathedral on the north side, some remnants of the town's 4th-century ramparts have been uncovered.

Eglise St-Aignan

One thousand years before Joan of Arc saved Orléans from the English, Aignan saved it from the Huns. He, too, became the object of intense reverence and was made the city's patron saint. The Gothic church dedicated to him is now much damaged, but the 11th-century Romanesque crypt is well preserved. It resembles a church in its own right. Some of its capitals have preserved the original colour with which they were painted in 1029. The crypt contains bones believed to be those of Aignan.

Hôtel Groslot

Set back within a courtyard, almost opposite the cathedral, stands this red-brick Renaissance masterpiece erected in 1550 by Jacques Groslot. It became the principal residence of royalty in Orléans: François II died while staying here, and Charles IX, Henri III and Henri IV all had periods of residence here. After the Revolution the mansion became the town hall, and remained so until the 1960s. It was extensively refurbished in the 19th century. Now open to the public, Hôtel Groslot not only gives a good insight into the extravagance of 19th-century French décor, it has also become a popular place for the town's grandest weddings and receptions. The Grand Salon d'Honneur is lavishly decorated, with gilded coloured walls, decorative coffered ceiling and chandeliers. The Council Chamber is especially richly decorated. The charming **gardens** are also open to the public.

Maison Jeanne d'Arc

This is a picture-perfect medieval house of brick and timber. Joan of Arc spent ten days in Orléans, in May 1429, lodged at the home of Jacques Boucher, a treasurer of the Duke of Orléans. The house disappeared centuries ago, and even the area in which it had stood was entirely destroyed by bombing in 1940. In 1965 the Maison Jeanne d'Arc was constructed from materials taken from various local old houses that had been demolished. The house contains a permanent exhibition honouring the girl soldier and saint (*see page 231*).

Musée Historique et Archéologique

The lovely Renaissance mansion Hôtel Cabu, which houses an extensive collection of local historical artefacts, was badly damaged during the 1940 bombing. Its ornate, beautifully proportioned three-storey façade has been well restored. The museum displays a wide variety of items dating back to the Roman period, with many medieval wooden religious pieces and interesting pre-industrial domestic household objects. The highlight is a large number of **Gallo-Roman bronzes** found at Neuvey-en-Sullias (east of Orléans).

Musée des Beaux-Arts

One of the best provincial collections of French painting is housed across the road from the cathedral. Some of the works are those confiscated from religious establishments during the Revolution. Subsequently, Orléans' Fine Arts Museum became a repository for many great state-owned works, as well as being given numerous donations. This priceless collection was partly destroyed during the bombing of the town during World War II, but thousands of important works remain. In total the museum possesses some 52,000 works, although it can only display about 700 at any one time. While French works from the 16th century to the 19th, displayed on the second floor, form the greater part of the collection, the first floor is devoted to other European schools, notably Italian, Spanish and especially 17th-century Flemish. In the basement is a good modern collection, starting with Gauguin's *Fête Gloanec*, including a room devoted to Max Jacob, and with a contemporary collection focusing on the 1980s. There is also a considerable sculpture collection, including works by Rodin and Maillol.

> **Musée des Beaux-Arts** € *pl. Ste-Croix; tel: 02 38 79 21 55; fax: 02 38 79 20 08; email: museesba@ville-orleans.fr. Open Tue–Sat 0930–1215 and 1330–1745, Sun 1400–1830. Closed Mon and some national hols.*

Parc Floral de la Source

These pleasant and interesting gardens of some 35ha lie south of the city at suburban Olivet. They were originally laid out in 1967 in the grounds of a château for the Floralies gardens exhibition. Neat gravel paths meander among flowerbeds and lawns shaded by some unusual trees. Botanists will be fascinated, while others may enjoy a visit for the agreeable setting around the source of the River Loiret (which in reality is not a separate river but an underground branch of the Loire that resurfaces here). One of the most surprising features is the giant-butterfly house, with interior heat and humidity mimicking the tropics, and exotic butterflies with 15cm wingspans. The park also includes a vegetable section, an animal farm, a little railway and other attractions such as mini-golf and a play area. Emu, deer and flamingos can also be seen.

> **Parc Floral de la Source** €€ *Olivet, about 5km S of the Loire, accessible by tram; tel: 02 38 49 30 00; fax: 02 38 49 30 19; www.parc-floral-la-source.com; email: info@parc-floral-la-source.com. Open Apr–Nov 1000–1900, rest of year 1400–1700 (the park remains open until one hr after final entry time). Guided tours are available.*

Accommodation and food in Orléans

Chain hotels in all price ranges are well represented at Orléans, but are often several kilometres from the city centre on the N20 or close to the *autoroute* exits.

Brin de Zinc € *62 r. Ste-Catherine; tel: 02 38 53 38 77; www.brindezinc.com.* On this pedestrian section of r. Ste-Catherine, just off pl. du Martroi, several inexpensive brasseries specialise in quick, low-cost meals served at outdoor tables, which almost fill the narrow street. This one offers not just a range of drinks and snacks, but interesting art exhibits, a piano free to all, regional products, gifts, Internet access, games, books and an inviting atmosphere.

Les Antiquaires €€ *2 r. au Lin; tel: 02 38 53 63 48; fax: 02 38 62 06 95; www.restaurantlesantiquaires.com.* In a backstreet close to the river, Philippe Bardeau's restaurant is the best in town, noted for an exceptionally light, deft touch with seafoods, sauces and seasoning, and excellent local farm-made ingredients. Good selection of Loire wines.

Hôtel d'Arc €€ *37 r. de la République; tel: 02 38 53 10 94; fax: 02 38 14 77 47; www.hoteldarc.fr.* Convenient for the railway station, this rather old-fashioned and basic hotel (with no restaurant) makes an adequate base and is just a short walk from the main square and the sights of Orléans. It's in a section of street with no traffic except for the tram.

La Vieille Auberge €€ *2 Faubourg St-Vincent; tel: 02 38 53 55 81; www.lavieilleauberge.fr.* Between the station and the theatre, enjoy good traditional cooking at outdoor tables or in the charming timbered interior of this 17th-century house.

Entertainment

Orléans has a full programme of shows, exhibitions, concerts and other events throughout the year. Major venues include the Zénith (*tel: 02 38 25 04 29; email: zenith@orleans-spectacles.fr; www.parc-expo-orleans.fr*), the Scène Nationale d'Orléans (*tel: 02 38 62 45 68; www.theatredorleans.fr*) at the Carré St-Vincent complex, and the Astrolabe concert hall (*tel: 02 38 54 20 06; www.lastrolabe.org*). For listings of discos, late-night bars with music, cabaret and other nightlife, ask the tourist office for a copy of the latest edition of *Orléans Jour et Nuit*, which also includes hotels and restaurants.

Suggested walk

Total distance: About 2km, or 8km including the tram detour.

Time: Allow 2–3 hours, or a full day with the detour.

Route: Start at **pl. du Martroi**, the main square. It has cafés, a carousel and a central equestrian statue of Joan of Arc in armour. Walk a few paces down arcaded 18th-century **r. Royale**, where William Wordsworth lodged in 1791 (he and a girlfriend, Annette Vallon, had an illegitimate child here). Reaching the handsome main street, r. Jeanne d'Arc, which runs majestically towards the cathedral, turn right (away from the cathedral) to pl. du Général de Gaulle and the **MAISON JEANNE D'ARC ❶**.

Turn down r. du Tabour, passing, on the right, the Centre Charles Péguy in a fine Gothic-Renaissance mansion. The centre is devoted to the study of the life and work of this Catholic Socialist thinker (1873–1914). Reaching r. Royale again, cross over to continue into **r. de Bourgogne**; this is the oldest street in the city, running through the middle of the once-walled 5th-century Orléans. A mainly pedestrianised shopping street today, it has many interesting old buildings. Turn to the right for the **Eglise St-Pierre le Puellier**, a deconsecrated church that originally dated from the 6th century. The much-renovated interior now provides a light, clear, white space used for exhibitions and concerts. The deserted area all around it was once a very active part of medieval Orléans, busy with river traders and students. Continue along r. des Africains and **r. Coligny** to the **EGLISE ST-AIGNAN ❷**.

Return to Eglise St-Pierre le Puellier and turn back away from the river on r. de la Poterne and **r. Parisie** until you reach the south side of the **CATHEDRALE STE-CROIX ❸**. On the north side of the building, the **MUSEE DES BEAUX-ARTS ❹** is across the road. A short distance behind it is the **CAMPO SANTO ❺**. Also adjacent to the north side of the cathedral, diagonally across the road from the west front, is **HOTEL GROSLOT ❻**.

Take r. Jeanne d'Arc away from the cathedral. Turn left into r. Charles Sanglier to see Hôtel Cabu, with its **MUSEE HISTORIQUE ET ARCHEOLOGIQUE ❼**. There are many other Gothic-Renaissance houses in this area. Turn right along r. des Albanais to reach **pl. du Martroi**.

Detour: From pl. du Martroi, catch a tram to **PARC FLORAL DE LA SOURCE ❽**. The tram stop is called Université-Parc Floral; the entrance to the park is a well-signposted 300m walk.

1 ....Attraction
.....Important Building
.............Park
.............Main Road
.............Other Road
i ....Information
.............Railway

RUE EUXODE MARCILLE

AVENUE DE PARIS

Railway Station

RUE ÉMILE ZOLA

RUE EUGÈNE VIGNAT

Parc Louis Pasteur

RUE FERDINAND BUISSON

BOULEVARD DE VERDUN

PLACE GAMBETTA

BLVD DE VERDUN

BOULEVARD ALEXANDRE MARTIN

RUE JULES LEMAITRE

RUE DU FAUBOURG SAINT-VINCENT

N

RUE DE LA BRETONNERIE

RUE D'ALSACE-LORRAINE

BOULEVARD ALEXANDRE MARTIN

RUE BANNIER

RUE DE LA BRETONNERIE

RUE THÉOPHILE CHOLLET

RUE DE LIONNE

RUE DE LA RÉPUBLIQUE

RUE SAINTE-ANNE

RUE DU COLUMBIER

RUE SERPENTE

i

RUE D'ESCURES

5
Campo Santo

RUE DES BOUTEILLES

Musée des Beaux-Arts

6 **4**

Hôtel Groslot

PLACE STE-CROIX

Cathédrale Ste-Croix

3

RUE BOURDON BLANC

RUE DESFRICHES

PLACE DU MARTROI

RUE JEANNE D'ARC

PLACE DU GÉNÉRAL DE GAULLE

Musée Historique et Archéologique

RUE ROYALE

7

RUE SAINTE-CATHERINE

RUE SAINT-ÉTIENNE

1
Maison Jeanne d'Arc

RUE DU TABOUR

RUE ÉTIENNE DOLET

RUE PARISIE

RUE DE BOURGOGNE

PLACE VIEUX-MARCHÉ

RUE DU POIRIER

Eglise St-Pierre le Puellier

RUE SAINT-FLOU

RUE DE LA TOUR NEUVE

SQUARE DU CHATELET

RUE DE LA CHARPENTERIE

RUE COLIGNY

2
Eglise St-Aignan

RUE DES HALLES

QUAI CYPIERRE

QUAI DU CHATELET

QUAI DU FORT ALLEAUME

PONT GEORGE V

Loire

8
Parc Floral de la Source (by tram)

Orléans

0 _____ 200 metres
0 _____ 200 yards

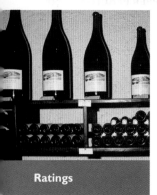

The Upper Reaches

Ratings

History	●●●●●
River views	●●●●●
Wildlife	●●●●○
Wine tasting	●●●●○
Activities	●●●○○
Architecture	●●●○○
Children	●●●○○
Gastronomy	●●●○○

Upstream from Orléans, the Loire Valley has a different character. Instead of the broad, meandering Loire of flood plains, opulent châteaux and royal history, the river flows with determination between the stone embankments of handsome old towns. All the way up to Sancerre, the river is wide and brisk, spanned by fine old bridges, edged by industrious small towns with dignified mansions and quaysides. Once teeming with small businesses and busy docks, and inhabited by boatmen with their own colourful lifestyle, today the upper Loire runs peacefully under its pearly skies. To either side the land rises into green hills. Nature lovers find plenty of birdlife on the way, while gourmets delight in discovering the elegant wines of the Loire Valley's oldest vineyards. Most of the route is in the Sancerre district, known especially for its great whites, and occasionally crosses the Loire into Burgundy to taste the local vintages on that side of the river.

BRIARE

ⓘ Briare Tourist Office / pl. Charles de Gaulle; tel: 02 38 31 24 51; fax: 02 38 37 15 16; www.Briare-le-Canal.com. Open Apr–Sept Mon–Sat 1000–1800, Sun 1000–1200; Oct–Mar Mon–Sat 1000–1200 and 1400–1700.

A tranquil little town clinging to the east bank of the Loire, at the meeting point of handsome 17th-century canals, Briare (now calling itself, sometimes, Briare-le-Canal) has become a centre for boating. Its loveliest sight is the great **Pont-Canal (Canal Bridge)** that carries the calm waters of a canal over the fast swirl of the River Loire. Some 662m long, the imposing wrought-iron bridge dates from 1890, and has an elegance and style that belies its purely functional purpose. The waterside pavement makes a pleasing and unusual stroll to the other side of the Loire and back.

The waterways, which linked the Atlantic, the Mediterranean and Paris, made Briare a prosperous small town. **La Maison des Deux Marines (House of the Two Waterways)** is all about the role of the canals and the river in the fortunes of the town, which, in the 18th and 19th centuries, became a great centre of trade and transport as every type of merchandise was carried through here. The museum

The Upper Reaches
France

The Upper Reaches

●	..............Attraction	
◉	..............City	
◎	..............Large Town	
○	..............Small Town	
▪	..............POI	
▬	..............Motorway	
━	..............Main Road	
━	..............Minor Road	
┄	..............Railway	

0 — 20km
0 — 10 miles

N

Nemours
Outarville
Toury
Pithiviers
Puiseaux
Souppes-sur-Loing
Château-Landon
ÎLE-DE-FRANCE
Bazoches-les-Gallerandes
Boynes
Dordives
Aschères-le-Marché
Ferrières
Neuville-aux-Bois
Chilleurs-aux-Bois
Beaune-La Rolande
Corbeilles
Châlette-sur-Loing
Orléanais
Boiscommun
Pannes
Ladon
Montargis
Loury
Traînou
Bellegarde
Villemandeur
Amilly
Triguères
Fleury-les-Aubrais
St-Jean-de-Braye
Fay-aux-Loges
Canal d'Orléans
Vimory
Châteaurenard
ORLEANS
Chécy
Châteauneuf-sur-Loire
Lorris
Montcresson
Olivet
Jargeau
Loire
Varennes-Changy
Châtillon-Coligny
Sandillon
Germigny-des-Prés
Les Bordes
Nogent-sur-Vernisson
Val d'Orléans
St-Benoît-sur-Loire
Tigy
Sully-sur-Loire
Ouzouer-sur-Loire
Marcilly-en-Villette
La Bussière
Bléneau
La Forté-St-Aubin
Sologne
Isdes
CENTRE
Loire
Gien
Canal de Briare
Loing
Vouzon
Cerdon
Coullons
Briare
Lamotte-Beuvron
Châtillon-sur-Loire
Beuvron
Brinon-sur-Sauldre
Bonny-sur-Loire
Nouan-le-Fuzelier
Argent-sur-Sauldre
Beaulieu-sur-Loire
Blancafort
Vrille
Aubigny-sur-Nère
Belleville-sur-Loire
BOURGOGNE
Sousmes
Vailly-sur-Sauldre
Léré
Salbris
Oizon
Savigny-en-Sancerre
Nançay
La Chapelle-d'Angillon
Cosne-Cours-sur-Loire
Bannay
Pougny
Theillay
Neuvy-sur-Barangeon
Henrichemont
Collines du Sancerrois
434
Sancerre
Tracy-sur-Loire
Allogny
Menetou-Salon
Pouilly-sur-Loire
Mesves-sur-Loire
Les Aix-d'Angillon
Herry

La Maison des Deux Marines € 58 *blvd Buyser; tel: 02 38 31 28 27; fax: 02 38 37 07 45; www.coeur-de-france.com/ briare-marine.html. Open Jun–Sept 1000–1230 and 1400–1830, Oct–Dec & Mar–May 1400–1800.*

Musée de la Mosaïque et des Emaux €€ *blvd Loreau; tel: 02 38 37 08 28; www.emauxdebriare.com. Open daily Jun–Sept 1000–1830, Oct–Dec & Mar–May 1400–1800.*

looks at the canal culture and boating trades of the people of Briare up to the time of the steamships. About a century ago, Briare's wealth came from high-quality enamelware. In particular, it had a factory that could mass-produce buttons – an innovation with which other firms around the world could not compete. Another development here was the use of machinery to create artworks, especially in ironwork and in mosaic, heralding the beginnings of Art Nouveau. A still-operating enamel factory is the setting for the town's interesting **Musée de la Mosaïque et des Emaux (Museum of Mosaic and Enamel)**, including a mosaic by Art Nouveau artist Eugène Grasset.

Accommodation and food near Briare

Hôtel des Voyageurs €–€€ *10 Grande Rue, Bonny-sur-Loire (12km south, on the right bank); tel: 02 38 27 01 45; fax: 02 38 27 01 46. Closed 27 Aug–10 Sept, 19 Feb–12 Mar and Mon.* Enjoy astonishing value for money at this simple, traditional, family-run country hotel, and excellent dining in its restaurant. Imaginative presentation of classic dishes, and good local wines.

Wildlife on the Loire

The Loire, threatened by upriver dams and development, is home to 240 species of birds. River swallows dart from the banks, crested warblers drift on the stream, herons and partridges and hoopoes fly by. Under the surface, catfish, eels, bream and perch number among the many fish. Beside the river, wildlife thrives in shallow lakes and streams and deciduous woods. The Forêt de Bertranges, upriver from Sancerre, is a forest of oak, beech, maple, cherry and other varieties, providing shelter for deer, wild boar, badgers and wild cats.

Above right
Briare Pont-Canal

Right
Musée de la Marine de la
Loire, Châteauneuf-sur-Loire

CHÂTEAUNEUF-SUR-LOIRE

ℹ️ Châteauneuf-sur-
Loire Tourist
Office 3 pl. Aristide Briand;
tel: 02 38 58 44 79; fax: 02
38 58 52 83;
www.chateauneuf-sur-
loire.com. Open all year
Mon–Sat 0930–1230 and
1400–1800 (in summer
closes at 1900, and is also
open Sun 0930–1230).

🏛️ Musée de la
Marine de la Loire
In château stables; tel: 02 38
46 84 46; fax: 02 38 46 41
01. Open Apr–Oct 1000–
1800; Nov–Mar 1400–
1800. Closed Tue.

A pleasant market town, Châteauneuf is named after a castle that no
longer exists. On the site of it, an exact copy of Versailles was built in
miniature, but that, too, was partly demolished in the Revolution.
Among what survives are a fine rotunda, gallery and pavilions (now
housing the town hall). The former château stables are occupied by
the **Musée de la Marine de la Loire (Loire Nautical Museum)**, which
contains a mass of interesting material about the Loire boatmen and
their way of life. The château grounds are now a moated park with a
fine display of rhododendrons. In the town's church lies the superb
Baroque marble tomb of Phélypeaux de la Vrillière (d. 1681), who had
the château built.

GIEN

Gien Tourist Office *Centre Anne de Beaujeu, pl. Jean Jaurès; tel: 02 38 67 25 28 or 02 38 67 88 88; fax: 02 38 38 23 16; www.gien.fr. Open all year (Sun, am only). Closed Sun in winter.*

Markets *Wed am in pl. Jean Jaurès, Sat am in pl. de la Victoire.*

Festival *Carnaval – third weekend in Jul.*

Musée de la Faïencerie €€ *78 pl. de la Victoire; tel: 02 38 38 23 16; www.coeur-de-france. com/gien-faiencerie.html. Open Jan–Feb Sun–Fri 1400–1800, Sat 0900–1200 and 1400–1800; Mar–Apr & Oct–Dec Mon–Sat 0900–1200 and 1400–1800, Sun 1000–1200 and 1400–1800; May–Sept Mon–Sat 0900–1230 and 1330–1830, Sun 1000–1230 and 1330–1830.*

Château de Gien and Musée International de la Chasse €€ *pl. du Château; tel: 02 38 67 69 69; fax: 02 38 38 07 32. Open daily Nov–Apr 0900–1200 and 1400–1800, May–Oct 0900–1800.*

Eglise Ste-Jeanne d'Arc € *pl. du Château. Open daily.*

Curiously, the town's noble château is built mainly of bricks, while the ordinary houses and cottages all around are built mainly of handsome stone. Flower-filled cobbled streets and restored historic town houses – all re-created after heavy wartime destruction – make the town attractive. The best view is from the handsome pale stone bridge that spans the Loire. The river is at its best here, stately and wide, yet not inaccessibly vast. Ordinary little bars line its quayside, and you can walk right beside the flowing river.

Traditionally, the Gien Faïence Works was one of the world's leading manufacturers of *faience*, or glazed earthenware. The factory is still in business, and this important part of the town's art and history can be explored at its excellent **Musée de la Faïencerie (Earthenware Museum)**. Housed in atmospheric cellars beneath the workshops, the museum explores the range from inexpensive household crockery to the most elegant chinaware commissioned by aristocratic families. Little other industry survives at this once busy town, and there are surprisingly few tourists.

Flights of steps lead up to Gien's star attraction, the very striking 15th-century **Château de Gien** with its geometric pattern of red and black brickwork. Originally 9th century, the castle was reconstructed in this way by Anne of Beaujeu, daughter of Louis XI, in 1484. Here, young King Louis XIV, along with his new queen, Anne of Austria, took shelter during the turmoil of the aristocratic Fronde rebellion of 1652. Inside the castle today is a comprehensive **Musée International de la Chasse (International Hunting Museum)**. If hunting upsets you, don't go in – the museum looks lovingly at the whole process of chasing and killing animals and birds, how it has inspired, entertained and fed people, which creatures have been hunted, and the methods and weapons used. Over 3,000 artworks depicting the hunt are displayed, as well as numerous stuffed specimens. Don't miss the entrance hall, however, with its 17th-century painting of St Hubert – hunting's patron saint – and his vision of a 'holy stag'.

While in the town, also visit the modern reconstruction of the 15th-century **Eglise Ste-Jeanne d'Arc** (incorporating a tower from its bombed predecessor), which has beautiful stained glass by Max Ingrand.

Accommodation and food in Gien

Hotel-restaurant du Rivage €€ *1 quai de Nice; tel: 02 38 37 79 00; fax: 02 38 38 10 21.* Have a cocktail at the bar and enjoy dinner on the terrace at this outstanding restaurant specialising in local dishes skilfully made from the best of fresh ingredients. It's also a small hotel, set in a handsome building a few minutes from the town centre and looking out across the Loire.

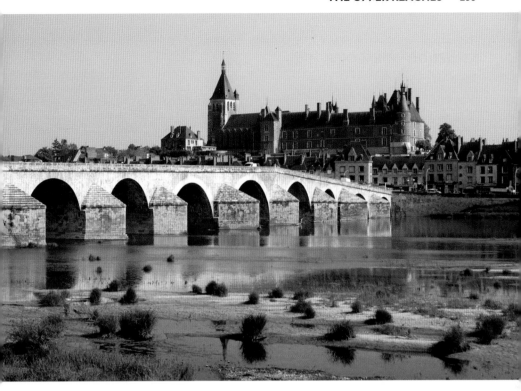

Above
Stone bridge over the Loire at Gien

POUILLY-SUR-LOIRE

Pouilly-sur-Loire Tourist Office 17 quai Jules Pabiot; tel: 03 86 39 54 54; fax: 03 86 39 54 55; www.pouillysurloire.fr. Open Mon–Sat 1000–1200 (except Jul–Aug daily 1000–1200 and 1500–1800). Closed Oct.

Caves de Pouilly Le Moulin à Vent av. de la Tuilerie; tel: 03 86 39 10 99; www.cavespouillysurloire. com. Open Mon–Sat 0800–1200 and 1400–1800.

Festival Foire aux Vins (a major festival of wine and food) 15 Aug.

Market Fri am.

Though the unassuming little town of Pouilly-sur-Loire is technically in Burgundy, it has vineyards on both sides of the river and its wine is considered a 'Loire'. Don't confuse it with the other Pouilly, near Mâcon, whose wine really is Burgundy. The town's name is given to its lesser wine, made using Chasselas grapes. Its better wines, using Sauvignon, are called Pouilly-Fumé. Compare the two at the **Caves de Pouilly** wine cellars.

Accommodation and food in Pouilly-sur-Loire

Le Coq Hardi €€ 42 av. de la Tuilerie; tel: 03 86 39 12 99; fax: 03 86 39 14 15; www.lecoqhardi.fr. Good classic cooking without pretensions, and a dozen comfortable rooms at this reliable, well-established, family-run *Logis*. Once a popular inn on the busy N6, it has become quieter now that through-traffic has been diverted around the edge of town.

St-Benoît-sur-Loire

Specialities

Les Moinillons are boiled-sugar sweets first devised by the monks (*moines*) at the abbey.

ⓘ St-Benoît-sur-Loire Tourist Office *Maison Max Jacob, 44 r. Orléanaise; tel: 02 38 35 79 00; fax: 02 38 35 10 45. Open all year Mon–Sat 0900–1230 and 1430–1730.*

Ⓦ *www.tourisme-loire-foret.com (St Benoît and its region)*

Below
A capital in St-Benoît-sur-Loire's Basilica

At this ancient riverside village stands one of France's finest Romanesque treasures, the imposing **basilica of the Abbaye de Fleury** dedicated to St Benoît (St Benedict in English). Known as the 'Father of Monasticism', St Benoît (d. 547) was the founder of the Benedictine Order, which had vast influence throughout Europe during the Middle Ages. Curious, diverse, richly carved capitals in the belfry-porch, which originally stood apart from the rest of the building, are considered a masterpiece of Romanesque stonework. Originally founded in the 7th century, an abbey was constructed on a site of great importance for the pre-Christian Druidic religion. Most of the existing majestic abbey church in pale stone dates from the 11th century, though an older crypt contains the remains of Benedict himself. Benedict had no associations with this place, and did not die here; 125 years after his death his remains were brought here from Italy with a view to attracting pilgrims and prosperity. The abbey was sacked by Protestants during the Wars of Religion, and its treasures sold – including a 700-year-old library of manuscripts. After the Revolution, the abbey was destroyed, leaving only the church, but the buildings were restored in the 19th century, and the abbey itself revived in 1944. The distinguished poet and artist Max Jacob lived for several years in the village. A permanent exhibition of his work is now on display at the **Maison Max Jacob**, which today also houses the tourist office, and he is buried in the local cemetery.

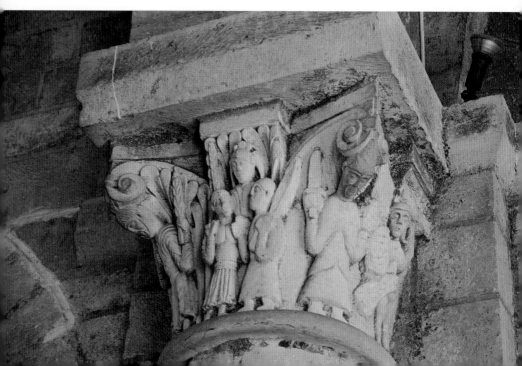

Abbaye de Fleury
tel: 02 38 35 72 43; www.coeur-de-france.com/ st-benoit.html, www.abbaye-fleury.com. Open 0630–2200, with 45min guided visits usually at 1030, 1500 & 1630, spring & summer daily (except during services, in Holy Week), winter Sun only. Closed Jan, Feb & first Fri each month.

Maison Max Jacob €
See tourist office.

Max Jacob at St-Benoît-sur-Loire

Born in 1876 and brought up as a Jew, Max Jacob became a convert to Catholicism in 1915. He moved to the village of St-Benoît and, when monks returned to the abbey in 1944, he took up residence there. Almost at once, he was arrested for being of Jewish descent and sent to Drancy, the Nazi detention camp for Jews. Many famous writers and artists of the day launched a petition for his release – it was notable that his close friend Picasso refused to sign, being fearful of the consequences for his own safety – but by the time it had been agreed to release him, Jacob was already dead as a result of the brutal conditions of the camp. As an acknowledgement of the order for his release, his body was returned to St-Benoît for burial.

Accommodation and food in St-Benoît-sur-Loire

Hotel du Labrador €€ *7 pl. Abbaye; tel: 02 38 35 74 38* and **Restaurant du Grand Benoît €€** *tel: 02 38 35 11 92; fax: 02 38 35 13 79; www.hoteldulabrador.com.* The quiet, comfortable hotel occupies several buildings facing the basilica, while its restaurant is one of the better eating places here, with good menus at very reasonable prices.

SANCERRE

Sancerre Tourist Office *Esplanade Porte César; tel: 02 48 54 08 21; email: officedetourisme@ ville-sancerre.fr. Open Mar, Oct & Nov Mon–Fri 1430–1700, Sat, Sun & national hols 1000–1230 and 1430–1700; Apr–Sept daily 1000–1230 and 1400–1730. Closed rest of year.*

www.ville-sancerre.fr

Markets *Mon and Sat am.*

Events and exhibitions *Fête du Crottin de Chavignol – weekend nearest 1 May; Sancerre Wine Fair – Pentecost (Whitsun); French Wine Festival – last weekend in Aug; Oyster Fair – last weekend in Oct.*

This exceptionally good-looking town is poised on a round hill gazing across the expanse of its neat vineyards, its tangled old streets and lanes guarded by a 14th-century tower. It's well known for world-class fragrant dry white wines, fortunately regarded as the local wine everywhere along this route. It can be tasted at wine cellars in and near the town. Try, too, some of the district's highly praised goat's cheese called Crottins de Chavignol, perfectly delicious despite the name (*crottins* means 'goat droppings').

Food in Sancerre

Restaurant La Pomme d'Or €-€€ *1 r. Panneterie / pl. de la Mairie; tel: 02 48 54 13 30; fax: 02 48 54 19 22.* Straightforward menus of classic local fare, expertly prepared, are served here. Wines of Sancerre and Pouilly are a speciality, and available by the glass – a good way of trying out a few. Very good value.

Restaurant de la Tour €€ *31 Nouvelle Place; tel: 02 48 54 00 81; fax: 02 48 78 01 54; www.la-tour-sancerre.fr.* An attractive local gastronomic favourite, and a long-established feature of Sancerre, the Tour has an easy, reliable way with traditional regional dishes, and represents exceptional value for money.

SULLY-SUR-LOIRE

ℹ Sully-sur-Loire Tourist Office *pl. de Gaulle; tel: 02 38 36 23 70; fax: 02 38 36 32 21; www.sully-sur-loire.fr. Open May–Sept Mon–Sat 0945–1215 and 1430–1830, Sun 1030–1300 (until end Aug); Oct–Apr 1000–1200 and 1400–1800, closed Mon pm, Thur am, Sun, Christmas & New Year.*

🏛 Château *tel: 02 38 36 36 86; email: chateau.sully@cg45.fr*

🅿 Market *All day Mon.*

🎭 Festivals *St-François Fair – Easter weekend; International Classical Music Festival – weekends in Jun.*

This pretty little town is a popular holiday spot and riverside resort, conveniently and attractively placed close to the forests of Orléans and Sologne, offering fishing, walking and river trips. It has a splendid 14th-century **château**, solidly rectangular, guarded by mighty towers and turrets, and cleverly 'moated' by the River Sange. Voltaire spent long periods here as a guest of the Duke of Sully. The keep has a remarkable 600-year-old wooden roof. Designed by the Louvre's architect, Raymond du Temple, the castle fell into ruin and has been impeccably restored since World War II, when the town suffered much damage from bombing – once by the Germans and once by the Allies. The château makes a wonderful setting for frequent indoor and outdoor evening entertainments held throughout the summer months.

Accommodation and food in Sully-sur-Loire

Hôtel Restaurant du Grand Sully €€ *10 blvd Champ de Foire; tel: 02 38 36 27 56; www.grandsully.com.* This smart and comfortable classic little family-run hotel is in the town centre, just minutes from the château. Its restaurant is a favourite with locals, who come for its imaginative set menus. Rooms with authentic furniture and rich fabrics are good value.

Opposite
Château, Sully-sur-Loire

Suggested tour

Total distance: 120km.

Time: Allow 1–2 days.

Links: At Orléans (*see page 240*) this tour links with the Blois–Orléans route (*see page 228*).

ℹ Regional tourist offices

Comité Départemental de Tourisme du Cher
5 r. de Séraucourt, Bourges; tel: 02 48 48 00 10; fax: 02 48 48 00 20; www.berrylecher.com

Comité Départemental de Tourisme de Loiret
8 r. d'Escures, Orléans; tel: 02 38 78 04 04; fax: 02 38 77 04 12; www.tourismeloiret.com

Comité Départemental de Tourisme de la Nièvre *(in Burgundy) 3 r. du Sort, Nevers; tel: 03 86 36 39 80; fax: 03 86 36 36 63; www.nievre-tourisme.com*

Route: Start out from **Orléans**, taking the N460 (or bigger N60), or perhaps the small and pretty south bank riverside road, to **CHATEAUNEUF-SUR-LOIRE ①**. Close by, at **Germigny-des-Prés** on the D60, there's a lovely small church which, astonishingly, dates from the year 806. It was originally built as a private chapel adjoining the home of Theodulf, Abbot of St-Benoît. On the roof of the east apse, there's a superb mosaic believed to be as old as the oldest parts of the building. Stay on the D60 to reach **ST-BENOIT-SUR-LOIRE ②**. Continue on the same road, and cross the river into **SULLY-SUR-LOIRE ③**. Stay on the south side of the river, on the D951 (there's a nuclear power station on the other side), as far as the bridge into **GIEN ④**, on the north bank.

From Gien, take the D952 to **BRIARE ⑤**. After seeing the canal-bridge, drive as far as the next river bridge, into **Châtillon-sur-Loire**, 7km from

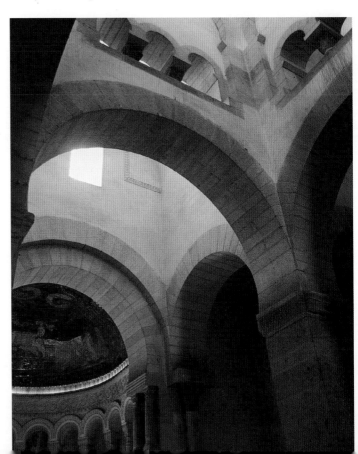

Right
Church interior,
Germigny-des-Prés

www.rivernet.org/loire/loire.htm (economics, politics and ecology are the issues here – English and French); *www.lvo.com* (Loire Valley Online, a commercial site about the whole region, in English).

The main highway N7 and the *autoroute* A77, coming from Paris, meet the Loire at Briare. TGVs run direct from Paris to Orléans, taking 1hr 30min. Frequent local trains run from town to town along the Loire. There are internal flights to Orléans.

Briare. This is a likeable and picturesque historic town with many charming old houses of stone or timber, and rooftops at chaotic angles. Follow the river road on either side of the river – on the right bank the busy N7 or, on the left bank, the quieter D951, pretty in parts – to **Cosne-Cours-sur-Loire**, a largish and busy but likeable riverside town (*www.mairie-cosnesurloire.fr* is the official Cosne website). Leave Cosne, cross the river if necessary, and take the attractive vine road into **SANCERRE ❻**.

The road continues up beyond Sancerre through vineyards and pretty countryside. Take the Loire's left bank road and cross the bridge into **POUILLY-SUR-LOIRE ❼**.

Also worth exploring: A little further upriver is La Charité-sur-Loire, a picturesque former monastic town, once a bustling river port, with old ramparts (*www.lacharitesurloire-tourisme.com* is its website). Here, a good red wine, rather than a typical Loire white, is produced. Quiet and attractive and well sited on the river's edge, La Charité is the last town, heading upriver, where the grandeur and beauty of the Loire Valley can be experienced.

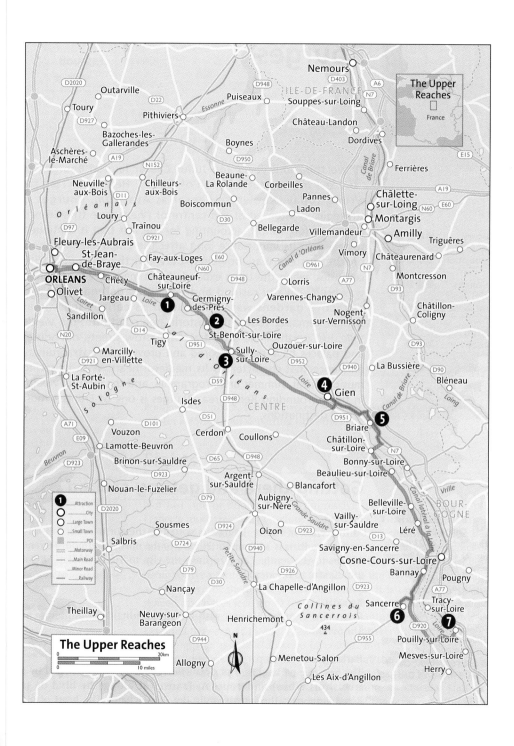

The Upper Reaches
France

D2020
Outarville
Toury
D927
Pithiviers
D22
Puiseaux
D948
ÎLE-DE-FRANCE
Nemours
D403
A6
N7
Souppes-sur-Loing
Château-Landon
Dordives
Essonne
Bazoches-les-Gallerandes
Aschères-le-Marché
A19
N152
Boynes
D950
Ferrières
E15
Canal de Briare
Neuville-aux-Bois
D11
Chilleurs-aux-Bois
Beaune-La Rolande
Corbeilles
Pannes
Châlette-sur-Loing
A19
E60
N60
o r l é a n a i s
Loury
D97
Traînou
D921
Boiscommun
D30
Ladon
Bellegarde
Villemandeur
Montargis
Amilly
Triguères
Fleury-les-Aubrais
St-Jean-de-Braye
ORLEANS
Olivet
Checy
Loiret
Fay-aux-Loges
E60
N60
Châteauneuf-sur-Loire
Germigny-des-Prés
Canal d'Orléans
Vimory
D961
N7
Châteaurenard
Montcresson
D93
Loire
Jargeau
Loire
Lorris
Varennes-Changy
A77
Châtillon-Coligny
Sandillon
N20
D14
Tigy
D951
St-Benoît-sur-Loire
Les Bordes
Nogent-sur-Vernisson
D93
Marcilly-en-Villette
D921
Sully-sur-Loire
Ouzouer-sur-Loire
D952
D940
La Bussière
D90
La Forté-St-Aubin
S o l o g n e
v a l   d '   o r l é a n s
D59
Loire
Gien
Bléneau
Loing
Isdes
D948
CENTRE
D51
A71
E09
Vouzon
D101
Cerdon
Coullons
D951
Briare
Châtillon-sur-Loire
N7
Canal de Briare
Vrille
BOUR-GOGNE
Lamotte-Beuvron
Brinon-sur-Sauldre
D923
D65
D948
Bonny-sur-Loire
Beaulieu-sur-Loire
Beuvron
D923
Nouan-le-Fuzelier
Argent-sur-Sauldre
D79
Blancafort
Aubigny-sur-Nère
Grande Sauldre
Belleville-sur-Loire
Vailly-sur-Sauldre
Canal latéral à la Loire

1 ....Attraction
○ ....City
○ ....Large Town
○ ....Small Town
■ ....POI
.........Motorway
.........Main Road
.........Minor Road
.........Railway

D2020
Sousmes
D924
Salbris
D724
Oizon
D923
Léré
D13
Petite Sauldre
D79
D940
Savigny-en-Sancerre
Cosne-Cours-sur-Loire
Bannay
Pougny
A77
Nançay
D30
La Chapelle-d'Angillon
D923
C o l l i n e s   d u
S a n c e r r o i s
Sancerre
Tracy-sur-Loire
Theillay
Neuvy-sur-Barangeon
Henrichemont
434
D955
D920
Loire
Pouilly-sur-Loire

The Upper Reaches
0 _____ 20km
0 _____ 10 miles

D944
N
Allogny
Menetou-Salon
Les Aix-d'Angillon
Mesves-sur-Loire
Herry

Bourges by Night

This is a unique *son-et-lumière* experience. During summer and over holiday weekends at other times, Bourges diffuses music and illuminates parts of its major monuments (and the gardens of the Archbishopric), giving the city quite a different feel. The route between the main monuments is much the same as our suggested walk (*see page 265*). If you have the chance, do it by night (*from 2130 in autumn and from 2200 or 2230 in spring and summer*) as well as by day.

ⓘ Cathédrale de St-Etienne € *tel: 02 48 65 49 44. Open Oct–Mar daily 0900–1745; Apr–Sept daily 0830–1915.* **Crypt and North Tower €€** *Crypt open daily (except Sun am) for guided visits at 0945, 1100, 1415, 1515, 1545, 1645 & 1700 and mid-Jul–mid-Aug for individual visits; North Tower open daily, times as cathedral. Both closed 1 Jan, 1 May, 1 Nov, 11 Nov & 25 Dec.*

Jardins de l'Archevêché € *Open 0700–2400.*

Musée des Arts Décoratifs € *6 r. Bourbonnoux; tel: 02 48 57 81 17. Open daily except Sun am & Mon 1000–1230 and 1330–1830; Jul–Aug 1000–1830. Closed 1 Jan, 1 May, 1 Nov, 11 Nov & 25 Dec.*

Above
Portal, Cathédrale de St-Etienne

de Berry lies) will also offer access to the Renaissance North Tower. After climbing 396 steps in corkscrew fashion to a height of 65m, you'll have a great view over the *Vieille Ville* and the marshy Marais area to the northeast.

Jardins de l'Archevêché

On the southeast flanks of the apse are the lozenge-shaped gardens of the Archbishopric. Beautifully laid out over 300 years ago, full of shady walks, and containing a delightful little bandstand, the gardens are a fine place to relax. The views of the cathedral's apse and south flank are particularly good.

Musée des Arts Décoratifs

This interesting museum, dedicated to the decorative arts, is housed in the fine Hôtel Lallemant. Note its elegant façade (a beautiful, and finely proportioned, early Renaissance work) before wandering through the collections of French furniture, 16th- and 17th-century tapestries, cabinets intricately inlaid with wood, oriental lacquerwork and some exquisite examples of faience and ivorywork.

Musée des Meilleurs Ouvriers de France

The former Archbishop's Palace, an imposing building from the 17th century, shelters this unusual and fascinating collection of crafts which changes as top craftspeople from some 200 disciplines enter the museum's prestigious yearly competition.

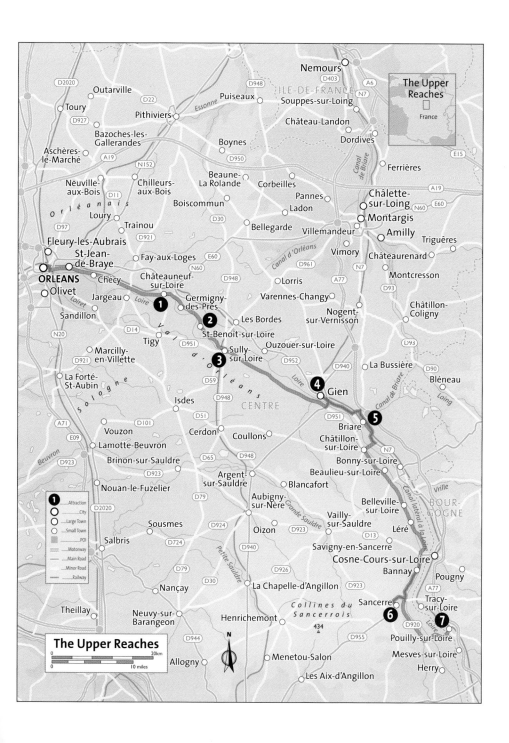

The Upper Reaches
France

The Upper Reaches

0   20km
0   10 miles

Legend:
- ● Attraction
- ○ City
- ○ Large Town
- ○ Small Town
- ■ POI
- ▬ Motorway
- ▬ Main Road
- ▬ Minor Road
- ▬ Railway

Place names:
Nemours, Outarville, Toury, Puiseaux, Souppes-sur-Loing, ILE-DE-FRANCE, Pithiviers, Essonne, Château-Landon, Bazoches-les-Gallerandes, Boynes, Dordives, Aschères-le-Marché, Neuville-aux-Bois, Chilleurs-aux-Bois, Beaune-La Rolande, Corbeilles, Ferrières, Orléanais, Boiscommun, Pannes, Châlette-sur-Loing, Loury, Ladon, Montargis, Traînou, Bellegarde, Villemandeur, Amilly, Triguères, Fleury-les-Aubrais, Fay-aux-Loges, Vimory, Châteaurenard, St-Jean-de-Braye, ORLEANS, Checy, Châteauneuf-sur-Loire, Lorris, Montcresson, Olivet, Jargeau, Loire, Germigny-des-Prés, Varennes-Changy, Nogent-sur-Vernisson, Châtillon-Coligny, Sandillon, Les Bordes, Marcilly-en-Villette, St-Benoît-sur-Loire, Ouzouer-sur-Loire, Tigy, Sully-sur-Loire, La Bussière, Bléneau, La Forté-St-Aubin, Isdes, Gien, Vouzon, Cerdon, Coullons, Briare, Châtillon-sur-Loire, Lamotte-Beuvron, Bonny-sur-Loire, Brinon-sur-Sauldre, Argent-sur-Sauldre, Blancafort, Beaulieu-sur-Loire, BOURGOGNE, Nouan-le-Fuzelier, Aubigny-sur-Nère, Belleville-sur-Loire, Sousmes, Vailly-sur-Sauldre, Léré, Salbris, Oizon, Savigny-en-Sancerre, Cosne-Cours-sur-Loire, Nançay, Bannay, Pougny, Theillay, Neuvy-sur-Barangeon, Henrichemont, Collines du Sancerrois, Sancerre, Tracy-sur-Loire, Allogny, Menetou-Salon, Pouilly-sur-Loire, Mesves-sur-Loire, Les Aix-d'Angillon, Herry, La Chapelle-d'Angillon

Map markers: ①②③④⑤⑥⑦

Bourges

Two thousand years ago Julius Caesar lauded Bourges as '...the most beautiful in all of Gaul...'. He wouldn't be far wrong today. Known to Caesar as *Avaricum*, Bourges is strategically situated at the centre of *l'hexagone* (the French nickname for France), accounting for the fact that it continued to maintain its importance long after the Empire fell. Its most prosperous era was, however, between the 13th and 16th centuries, when the town expanded, the magnificent cathedral was built, royalty resided and when palatial mansions and attractive gardens were laid out on its earlier, sometimes Roman, remains. Today, this historic area constitutes the *Vieille Ville*, just north of the cathedral. On narrow streets, old houses and palaces have been restored and provide the extraordinary ambience that characterises its medieval heart. With its spring music festival, summer arts programme, and the cultural wealth in the surrounding Berry area, Bourges is one of France's most prized destinations.

Getting there and getting around

Bourges Tourist Office *21 r. Victor Hugo; tel: 02 48 23 02 60; fax: 02 48 23 02 69; email: accueil@bourgestourisme. com. Open Oct–Mar Mon–Sat 0900–1800, Sun & hols 1400–1700; Apr–Jun & Sept Mon–Sat 0900–1900, Sun & hols 1000–1900; Jul–Aug Mon–Sat 0900–1930, Sun & hols 1000–1900. Closed 1 Jan, 5 May & 25 Dec.*

By road
At the centre of France, Bourges is skirted by the north–south A71–E11 motorway. Paris is 246km (2hr 30min) to the north, Clermont-Ferrand 178km to the south. The N76 links the city to Tours (155km, about 2hr 30min) to the west.

By rail
Fast trains connect Bourges with Paris (Austerlitz) in a minimum of 1hr 50min.

Parking
The best free parking is in pl. Séraucourt (linked to the cathedral by a free shuttle bus) and cours A. France, or along the blvd de la République near the superb Jardin des Prés-Fichaux. The heart of old

Note that five of Bourges' museums are free of charge (a welcome surprise), while there is a combined ticket (€€–€€€) which gives access to the cathedral's North Tower, crypt and Palais Jacques Cœur.

W www.bourgestourisme. com

Markets *Halle Saint-Bonnet am except Mon, Maronniers Thur am, pl. de la Nation Sat am, and Chancellerie Wed am.*

Bourges is compact. Having parked, walk or take the *Train Touristique* (€€) for a 45min tour departing from the cathedral.

Sights

Cathédrale de St-Etienne

Not just one of Bourges' most impressive monuments, but one of France's most treasured religious works and a UNESCO heritage site, this cathedral was begun at the turn of the 12th century. Take in its western portal first – not just one but five finely carved entrances, decorated with saints and Apostles, pencil-thin columns and arcades rising to five-pointed arches. These lead into the five-nave cathedral, an anomaly, for the building has no transept. It is essentially bullet-shaped: the naves lead up to the choir and the rounded apse behind. In these apse chapels are the fabulous stained-glass windows. Executed between 1215 and 1225 by three different workshops, they at first appear as a kaleidoscope of colour. But as you look up and begin to discern the windows, you'll pick out the individual figures from both the Old and New Testaments. Before exiting the cathedral, pass by the Chapelle Jacques Cœur with more spectacular stained glass. A ticket to the crypt (where an effigy of the once-powerful Duc

Cathédrale de St-Etienne € *tel: 02 48 65 49 44. Open Oct–Mar daily 0900–1745; Apr–Sept daily 0830–1915.* **Crypt and North Tower** €€ *Crypt open daily (except Sun am) for guided visits at 0945, 1100, 1415, 1515, 1545, 1645 & 1700 and mid-Jul–mid-Aug for individual visits; North Tower open daily, times as cathedral. Both closed 1 Jan, 1 May, 1 Nov, 11 Nov & 25 Dec.*

Jardins de l'Archevêché € *Open 0700–2400.*

Musée des Arts Décoratifs € *6 r. Bourbonnoux; tel: 02 48 57 81 17. Open daily except Sun am & Mon 1000–1230 and 1330–1830; Jul–Aug 1000–1830. Closed 1 Jan, 1 May, 1 Nov, 11 Nov & 25 Dec.*

Above
Portal, Cathédrale de St-Etienne

de Berry lies) will also offer access to the Renaissance North Tower. After climbing 396 steps in corkscrew fashion to a height of 65m, you'll have a great view over the *Vieille Ville* and the marshy Marais area to the northeast.

Jardins de l'Archevêché

On the southeast flanks of the apse are the lozenge-shaped gardens of the Archbishopric. Beautifully laid out over 300 years ago, full of shady walks, and containing a delightful little bandstand, the gardens are a fine place to relax. The views of the cathedral's apse and south flank are particularly good.

Musée des Arts Décoratifs

This interesting museum, dedicated to the decorative arts, is housed in the fine Hôtel Lallemant. Note its elegant façade (a beautiful, and finely proportioned, early Renaissance work) before wandering through the collections of French furniture, 16th- and 17th-century tapestries, cabinets intricately inlaid with wood, oriental lacquerwork and some exquisite examples of faience and ivorywork.

Musée des Meilleurs Ouvriers de France

The former Archbishop's Palace, an imposing building from the 17th century, shelters this unusual and fascinating collection of crafts which changes as top craftspeople from some 200 disciplines enter the museum's prestigious yearly competition.

Right
Musée des Arts Décoratifs, interior

Musée des Meilleurs Ouvriers de France pl. Etienne Dolet; tel: 02 48 57 82 45. Open daily except Sun am & Mon 1000–1230 and 1330–1800, Jul–Aug 1000–1830. Closed 1 Jan, 1 May, 1 Nov, 11 Nov & 25 Dec.

Musée du Berry
4 r. des Arènes; tel: 02 48 57 81 15. Open daily except Sun am & Tue 1000–1230 and 1330–1800, in Jul & Aug 1000–1830. Closed 1 Jan, 1 May, 1 Nov, 11 Nov & 25 Dec.

Musée Estève
13 r. Edouard Branly; tel: 02 48 24 75 38; fax: 02 48 24 29 48. Open daily except Sun am & Tue 1000–1230 and 1330–1800, in Jul & Aug 1000–1830. Closed 1 Jan, 1 May, 1 Nov, 11 Nov & 25 Dec.

Palais Jacques Cœur €€
10bis r. Jacques Cœur; tel: 02 48 24 06 87. Open daily for guided visits 0930–1745. Closed 1 Jan, 1 May, 1 Nov, 11 Nov & 25 Dec.

Musée du Berry

Located in the impressive Hôtel Cujas, a Renaissance mansion (look at the wonderful bulging corner towers – so popular at that period – capped by their slate pepperpot roofs), houses relics from the Roman days of *Avaricum*, parts of the Duc de Berry's mausoleum and a large collection of pottery.

Musée Estève

This is a museum – in old surroundings – for modern art lovers. The Hôtel des Echevins was used for over three centuries as the municipal headquarters. Its stairwell, in the form of a tower with light, lacy sculptural decoration on its monochrome exterior, does little to prepare one for the vast and colourful works of a French contemporary artist. Maurice Estève (1904–2001) was a self-taught painter who, influenced by Braque and Cézanne, hovered between the figurative and abstract, before heading in the 1950s towards a highly colourful, abstract world of painting. The 130 oil paintings, watercolours and sketches in this museum are imbued with the vibrant colours and strong sense of form that made his reputation.

Palais Jacques Cœur

Charles VII's protégé silversmith, Jacques Cœur (*see page 279*), rose to fame and considerable wealth from a humble start in life. He commissioned this lovely Gothic mansion for himself. Delicate stone tracery, ornate towers and beautiful balustrades enhance the creamy stone façade, while the interior is richly decorated with superb sculptural elements around its chimneys and doors, and paintings, woodwork and ceilings. Cœur invested lavishly and introduced decorative elements gathered on his considerable travels in the East. It was finished in 1451 but, as Cœur was by then in exile, he never inhabited it and the palace passed to his heirs on his death in 1457.

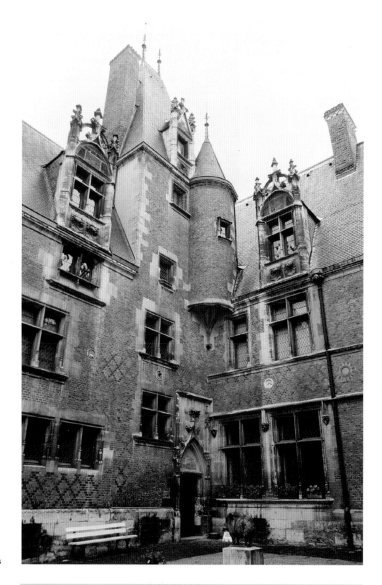

Right
Musée du Berry – Hôtel Cujas

Vercingétorix versus Caesar

The nigh-indomitable Gaul leader, Vercingétorix, met his match in Julius Caesar. As the Romans moved north, conquering and absorbing the locals into their expanding empire, this leader stood his ground and, rather than relinquish Gaul to the invaders, burnt all the towns and villages. The citizens of Bourges begged him to spare the town and he made an exception. Bourges' safety was not long-lived, however. Caesar came and conquered, reputedly slaying all its 40,000 citizens.

Accommodation and food in Bourges

Cobbled r. Bourbonnoux and r. Coursarlon lead into pretty little **pl. Gordaine**, where several of the picturesque half-timbered houses are now food specialists. Look out for quality chocolates and local specialities, including *nonettes*, tasty little soft cakes in various flavours. All around the square are the tables of good, inexpensive restaurants that are busy every evening.

Hôtel d'Angleterre €€ *1 pl. des Quatre Piliers; tel: 02 48 24 68 51; fax: 02 48 65 21 41; www.bestwestern-angleterre-bourges.com.* In the middle of the *Vieille Ville*, this medium-sized hotel is located in an elegant 19th-century building. Comfortable, private (paying) parking and restaurant offering traditional French cuisine.

Inter-Hôtel Les Tilleuls €€ *7 pl. de la Pyrotechnie; tel: 02 48 20 49 04; fax: 02 48 50 61 73; email: lestilleuls.borges@wanadoo.fr; www.les-tilleuls.com.* Just ten minutes from the cathedral, this smallish hotel is comfortable, friendly and well maintained.

Restaurant Le Beauvoir €€ *1 av. Marx Dormoy; tel: 02 48 65 42 44; fax: 02 48 24 80 84; www.restaurant-lebeauvoir.com. Closed Sun pm.* In the direction of Les Marais, but not far from the centre, this restaurant with modern décor has established a reputation for high-quality and creative cuisine at reasonable prices.

Hôtel de Bourbon €€–€€€ *blvd de la République; tel: 02 48 70 70 00; fax: 02 48 70 21 22; email: h1888@accor-hotels.com.* Incorporating the remains of the Abbaye St-Ambroix, this fine hotel is exceptionally comfortable. The historic centre is within walking distance. The hotel restaurant (*see below*) is outstanding.

Abbaye St-Ambroix €€€ *Hôtel de Bourbon (see above).* In the remains of the nave of what was once the Abbaye St-Ambroix's church, this award-winning gastronomic restaurant has innovative modern cuisine and an outstanding wine cellar.

Suggested walk

Total distance: About 2km.

Time: 2 hours, not counting time spent in museums.

Route: Start in **pl. Etienne Dolet** in front of the south door of the **CATHEDRALE DE ST-ETIENNE ❶** and walk along its flanks to the magnificent western portals. Keep to its northern side, taking r. des 3 Maillets. On the left, between r. Molière and the pedestrian

r. Bourbonnoux, are the remains of Bourges' **Roman ramparts**. Continue via r. Bourbonnoux down to the Hôtel Lallemant, the **MUSEE DES ARTS DECORATIFS** ❷, on your left. From here, continue to **pl. Gordaine**, full of half-timbered houses, one of the most beautifully restored squares in town.

Detour: To the east of pl. Gordaine, via r. Joyeuse, r. de Croisy, blvd Clemenceau and r. Neuve des Bouchers, you'll reach the **Marais**, the marshland attached to the River Auron. This fascinating area, a breath of fresh air for the city, has been cultivated for over 300 years (*end of detour*).

Go back along the pedestrianised **r. Mirabeau** and turn left up the stairs, coming out in r. Edouard Branly. On your right is the Hôtel des Echevins, which houses the **MUSEE ESTEVE** ❸. Retrace your steps (and mind your head down the stairs) to r. Mirabeau and follow this

Right
Carved window and
figure, Bourges

lovely road with its half-timbered buildings around to **pl. de la Barre**, where you take the r. Pelvoysin, named for the local architect, through pl. Planchat to Hôtel Cujas, and the **MUSEE DU BERRY** ❹. Walk down **r. des Arènes**, which used to lead to the Roman amphitheatre, as far as the steep stairs, escalier Jacques Cœur, on your left, that climb up to the r. Jacques Cœur and, again on your left, the imposing **PALAIS JACQUES CŒUR** ❺.

Leaving the palace, walk past the escalier Jacques-Cœur, and into the **pl. des Quatre Piliers**, where imposing 17th- to 18th-century mansions are grouped around a fountain, and head down the **r. des Armuriers** towards the Prefecture. On the corner of **r. d'Auron** is a fine half-timbered house known, erroneously, as the 'house of Jacques Cœur': in fact, the house was built long after the silversmith's demise but was on the site of his birthplace. Cross the pl. M Plaisant and walk along r. Henri Ducrot, past the Prefecture, turning left into **r. V Hugo**, past the **tourist office** and back to the south side of the cathedral. Turn right, and you'll see the entrance to the **MUSEE DES MEILLEURS OUVRIERS DE FRANCE** ❻. After the last museum, it's time to relax. Turn right out of the museum and enter the **JARDINS DE l'ARCHEVECHE** ❼ to explore this pleasant park.

The Berry

Ratings

History	●●●●●
Medieval towns	●●●●○
Porcelain	●●●●○
Religious architecture	●●●●○
Gastronomy	●●●○○
Scenery	●●●○○
Children	●●○○○
Local produce	●●○○○

The Berry is a vast plateau area straddling central France – indeed, the geographical centre of the country falls within this region. It rises through forests and descends to marshes, extends through important agricultural land and touches the broad band of the Loire Valley in the east. It is not one of the country's most crowded tourist areas, so getting around is fairly easy. In fact, Berry does a fairly good job of hiding its assets. As one of its famous sons, Henri Alain-Fournier, wrote: you need to 'part the branches to get to know the area'. But the rewards of doing so are rich. Although the Romans conquered the Celtic tribes of the Berry, the most complete historical legacy here is from the 11th and 12th centuries, the Romanesque era. The religious architecture and the many wall paintings from this period form one of France's greatest treasures. Famous Berry residents include George Sand, Henri Alain-Fournier, Honoré de Balzac and contemporary actor, Gerard Dépardieu.

BOUGES-LE-CHÂTEAU

ⓘ Comité Départemental de Tourisme du Cher 5 r. de Séraucourt, Bourges; tel: 02 48 48 00 10; fax: 02 48 48 00 20; email: berrylecher tourisme@berry.fr; www.berrylecher.com. Open Mon–Fri 0900–1230 and 1330–1700.

Comité Départemental de Tourisme de l'Indre 1 pl. Eugène Rolland, Châteauroux; tel: 02 54 07 36 36; fax: 02 54 22 31 21; email: berrylindretourisme@ berry.fr; www.berrylindre.com.

It is something of a surprise to see the elegant, Italianate **Château de Bouges** rise amid Berry pastureland. But this rectangular stone building, devoid of towers and with grey slate roofs, has symmetry and proportion not usual in this part of France. It is often compared to the Petit Trianon, in Versailles, to which it has a strong resemblance. It was built in 1759, probably by architect Jacques-Ange Gabriel, for Charles Le Blanc de Marnaval, who was the manager of Châteauroux's royal factory for bed linen, and was later owned by Talleyrand. Smallish but very well furnished, the château doesn't have that musty, museum feel to it that some other small mansions do. During the guided visit you'll see a remarkable collection of good 18th-century furniture (added by the last private owner, Henri Viguier) and pass through Louis XVI's bedroom. The well-maintained 80ha park also has a formal French garden, while the courtyard, with its elegant stone buildings capped by steep, slate-tiled Mansard roofs, contains the

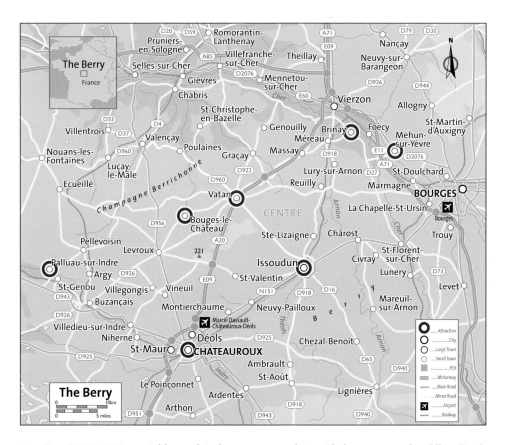

Open Mon–Fri 0900–1200 and 1400–1800. Closed national hols.

🅱 **Château de Bouges** €–€€ tel: 02 54 35 88 26; fax: 02 54 35 16 96. Open for guided tours, Mar, Jun & Nov 1100, 1500 & 1600; Apr, May, Sept & Oct 1100, 1500, 1600 & 1700; Jul–Aug 1000, 1200, 1500, 1600, 1700 & 1800. Closed Dec–Feb & 1 May.

stables and tack rooms, complete with harnesses and saddles. Don't miss the good collection of horse-drawn carriages.

Food in Bouges-le-Château

La Petite Auberge du Château € *14 r. Château; tel: 02 54 35 68 73; email: aubergeduchateau.bouges@wanadoo.fr.* A simple but pleasant and inexpensive place to stop for a bite.

Berry lentils

Seven times richer in iron than spinach, full of protein, vitamins, fibre and natural sugar, green Berry lentils are of excellent quality. The best lentils carry the *Label Rouge* denoting adherence to stringent criteria of cultivation.

BRINAY

Eglise St-Aignan €
Open daily
0900–1900.

Market *Foëcy, Fri am.*

Highlight of this tiny Berrichonne village is its 11th-century **Eglise St-Aignan**, hidden from immediate view by the prolific shrubbery and old trees. This small Romanesque building, with a somewhat triangular façade and topped by an odd little steeple, was sited on the remains of a former proto-Christian church and is in the simplest of forms: a rectangular nave and a smaller rectangular choir. It has a wooden barrel-vault ceiling held in place by crossbars, ancient wooden pew stalls and a well-worn brick floor. However, its highlights are the substantial remains of its frescoes, decorating the apse in vivid hues of ochre, red, white, green and even some touches of blue. The paintings represent, among other subjects, the *Labours of the Months* (unique as it's the only complete Romanesque cycle of this subject still extant in France), *The Prophets and Apostles* and the *Life of Christ*. They are executed with unusual realism and certain vigour – a late Carolingian style with some Byzantine touches. The *Massacre of the Innocents*, a scene that is often represented in later art, is quite gruesome in its depiction and intentionally evokes emotion. Amazingly, the work has withstood the ravages of nine centuries, possibly because the wall paintings were covered with later layers of painting and the original 12th-century work was only discovered in 1911. It remains one of the finest examples of French Romanesque art.

Below
Frescoes, Eglise St-Aignan, Brinay

Route de Porcelaine

An itinerary has been organised in this area of the Berry to link the factories that produce porcelain. Known as the *Route de Porcelaine*, it gives information on 14 participating manufacturers, museums or workshops located in the 6 local communities between Vierzon and Bourges. Although only introduced in the beginning of the 19th century, the industry has prospered and garnered a reputable name for its decorative and household products.

CHÂTEAUROUX

ⓘ Châteauroux Tourist Office 1 pl. de la Gare; tel: 02 54 34 10 74; fax: 02 54 27 57 97. Open Jun–Sept Mon–Sat 0900–1900, Sun & hols 1000–1530; Oct–May Mon–Sat 0900–1230 and 1400–1815.

Déols Tourist Office 7 r. de l'Abbaye; tel: 02 54 07 58 87; fax: 02 54 34 54 19; www.ville-deols.fr. Open Mon–Sat 0900–1200 and 1400–1900.

Ⓦ www.ville-chateauroux.fr (the town's official site); www.chateauroux-tourisme.fr (the tourist office site).

ⓗ Hôtel Bertrand; 2 r. Descente des Cordeliers, Châteauroux; tel: 02 54 61 12 30; fax: 02 54 61 12 31; email: musees@ ville-chateauroux.fr. Open Jun–Aug Tue–Fri 1000–1200 and 1400–1800, Sat–Sun 1000–1200 and 1400–1900; Sept–May Tue–Sun 1400–1800. Closed national hols.

Maison des Arts et Traditions Populaires du Berry Parc Balsan, 44 av. François Mitterrand; tel: 02 54 61 12 30; email: musees@ville-chateauroux.fr. Open Tue–Sun 1400–1800. A fine collection of items relating to the local arts, crafts and cultural traditions in the Berry.

Eglise de St-Etienne € Déols; tel: 02 54 34 43 62. Open daily for guided tour mid-Jun–mid-Sept 1500, rest of year open daily 0900–1700.

As the regional capital of southern Berry, the substantial hilltop town of Châteauroux is imposing. It rises above the large oak forests to the south and the vast stretches of agricultural land that gave it prosperity, and sits at an important north–south crossroads. It grew around the fortress built at the end of the 10th century by the seigneur of Déols, who required a safer address than his previous one. The site at Châteauroux was a great improvement. The oldest – and most pleasant – part of Châteauroux is around the former main street, the r. Grande, which runs into the r. de l'Indre, one-time haunt of the town's tanners, weavers and dyers. The town's **Hôtel Bertrand** (also known as the Musée de Châteauroux) is in a fine 18th-century mansion that belonged to Napoleon's faithful companion, General Henri-Gatien Bertrand. It is notable for its Napoleonic memorabilia, including paintings and decorative arts. Looking out over the countryside at one edge of the old town is the handsome Couvent des Cordeliers, now a venue for local exhibitions. Not to be missed, either, is the **Maison des Arts et Traditions Populaires du Berry**.

The town of **Déols**, across the river, has been absorbed into the suburbs of Châteauroux with the result that there is no obvious distinction for tourists. The heart of ancient Déols fans out from the sparse remains of its Abbaye Notre-Dame dating from 917. The gracious stonework of its clock tower is all that still stands of a once-important abbey (a sister abbey to the great Abbaye de Cluny and the most important monastery in the Berry), though current excavations are revealing the foundations of the former complex. Part of the remains can be seen in the **Hôtel Bertrand**. If early Christian sculpture fascinates, then don't miss the parish church of **St-Etienne** on pl. Carnot (a short walk northwards from the abbey remains), for here there is an extraordinarily beautifully carved sarcophagus belonging to Saints Ludre and Léocarde, dating from the 4th century. The delicacy and realism of its figures harks back to the best sculpture of the Roman Empire some 300 years earlier.

Back in the centre, the 15th-century Porte du Pont-Perrin is an elegant entrance town gate that once guarded the Pont-Perrin, crossing point over the Indre, while, at the other end of the street, the fine twin-towered Porte de l'Horloge has, for over 550 years, housed the town clock.

Accommodation and food in and around Châteauroux

Jeux 2 Gouts €–€€ 42 r. Grande; tel/fax: 02 54 27 66 28. A central address and attractive rustic décor in this restaurant serving a wide choice of French dishes with some tasty oriental touches. Good wine list.

Le Relais Saint Jacques €€ On D920 at exit 12 from A20; tel: 02 54 60 44 44; fax: 02 54 60 44 00; email: contact@relais-st-jacques.com;

Markets *pl. Voltaire, Châteauroux, Sat all day; Déols, Tue & Fri all day.*

www.relais-st-jacques.com. Open year-round. Nearer Déols than the centre of Châteauroux (5km), this good, modern hotel and restaurant is a favourite with locals.

ISSOUDUN

Issoudun Tourist Office *pl. St-Cyr; tel: 02 54 21 74 02; fax: 02 54 03 03 36; www.issoudun.fr. Open Jul–Aug Mon–Sat 0900–1230 and 1400–1800 (1700 Sun), Sept–Jun Mon–Sat 0900–1200 and 1430–1800.*

La Tour Blanche € *tel: 02 54 03 22 15. Open Apr–Jun & Sept Tue–Sat 1400–1800, Sun 1400–1900; Jul–Aug Mon–Sat 1400–1800, Sun 1400–1900. Night-time opening Jul–Aug Thur–Sat from sunset to midnight.*

Issoudun is a pleasant, unhurried town in the midst of farming land and oak woods. As you climb up into the old town, its sense of history begins to unfurl. Because of its strategic location, Issoudun prospered in the Middle Ages as the capital of Lower Berry and became a royal city in 1240. Its 27m-high **Tour Blanche** (not really white but of light-coloured stone) is an imposing, medieval tower begun in 1195 and, as part of Issoudun's defensive system, rises high above the town, piercing its skyline. It was once part of English-occupied France; Richard the Lionheart and Philippe-Auguste came to blows (yet again) here, but Philippe-Auguste won the town back on Richard's death in 1199, and finished constructing the tower. On summer evenings it can be visited after dark, made mysterious and romantic by illuminations and music. Next door is a fine topiary garden, with yew trees manicured into the form of chess pieces. The belfry also dates from a similar era and, despite its use as a prison and a later renovation, remains a fine building. The Eglise St Seer stands a stone's throw from the main square (it's just beside the half-timbered tourist office) and

Right
Tour Blanche, Issoudun

🏛 **Museé de l'Hospice St-Roch** € 23 r. de l'Hospice St-Roch; tel: 02 54 21 01 76; fax: 02 54 21 88 56. Open Nov–Mar Mon, Wed, Thur & Fri 1400–1800, Sat & Sun 1000–1200 and 1400–1800; Apr–Oct Mon & Tue 1400–1900, Wed–Sun 1000–1200 and 1400–1900. Closed 1 May, 1 & 11 Nov.

🔵 **Market** Fri am, Sat all day.

dates from the 10th to the 12th century. It has an unusually long nave and, above the west door (where you enter), a good, but poorly lit, *Descent from the Cross* by Jean Boucher dating from 1625. The modern building (housing temporary exhibits) that forms part of the **Museé de l'Hospice St-Roch** is a surprise beside the handsome almshouse that, as the Hôtel-Dieu de Issoudun, once sheltered pilgrims and beggars on their way to Santiago de Compostela. This 15th- to 18th-century building now houses the eclectic but interesting museum tracing Issoudun's Roman and Renaissance heritage. The almshouse's chapel is decorated with two magnificent sculptural interpretations of the *Tree of Jesse*, a unique feat of three-dimensional workmanship, while another section holds the hospice's fascinating 17th- to 19th-century pharmacy. The surgical instruments once used in the hospice are a salutary reminder of the progress made in medicine. Lastly, don't miss the modern painting of the medieval healing saint, Roch (*see page 274*), complete with his life-saving dog. He's dressed rather like a brasserie waiter and has dropped his trousers to show the plague pustules!

Accommodation and food in Issoudun

Hotel-Restaurant La Cognette €€ *Hotel: 6 blvd Stalingrad; Restaurant: 26 r. Minimes; tel: 02 54 03 59 59; fax: 02 54 03 13 03; www.la-cognette.com.* Built in 1789 as an inn, and frequented by Balzac. The renowned restaurant offers Berry specialities and contemporary dishes in a refined atmosphere.

Saint Roch

Saint Roch is a popular holy man, hailing from Montpellier, in the south of France. During the plague years in the mid-14th century, he renounced his worldly goods and set off on a pilgrimage to Rome. He healed many fellow pilgrims en route by making the sign of the cross over their ailing bodies. He, too, succumbed to the plague and famine and collapsed in a wood. Roch was kept alive by a dog who brought him a hunk of bread daily until its owner discovered the man and sheltered him. His short life ended in prison in 1379. He has been adopted as the patron saint of beasts by many guilds and is often depicted in paintings accompanied by a dog.

MEHUN-SUR-YÈVRE

ℹ **Mehun Tourist Office** pl. du 14 juillet; tel: 02 48 57 35 51; fax: 02 48 57 13 40. Open Jun–Aug Mon–Sat 1000–1200 and 1400–1800, Sun 1000–1200.

🏛 **Eglise Notre-Dame** € Open daily 0830–1800.

Pôle de la Porcelaine € r. des Grands Moulins; tel: 02 48 57 06 19; fax: 02 48 57 34 16; email: pole-de-la-porcelaine@ wanadoo.fr. Open May, Jun & Sept 1400–1800, except Mon; Jul–Aug 1000–1200 and 1400–1800; Mar–Apr & Oct–Nov weekends only 1400–1800.

🛒 **Market** Wed am.

It was Jean, Duke of Berry, son of King Jean II le Bon, who reconstructed the château in Mehun in the late 14th century. Perhaps better known as a patron of arts, Jean de Berry commissioned the famous *Les Très Riches Heures* (*see page 276*), one of Europe's most beautiful illustrated medieval manuscripts. At his death in 1416, the castle passed into the hands of his nephew, King Charles VII, who was to receive here, among others, Joan of Arc in 1429 and 1430. The king died in Mehun, and the castle survived another couple of centuries before being dismantled during the Revolution. What is left is minimal – however, it must have been a sumptuous castle if the illustration in *Les Très Riches Heures* is accurate. The Tour Charles VII is one of the last remaining towers of the castle and can also be visited. Medieval Mehun is rather scant, too, although the **Eglise Notre-Dame**, former collegiate church dating from the mid-1000s, still stands, and the attractive r. Jeanne d'Arc, named after the heroine who stayed in this street, still has some historic homes. At its end is the dignified town gateway Porte de l'Horloge, which dates from the 14th century. Mehun is best known today for its porcelain industry – it has some porcelain companies that welcome visitors. Since this industry was established 200 years ago in the valley of the Yèvre it has prospered, making this one of France's prime areas of production. Apart from visiting exhibitions and museums that trace the history, the bonus for visitors is the possibility of buying items at factory outlets. The **Pôle de la Porcelaine** in Mehun displays some beautiful items that aptly capture the breadth of this craft.

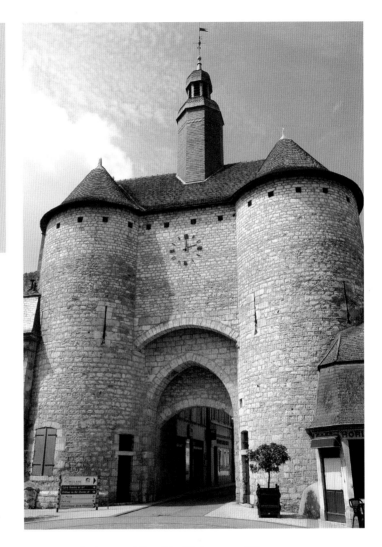

Right
The town gate at Mehun-sur-Yèvre

Accommodation and food in Mehun-sur-Yèvre

L'Eole € *13 r. André Brému; tel: 02 48 57 14 12; email: eole.mehun@ neuf.fr; www.royal-musichall-cabaret.com.* This popular convivial restaurant and crêperie has a terrace and offers a good-value dish of the day. At weekends it stages very glamorous Music Hall-style live shows with can-can dancers and cabaret (*bookings tel: 02 48 57 06 54*), accompanied by set menus.

> ## Les Très Riches Heures du Duc de Berry
>
> This exquisite work was commissioned by the duke and executed by the three Limbourg brothers, Paul, Hermann and Jean, a trio of celebrated illustrators from Flanders who had also worked for the Duke of Burgundy. This Book of Hours outlines the liturgical text for each hour of the day and includes psalms, prayers and calendars. The finely executed illustrations in the calendar part of these *Très Riches Heures* probably comprise the book's finest section, and the importance of this example of medieval art is arguably on a par with any of Raphael's or Leonardo da Vinci's works. The original is now kept at Chantilly in northern France.

PALLUAU-SUR-INDRE

ℹ Palluau-sur-Indre Tourist Office *19 pl. Frontenac; tel: 02 54 53 03; www.palluau-sur-indre.com. Open mid-Jun–mid-Sept except Mon 0900–1200 and 1430–1830. Other times contact the Mairie, tel: 02 54 38 45 55.*

⊖ Market *Sun am, pl. des Marronniers.*

🏛 Eglise St-Laurent € *Open 0745–1930. To visit, ask for key either at the nearby shops, at the tourist office or from the Mairie.*

Palud means *swamp* in Latin, and no doubt the marshy areas around the Indre gave their name to this small medieval village built above the river. Its history is traceable with certainty to the 9th century, but most of what one sees today is 15th century and later. The stone Château de Palluau (not open to the public) was built by the Count of Anjou, Foulques le Rechin, at a strategic position on the Indre. It was a much sought-after castle and gave rise to many a battle, the most notable of which was the successful siege against the English in 1188, when Philippe-Auguste managed to outwit Richard the Lionheart's men by cutting off their water supplies. The deconsecrated **Eglise St-Laurent**, once part of the Prieuré St-Laurent, has extremely fine frescoes in its apse. The church has been divided up, and parts of it are used for domestic purposes.

VATAN

ℹ Vatan Tourist Office *pl. de la République; tel/fax: 02 54 49 71 69; www.vatan-en-berry.com. Open May–Sept 0900–1200 and 1400–1800 (closed Sun pm); Oct–Apr Mon–Fri 1000–1200 and 1400–1700.*

Amid kilometres of undulating hills defined by golden cereals or rapeseed flowers lies the agricultural town of Vatan. It has one of the country's most unusual museums: the **Musée du Cirque**. It grew from the private collection of Dr Alain Frère who had amassed an extraordinary assortment of posters, costumes, maquettes and accessories. Through video footage, visitors learn much about the behind-the-scenes life of itinerant circus artists. In the centre of town the pl. de la République is where the old Wheat Hall is still located. Once used for the public auctions of grain, and for public festivals, it now houses the tourist office. In the north of town the 15th-century Eglise St-Laurian faces the ancient Granary. This was used to store

Musée du Cirque €
square de la Libération;
tel: 02 54 49 77 78;
www.musee-du-cirque.com.
*Open Wed–Sun 1000–1200
and 1400–1800, Tue pm
only. Closed Mon, 1 Jan,
1 May, 1 Nov & 25 Dec.*

Market *Wed am.*

tithed grain representing a levy of 10 per cent of a farmer's annual output, which had to be given to the Church.

Accommodation and food in Vatan

Hôtel de la France € *16 pl. de la République; tel: 02 54 49 74 11. Open year-round except first week in Dec, last 2 weeks in Feb, first week in Sept. Restaurant closed as above and each Tue pm and Wed, excepting national hols.* A simple but pleasant place to lodge or eat. The restaurant serves local specialities.

Suggested tour

Total distance: About 240km or, with the detour, 300km.

Time: 1 or 2 days, depending on how much time you want to spend at each stop.

Links: From Vatan, it is 24km on the D960 between this market town and Valençay, on the tour of South Touraine (*see page 90*), while Palluau is around 14km from Châtillon-sur-Indre on the same tour.

Route: Exit **Bourges** (*see page 260*) by the main road to Vierzon, and you'll arrive in **MEHUN-SUR-YEVRE ❶**, one of the major stops on the **Route de Porcelaine**, the Porcelain Route. Continue on the same road towards Vierzon but turn off to the left as you enter Vignoux-sur-Barangeon on to the D30, which crosses both the Yèvre and the motorway and enters the village of **Foëcy**, site of an important porcelain factory. Continue on the D30 for a couple of kilometres, crossing the Cher, and take the D27 road off to the right at Beauregard, marked Vierzon and **BRINAY ❷**. It is a winding set of roads that leads onwards.

**Porcelaines Philip
Deshoulières** *5 r.
Louis Grandjean, Foëcy; tel:
02 48 53 04 55; fax: 02 48
52 60 50. Shop open
Mon–Sat 1000–1830.*

Leave Brinay on the D18E via the village of **Méreau**, passing the large and impressive Abbaye St-Martin-de-Massay, with its interesting Eglise St-Martin in the village of **Massay**, before taking the small, and not particularly busy, D320, which hugs the motorway, passing from side to side until it enters **VATAN ❸**.

The D926 towards Levroux is a fast road. Dolmens are off the road to the left just before entering the village of Liniez. Here, you take the D66 to the right, marked **BOUGES-LE-CHATEAU ❹**. The château itself is just on the north side of the village. From Bouges, the D2, southwards, follows the valley of the River Renon and goes via **Levroux**. Continue on the D926 in the direction of Châteauroux before turning off 7km later on to the D27, which leads to the **Villegongis**, site of a Renaissance château, closed for the foreseeable

The 'village of lovers'

In the triangle between Vatan, Châteauroux and Issoudun is the small village of **St-Valentin**, the only village in the country bearing the saint's name. Dubbed *Le Village des Amoureux*, it trades on its sobriquet to hold an annual festival for sweethearts and attracts visitors from all over France. The date? 14 February, St Valentine's Day, of course.

future. This road changes into the D73 and then D63 as it skirts the Forêt de Villegongis, passing through the hamlet of Fouillereau and crossing the D926 in the direction of **Argy**, noted for its 15th- to 16th-century château. Turn right here on to the D11 in the direction of Ecueillé and pass through **Pellevoisin** where the D15 leads to **PALLUAU-SUR-INDRE ❺**, situated on the northern banks of the Indre. The best views of this medieval hillside town are as you cross the Indre, leaving for the D943 (former N143) to the south. Turn left on this highway and follow the directions to **CHATEAUROUX ❻**.

Maison de George Sand € tel: 02 54 31 06 04; fax: 02 54 31 18 48. *Open daily Jul–Aug 0930–1830; Sept & Apr 1000–1230 and 1400–1800; May & Jun 0930–1200 and 1400–1830; Oct–Mar 1000–1230 and 1330–1700. Closed 1 Jan, 1 May, 1 Nov, 11 Nov & 25 Dec.*

Detour: Literary aficionados might like to include a tour to **Maison de George Sand** at Nohant-Vic, 27km south of Châteauroux on the D943. The 19th-century author's home is arranged much as it was when she inhabited it, and now fulfils a role as an interesting museum of memorabilia, from the life of this prominent man of letters. The house was originally constructed in the 12th century, but was restored and modernised in the 17th century. George Sand (born Aurore Dupin in 1804) spent her youth and adolescence here, and later inherited the large house, a *'modeste demeure'*, as she referred to it. It provided her with a much-loved refuge. Among the luminaries of the 19th-century music, artistic and literary world to visit her home were Balzac, Lizst, Delacroix, Gautier, Flaubert and, of course, her lover, Chopin. George Sand was also responsible for helping restore the exquisite Romanesque frescoes in Nohant-Vic's **Eglise St-Martin**, a church that was under the jurisdiction of the abbey at Déols. Take a few minutes to visit this well-known little church, *open daily (end of detour)*.

The old town of **Déols**, on the D151 to the north, was once a separate entity but has now been absorbed by the suburbs of Châteauroux. It is a straight road, onwards to the less busy but equally interesting town of **ISSOUDUN ❼**. Bourges is just 37km from here, back along the N151.

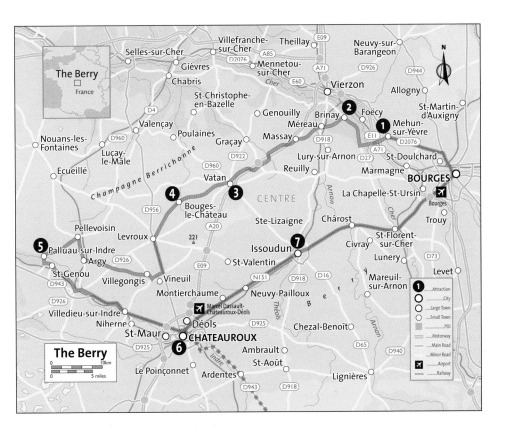

The Berry
France

The Berry

0   10km
0   5 miles

Reuilly wine

This tour encircles the Reuilly wine-producing district. Sauvignon, Pinot Noir and Pinot Gris are the three grape varieties used in the cultivation of AOC Reuilly wine. This area has a history of some 1,500 years of vinification, notably producing its fine Pinot Noir red wine, and now extends over 137ha with a total output of some 8,000hl annually.

Jacques Cœur

In the Berry region, north and south of Bourges, you'll come across the symbol marking the *Route de Jacques Cœur*. It might seem that you're following a child's comical cartoon character but in fact you're tracing the footsteps of Jacques Cœur, the wealthy merchant and master silversmith who was employed by King Charles VII. He was born in Bourges (see page 260) around 1400 and rose to prominence for his fine craftsmanship. Apart from being present in many of the royal châteaux along the Loire and in the heart of the Berry, he also travelled to the Orient to trade. In a hideous plot to discredit him, he was accused of treason and of poisoning the king's mistress, Agnès Sorel – offences punishable by the death sentence. In an unfair trial he was found guilty of subsidiary crimes but not guilty of the murder, and was exiled. He died on the Greek island of Chios.

Language

Although English is spoken in most tourist locations it is courteous to attempt to speak some French. The effort is generally appreciated, and may even elicit a reply in perfect English! The following is a very brief list of some useful words and phrases, with approximate pronunciation guides. For driver's vocabulary, see page 26. The Thomas Cook European Phrasebook: 12 Languages (£5.99) lists more than 350 travel phrases in French (and in 11 other European languages).

- **Hello/Goodbye**
  Bonjour/Au revoir *Bawngzhoor/Ohrevwahr*
- **Good evening/Goodnight**
  Bonsoir/Bonne nuit *Bawnswahr/Bon nwee*
- **Yes/No**
  Oui/Non *Wee/Nawn*
- **Please/Thank you (very much)**
  S'il vous plaît/Merci (beaucoup) *Seelvooplay/Mehrsee (bohkoo)*
- **Excuse me, can you help me, please?**
  Excusez-moi, pouvez-vous m'aider, s'il vous plaît? *Ekskewzehmwah, pooveh voo mehdyeh, seelvooplay?*
- **Do you speak English?**
  Parlez-vous anglais? *Pahrleh voo ahnglay?*
- **I'm sorry, I don't understand.**
  Pardon, je ne comprends pas. *Pahrdawn, jer ner kawnprawn pah.*
- **I am looking for the tourist information office.**
  Je cherche l'office de tourisme. *Jer shaersh lohfeece de tooreesm.*
- **Do you have a map of the town/area?**
  Avez-vous une carte de la ville/région? *Ahveh-voo ewn cart der lah veel/rehjeeawn?*
- **Do you have a list of hotels?**
  Avez-vous une liste d'hôtels? *Ahveh voo ewn leesst dohtehl?*
- **Do you have any rooms free?**
  Avez-vous des chambres disponibles? *Ahveh voo day shahngbr deesspohneebl?*
- **I would like to reserve a single/double room with/without bath/shower.**
  Je voudrais réserver une chambre pour une personne/pour deux personnes avec/sans salle de bain/douche. *Jer voodray rehsehrveh ewn shahngbr poor ewn pehrson/poor der pehrson avek/sawns sal der banne/doosh.*

- **I would like bed and breakfast/(room and) half board/(room and) full board.**
  Je voudrais le petit-déjeuner/la demi-pension/la pension complète. *Jer voodray ler pewtee-dehjerneh/lah dermee-pahngsyawng/lah pahngsyawng kawngplait.*
- **How much is it per night?**
  Quel est le prix pour une nuit? *Khel eh ler pree poor ewn nwee?*
- **I would like to stay for . . . nights.**
  Je voudrais rester . . . nuits. *Jer voodray resteh . . . nwee.*
- **Do you accept traveller's cheques/credit cards?**
  Acceptez-vous les chèques de voyages/les cartes de crédit? *Aksepteh voo leh sheck der vwoyaj/leh kart der krehdee?*
- **I would like a table for two.**
  Je voudrais une table pour deux personnes. *Jer voodray ewn tabl poor der pehrson.*
- **I would like a cup of/two cups of/another coffee/tea.**
  Je voudrais une tasse de/deux tasses de/encore une tasse de café/thé. *Jer voodray ewn tahss der/der tahss der/oncaw ewn tahss der kafeh/teh.*
- **I would like a bottle/glass/two glasses of mineral water/red wine/white wine, please.**
  Je voudrais une bouteille/un verre/deux verres d'eau minérale/de vin rouge/de vin blanc, s'il vous plaît. *Jer voodray ewn bootayy/ang vair/der vair doh mynehral/der vang roozh/der vang blahng, seelvooplay.*
- **Could I have it well cooked/medium/rare, please?**
  Je le voudrais bien cuit/à point/saignant, s'il vous plaît. *Jer ler voodray beeang kwee/ah pwahng/saynyang, seelvooplay.*
- **May I have the bill, please?**
  L'addition, s'il vous plaît. *Laddyssyawng, seelvooplay.*
- **Where is the toilet (restroom), please?**
  Où sont les toilettes, s'il vous plaît? *Oo sawng leh twahlaitt, seelvooplay?*
- **How much does it/this cost?**
  Quel est le prix? *Kehl eh ler pree?*
- **A (half-) kilo of . . . please.**
  Un (demi-) kilo de . . . s'il vous plaît. *Ang (dermee) keelo der . . . seelvooplay.*

Index

Acknowledgements

Project management: Cambridge Publishing Management Limited
Project editor: Tom Lee
Series design: Fox Design
Cover design: Liz Lyons Design
Layout: Cambridge Publishing Management Limited
Map work: PCGraphics (UK) Ltd
Repro and image setting: PDQ Digital Media Solutions Limited/Cambridge Publishing Management Limited
Printed and bound in India by: Replika Press Pvt Ltd

Thomas Cook Publishing wishes to thank **Ethel Davies**, to whom the copyright belongs, for the photographs in this book (except for the following images):

Alamy (pages 246 Ball Miwako; 253 and 275 David South) **Dreamstime.com** (pages 18 Christian Musat; 1A, 35 James Warren; 36 Edyta Pawlowska; 1B, 39, 121 David Hughes; 46, 55 S Finn; 58 Cuddlzandhugz; 187 José I Soto) **Getty Images** (page 37 Jean-Paul Nacivet) **John Heseltine** (page 149) **iStockphoto.com** (pages 36 Lillisphotography; 102 Richard Semik; 136 Kermarrec Aurelien; 184 Claudio Giovanni Colombo; 23 Richard Schmidt-Zuper) **www.loiredeschateaux.com** (page 202 Office de Tourisme de Blois) **Pictures Colour Library** (pages 36, 37, 102, 184, 232, 246 and 253) **Robert Harding World Imagery** (page 136) **Wikimedia Commons** (pages 155 Mandred Heyde; 176 David Merrett; 202 Patrick Giraud) **World Pictures/Photoshot** (page 45).

Feedback form

We're committed to providing the very best up-to-date information in our travel guides and constantly strive to make them as useful as they can be. You can help us to improve future editions by letting us have your feedback. Just take a few minutes to complete and return this form to us.

When did you buy this book? ....
....

Where did you buy it? (Please give town/city and, if possible, name of retailer)
....
....

When did you/do you intend to travel in the Loire Valley?...
....

For how long (approx)? ....

How many people in your party? ....

Which cities, national parks and other locations did you/do you intend mainly to visit?
....
....
....
....

Did you/will you:
❏ Make all your travel arrangements independently?
❏ Travel on a fly-drive package?
Please give brief details: ....
....

Did you/do you intend to use this book:
❏ For planning your trip?   ❏ Both?
❏ During the trip itself?

Did you/do you intend also to purchase any of the following travel publications for your trip?
A road map/atlas (please specify) ....
Other guidebooks (please specify) ....

Have you used any other Thomas Cook guidebooks in the past? If so, which?

....

....

Please rate the following features of *driving guides Loire Valley* for their value to you (circle VU for 'very useful', U for 'useful', NU for 'little or no use'):

The *Travel facts* section on pages 12–21	VU	U	NU
The *Driver's guide* section on pages 22–27	VU	U	NU
The touring itineraries	VU	U	NU
The recommended driving routes throughout the book	VU	U	NU
Information on towns and cities, châteaux, etc	VU	U	NU
The maps of towns and cities, etc	VU	U	NU

Please use this space to tell us about any features that in your opinion could be changed, improved, or added in future editions of the book, or any other comments you would like to make concerning the book:

....

....

....

....

....

....

....

....

Your age category: ❏ 21–30   ❏ 31–40   ❏ 41–50   ❏ over 50

Your name: Mr/Mrs/Miss/Ms ....

(First name or initials) ....

(Last name) ....

Your full address: (Please include postal or zip code)

....

....

....

....

Your daytime telephone number: ....

Please detach this page and send it to: driving guides Series Editor,
Thomas Cook Publishing, PO Box 227, Coningsby Road, Peterborough PE3 8SB.

Alternatively, you can email us at: *books@thomascook.com*